Epicurus in Lycia

Epicurus in Lycia

The Second-Century World of
Diogenes of Oenoanda

Pamela Gordon

Ann Arbor

THE UNIVERSITY OF MICHIGAN PRESS

1999   1998   1997   1996   4   3   2   1

A CIP catalog record for this book is available from the British Library

Library of Congress Cataloging-in-Publication Data

Gordon, Pamela, 1957–
     Epicurus in Lycia : the second-century world of Diogenes of
Oenoanda / Pamela Gordon.
        p.   cm.
     Includes bibliographical references and index.
     ISBN 0-472-10461-6 (cloth)
     1. Diogenes, of Oenoanda.   2. Epicureans (Greek philosophy)
I. Title.
B557.D564G67   1996
187—dc20   96-42968
                                                         CIP

To
Anthony E. Riccio
1957–91

Acknowledgments

I wish to express my gratitude to Julia Haig Gaisser and Harold Washington, who read many drafts of this book and were generous with their comments, and to Diskin Clay, who offered his advice when this project was in its very early stages many years ago. I also owe special thanks to Gregory Dickerson, Richard Hamilton, David Konstan, Mabel Lang, Abraham Malherbe, David Potter, and Amy Richlin. Audiences at talks I gave at Bryn Mawr College, Lehigh University, the University of Kansas, and the University of Tübingen and at the meetings of the American Philological Association, the Society of Biblical Literature, and the Classical Association of the Middle West and South also helped me clarify my views.

I could not have completed the project without Kathleen Whalen, who walked many miles for me in the University of Kansas libraries and tended my κηπίδιον while I traveled. Amy Welch also helped by carrying heavy tomes to my study. For their friendly interest, inspiration, and encouragement, I am also grateful to Deborah Altus, April Bremby, Maggie Childs, Caroline Jewers, Anthony E. Riccio, Bea Scott, Kitt Stone, Sara Winter, and my students and colleagues at Barnard College and the University of Kansas. This work was supported by the University of Kansas General Research Fund.

Contents

Introduction

εἰ δὲ μη[δὲν] ἔτι ὦν ἥκ[ε]τ[ε] εἰς γνῶσιν, τὰ τοσαῦτα ὑμεῖν ἐλιθο-
ποιήσαμεν γράμματα.

[It is in case [you] do not yet [possess] knowledge that we turned so
many letters to stone for you.]

—Diogenes of Oenoanda fr. 116 = NF 81

For a figure that the uninitiated consider a minor author, Diogenes of Oenoanda
has inspired an extraordinary number of editions and commentaries. In the
preparation of this book I have relied on the results of over a century of that
painstaking work, most of which has focused on the establishment of the text of
Diogenes' inscription and on the use of that text as a source for new knowledge
of the teachings of Epicurus.[1] My purpose here, however, is to bring a new approach to the study of Diogenes by reading Diogenes' inscription with a sustained concern for Diogenes' particular context in the bustling world of Asia
Minor during the Roman Empire. A few treatments of Diogenes have already
begun to consider his cultural and social milieu, but most have kept the Greek
renaissance and other developments of the second century far in the background.[2] For many of Diogenes' editors, Diogenes is a worthy subject not because he displays the Epicurean outlook of one particular believer in second-
century Lycia but because he is a good orthodox Epicurean. This view accords
well with modern scholarship on Hellenistic philosophy, which rarely describes
Epicureanism as a flexible and innovative system. In my reading, however,

---

Part of this introduction was originally written for my review of *Diogenes of Oinoanda: The
Epicurean Inscription,* ed. M.F. Smith, *AJP* 116 (1995): 662–64.

1. See M.F. Smith, ed., *Diogenes of Oenoanda: The Epicurean Inscription* (Naples, 1993),
19–32, and Smith, "A Bibliography of Work on Diogenes of Oenoanda (1892–1981)", in *Syzetesis:
Studi sull' epicureismo greco e romano offerti a Marcello Gigante* (Naples, 1983), 683–95. See also
A. Casanova, "Diogene d'Enoanda oggi," *Prometheus* 9 (1983): 111–38; and Casanova, ed.,
I frammenti di Diogene d'Enoanda, Studi e testi 6 (Florence, 1984).

2. A welcome exception is the work of Diskin Clay. See his article "A Lost Epicurean Community," *GRBS* 30 (1989): 313–35.

Diogenes is quite a bit more eccentric than the traditional view allows. In fact, I would argue that Diogenes has acquired so many modern readers neither simply because Epicurean texts are so rare nor because his limestone handbook is such a novelty, but because Diogenes manages to project—from stone—an inimitable voice. The premise of this book is that his voice deserves a hearing both within the context of the Second Sophistic and within the history of Epicureanism.

A Brief Introduction to Diogenes and His Modern Readers

Fragments of the inscription of Diogenes of Oenoanda were first discovered in the town of Oenoanda in Lycia (now in Turkey) in 1884. Although only five fragments were found that year, the unusual nature of the inscription was immediately obvious. One of the first limestone blocks discovered announces the author's desire to release his readers from fear and pain and to teach them the value of Epicurean tranquillity (ἀταραξία). Also included among that year's discoveries were the name of the author and his statement that he had chosen to inscribe his "remedies which bring salvation" on the walls of a stoa. As more fragments of Diogenes' dismantled stoa were found, it became clear that the original monument had displayed an entire handbook of Epicureanism, most of which was apparently composed especially for this inscription. To date approximately six thousand words have been recovered, but these are estimated to represent only one-fifth to one-fourth of the original inscription, which included several epistles, two collections of Epicurean aphorisms, and treatises on physics, ethics, and old age.[3] Since there has been no excavation in Oenoanda, the hope remains that the rest of Diogenes' inscription will be recovered.

Attempts to identify Diogenes with other Epicureans cited in external sources or with men called Diogenes in some of the many other inscriptions in Oenoanda have been inconclusive,[4] and the known fragments of Diogenes' inscription do not indicate exactly when the monument was erected. The structure that originally displayed the inscription was demolished sometime in antiquity, and the inscribed blocks have been discovered in various locations in

---

3. See Smith, *The Epicurean Inscription,* 83. For "a view of the whole," see also D. Clay, "The Philosophical Inscription of Diogenes of Oenoanda: New Discoveries 1969–1983," *ANRW* II 36.4 (1990): 2465–78.

4. See A. Grilli, ed., *Diogenis Oenoandensis Fragmenta* (Milan, 1960), 20; A.S. Hall, "Who Was Diogenes of Oenoanda?" *JHS* 99 (1979): 160–63; and Smith, *The Epicurean Inscription,* 35–48.

and near Oenoanda.[5] Some were found built into a city wall, which provides us with an approximate *terminus ante quem;* the wall was probably built during the second half of the third century C.E.[6]

Most attempts to date the inscription more precisely have depended on Diogenes' prose style and the style of the lettering. Early editors were led by Diogenes' verbose and affected style, his orthography, and his combination of Koine and atticizing constructions to conclude that he lived in late antiquity, possibly at the end of the second century C.E. They also recognized that the rounded epsilons, sigmas, and omegas, the broken crossbar of the alphas, and the use of ligatures, apexes, and serifs point to the same general era.[7]

These first impressions are supported by other observations. It was observed early on, for example, that a second-century date would coincide well with the documented revival of Epicureanism during that time.[8] The choice of medium is also relevant; epigraphy was immensely popular in the Roman Empire, and its use rose steadily during the period between Domitian and Septimius Severus.[9] Numerous other inscriptions and monumental buildings in Oenoanda can be dated to the period from Hadrian to the Severans, and Diogenes' stoa would fit in well with that era of prosperity.

Recently, however, evidence that the inscription can be dated closely to the reign of Hadrian (117–38) has surfaced: another inscription that may have been carved by one of the same stonecutters who worked for Diogenes has been found near Oenoanda. This other remarkable inscription from Oenoanda concerns the founding, by one C. Iulius Demosthenes, of an elaborate theatrical festival and competition in the year 124 C.E. Among other documents, it records a

---

5. Recently a few fragments have turned up around seven kilometers away, in the neighboring village of Zorban. See M.F. Smith, "Diogenes of Oenoanda, New Fragments 122–124," *AS* 34 (1984): 43–44; and Smith, *The Epicurean Inscription,* 73–74.

6. See A.S. Hall, "The Oenoanda Survey: 1974–1976," *AS* 21 (1976): 191–97. Smith now narrows the date of the fortification wall to the third quarter of the third century (*The Epicurean Inscription,* 56–57).

7. The first editor, G. Cousin, remarked in 1892, "pour la forme, elle est subtile, précieuse, pas toujours claire et pas toujours correcte" ("Inscriptions d'Oenoanda," *BCH* 16 [1892]: 66). Five years later R. Heberdey and E. Kalinka concluded: "Wenn man die im Vorausgehenden zusammengestellten graphischen und stilistischen Thatsachen ueberblickt, wird man das Ganze unbedenklich etwa dem Ende des zweiten nach-christlichen Jahrhunderts zuschreiben. Alles stimmt dazu, vor allem auch die Mischung atticistischer und gemeingriechischer Elemente in der Sprache" ("Die philosophische Inschrift von Oinoanda," *BCH* 21 [1897]: 442). Philippson accepted the date proposed by Heberdey and Kalinka but pointed out that the epigraphical and linguistic evidence is not at all conclusive ("Diogenes von Oinoanda," *RE* Suppl. 5 [1931]).

8. See H. Usener, "Epikureische Schriften auf Stein," *RhM* 47 (1892): 416.

9. See R. MacMullen, "The Epigraphic Habit in the Roman Empire," *AJP* 103 (1982): 232–46. MacMullen (242) documents the increase of production of inscriptions in Latin.

supporting letter, written in August 124, from the emperor Hadrian to the local inhabitants.[10] Both inscriptions exhibit the same peculiarities in orthography and letter styles, and both are distinguished by the stonecutter's habit of carving the omicrons smaller than usual and placing them under the horizontal lines of the preceding gamma or tau.[11] Identifying a stonecutter's hand is difficult, and not all epigraphists would acknowledge that one cutter can be distinguished from another. Several studies have demonstrated persuasively, however, that one can know the hand of a cutter "much the same way that one knows the handwriting of a close friend."[12] As soon as fragments of both inscriptions have been examined by experts in the identification of individual hands, we can hope to confirm a Hadrianic date for Diogenes of Oenoanda.[13] Meanwhile, the inscription that records the founding of the Demostheneia displays enough of the idiosyncrasies of Diogenes' inscription that, even without the identification of the particular epigraphical personality, it establishes that Diogenes' message was probably inscribed sometime during or close to the reign of Hadrian.[14]

Although Diogenes of Oenoanda does not fully belong to the rhetorical movement Philostratus called the "Second Sophistic," the sophistic movement

---

10. The inscription is published by Michael Wörrle, in *Stadt und Fest im kaiserzeitlichen Kleinasian: Studien zu einer agonistischen Stiftung aus Oinoanda* (Munich, 1988). The emperor's letter is addressed to the Termessians, and elsewhere in the inscription we hear of "Termessians-at-Oenoanda" as well as "Oenoandians." Heberdey and Kalinka have identified Termessus Minor (the presumed home of the "Termessians" mentioned in other inscriptions from Oenoanda) with a site two miles from Oenoanda ("Bericht über zwei Reisen im südwestlichen Kleinasien," *Denkschriften der Akademie der Wissenschaften in Wien* 45 [1897]: 55). If Termessus Minor was a separate town, Oenoanda must have served as its administrative center (at least in the second and third centuries) because official inscriptions of the Termessians are found at Oenoanda. See D. Magie, *Roman Rule in Asia Minor,* 2 vols. (Princeton, 1950), 1377 n. 22. Recently, in "Termessians at Oenoanda," *AS* 32 (1982): 115–31, Coulton argues that Termessus Minor must have been an alternative name for Oenoanda itself and suggests that the Termessians and Oenoandians shared a joint community at Oenoanda. See also Wörrle, 45–53.

11. The similarities between the two inscriptions are described by M.F. Smith in "Oenoanda: The Epicurean Inscription," in *Acta of the Tenth International Congress of Classical Antiquity* (Ankara, 1973): 846; "Diogenes of Oenoanda, New Fragments 122–124," *AS* 34 (1984): 43–56; and *The Epicurean Inscription,* 39–40.

12. S.V. Tracy, *The Lettering of an Athenian Mason, Hesperia* Suppl. 15 (Princeton, 1975), 2. See also Tracy, "Identifying Epigraphical Hands" *GRBS* 11 (1970): 321–33; H.T. Wade-Gery, "A Distinctive Attic Hand," *BSA* 33 (1935): 122–35; and H.B. Mattingly, "Some Fifth-Century Attic Epigraphic Hands," *ZPE* 83 (1990): 110–15.

13. Close study of the lettering may also help us reconstruct Diogenes' inscription: if, for example, more than one stonecutter can be securely identified, the lettering should help us attribute isolated fragments to particular treatises (assuming that each stonecutter worked on one continuous passage at a time). See Clay, "The Philosophical Inscription," 2472.

14. Smith sums up: "In view of the remarkably close similarity between the lettering of the two inscriptions, it seems very likely that both were carved at about the same time, and it may even be that the lapicide who carved the Termessus Minor inscription was employed by Diogenes. Cer-

influenced Diogenes profoundly. Philostratus, the greatest biographer and pro-
moter of the sophists, traced the Second Sophistic back to Aeschines in the
fourth century, but it has become conventional to use the term *Second Sophistic*
in reference to the sophists on whom Philostratus concentrates,[15] those who
achieved unprecedented fame in the Roman Empire in the second and early
third centuries. Wilamowitz once claimed that the Second Sophistic was the
"totally useless invention" of Philostratus, but scholarship in recent decades
has rejected that verdict and revived interest in previously despised authors and
the world in which they flourished.[16] Several recent studies have expanded the
term *sophist* to accommodate authors not mentioned by Philostratus. Thus,
the irreverent Lucian has been dubbed "a sophist's sophist"[17] and Tertullian

---

tainly it can no longer be argued that epigraphical considerations require that the Epicurean inscription be dated to about A.D. 200" ("Oenoanda: The Epicurean Inscription," 841). Cf. Wörrle's judgment: "Auf die grosse stilistische Ähnlichkeit mit den Schriftformen der Diogenes-Inschrift hat
Smith ganz zu Recht aufmerksam gemacht" (*Stadt und Fest,* 2 n. 4; see also 72 n. 131). Other recently suggested dates for Diogenes' inscription include Diskin Clay's suggestion that the partially
preserved name in fr. 70 (NF 10) is that of Avitus, the Roman legate to Bithynia and Pontus in 165
("A Lost Epicurean Community," 318).

15. For a recent discussion of the expression *Second Sophistic,* see G.W. Bowersock's article
"Philostratus and the Second Sophistic," in *Cambridge History of Classical Literature,* vol. 1, *Greek
Literature,* ed. P.E. Easterling and B.M. Knox (Cambridge, 1985), 655–62, where Bowersock writes
that Philostratus "successfully identified and recorded an important phenomenon in later Greek
rhetoric. It is ultimately immaterial whether the cumbrous phrase 'Second Sophistic' or some other
is used to refer to it" (656). Bowersock also points out that Philostratus traces the Second Sophistic
back to Aeschines in order "to anchor the movement of the Roman period in the classical age" (656).
In his earlier study *Greek Sophists in the Roman Empire* (Oxford, 1969) Bowersock overemphasized
the historical and political importance of the movement and underestimated its literary importance.
E.L. Bowie's article "The Importance of Sophists," *YCS* 27 (1982), exposes but perhaps overcor-
rects Bowersock's excesses. See also Graham Anderson, *Philostratus: Biography and Belles Lettres
in the Third Century* A.D. (London, Sydney, and Dover, N.H., 1986). Anderson's reassessment of the
quiddity of the Second Sophistic seems also to have been a reaction to Bowersock's overly political
emphasis. Anderson concludes: "The Second Sophistic is not a fiction; but it was the sort of grandi-
ose affectation which may have given rise to misleading distinctions" (13).

16. Wilamowitz called the Second Sophistic a "schlechthin unbrauchbare Erfindung" in a 1925
review of Boulanger's *Aelius Aristide;* the review is reprinted in *Kleine Schriften,* vol. 3 (Berlin,
1969), 421. Elsewhere, however, Wilamowitz found the term *Second Sophistic* quite useful. One
example is his use of it in "Asianismus und Atticismus," *Kleine Schriften* 3, 223 ff. For more recent
scholarship, see Graham Anderson, *The Second Sophistic: A Cultural Phenomenon in the Roman
Empire* (London and New York, 1993); and the following bibliographies: George Kennedy and
Mark Barnard, "A Selective Bibliography of the Second Sophistic," in *Approaches to the Second
Sophistic,* ed. G.W. Bowersock (University Park, Pa., 1974), appendix 1; and Barry Baldwin, "The
Second Century from Secular Sources," *Second Century* 1 (1981): 173–89. For a less appreciative
view see B.A. van Groningen, "General Literary Tendencies in the Second Century A.D.," *Mnemo-
syne* 18 (1965): 41–56.

17. Graham Anderson, "Lucian: A Sophist's Sophist," *YCS* 27 (1982): 61–92. In his conclusion
Anderson writes: "Various labels, or pairs of labels, such as 'sophist and satirist' or 'satirist and bel-

"the Christian sophist."[18] Similarly, several scholars have begun to investigate the impact of the Second Sophistic on other realms, such as philosophy, historiography, poetry, and the novel.[19] Some have shown that the Sophistic itself exemplified a broader cultural renaissance.[20] It is with such research in mind that I link Diogenes of Oenoanda with the Second Sophistic.

In chapter 1 of this book I establish the connection between the inscription of Diogenes of Oenoanda and the revival of ancient Greek culture in the second century C.E. I demonstrate that despite Diogenes' efforts to separate himself from the sophists and align himself with the philosophers, his inscription betrays a sophistic influence. In chapter 2 I explain why the inscription should not be adduced as evidence for the specific content of Epicurus' own writings. In chapter 3 one text from the inscription is shown to be indicative of the issues described in the first two chapters. In chapter 4 I elucidate some of the factors (such as the revival of oracular prophecy) behind Diogenes' decision to broadcast his second-century version of Epicureanism. Throughout this book I argue that in adopting the role of "new Epicurus" Diogenes is simultaneously at one with his contemporaries and against them. The educated elite among Diogenes' contemporaries shared his conviction that ancient Greek wisdom was the solution to the problems of their time, but Diogenes had chosen an unconventional model in Epicurus.

---

lettrist,' are not entirely satisfactory. . . . How then *is* Lucian to be characterized? . . . We can fall back on the title 'sophist's apprentice,' for a writer who plays with the raw materials of rhetoric and turns the sophist's lecture-room upside down at every opportunity, or we can say that his manipulations of sophistic material and techniques come closest to realizing the real literary potential of this uniquely well-equipped literary movement: we can call him a sophist's sophist" (92).

18. Timothy David Barnes, "The Christian Sophist," in *Tertullian: A Historical and Literary Study* (Oxford, 1971), chapter 14. Barnes calls Tertullian a sophist because he combined philosophy and theology with persuasive rhetoric, thereby using "the benefits of a traditional education and the fruits of his pagan erudition to defend and to propagate what he considered to be the truth" (210). The result was Christian treatises written as orations, with all the current stylistic devices.

19. Examples include the studies gathered in Bowersock's *Approaches to the Second Sophistic,* such as B.P. Reardon's "The Second Sophistic and the Novel" (23–29) and Phillip De Lacy's "Plato and the Intellectual Life of the Second Century A.D." (4–10). See also Graham Anderson, "The Second Sophistic: Some Problems of Perspective," in *Antonine Literature,* ed. D.A. Russell (Oxford, 1990), 91–110.

20. See, especially, the important article by E.L. Bowie, "Greeks and Their Past in the Second Sophistic," *Past and Present* 46 (1970); reprinted in *Studies in Ancient Society,* ed. M.I. Finley, *Past and Present* Series (London and Boston, 1974). Anderson remarks: "Philostratus calls his sophists the Second Sophistic. It is difficult to define precisely what he is claiming to chronicle: we seem to be dealing with an ethos or outlook rather than a movement, a self-confident Hellenism which flourished within the Roman Empire on the secure economic foundations provided by the *Pax Romana*" (*Philostratus,* 8).

A Note on the Greek Text

For the text of Diogenes of Oenoanda I have used Smith's 1993 edition of all the known fragments of Diogenes.[21] Because Smith's edition is not available in many college libraries, I have also included references to Chilton's widely available Teubner text (Ch)[22] or, in the case of discoveries that postdate Chilton's edition, to the "New Fragment" (NF) numeration system used by Smith in the various journals in which these fragments were first published. As Smith makes clear in the preface to his edition, all book-length editions of Diogenes besides his own (William 1907, Grilli 1960, Chilton 1967, and Casanova 1984) are based exclusively on earlier printed records (e.g., Cousin 1892, Usener 1892, and Heberdey and Kalinka 1897), and all except Casanova predate the discovery of more than half of the known fragments. For his 1993 edition, Smith reexamined all the stones that were found during the British investigation in Oenoanda (1968–83), and in the case of stones that have not resurfaced since they were recorded by Diogenes' first modern readers in the late nineteenth century, he consulted notebooks and epigraphic squeezes that are available in archives located in Athens at l'École française d'Athènes and in Vienna at the Kleinasiatische Kommission of the Österreichische Akademie der Wissenschaften. Smith is meticulous in his recording of lacunae, blank spaces, doubtful letters, letters erased by the stonecutter, dimensions of stones and letters, previous attempts at restoration, and other details about the inscription itself. Smith's 1993 text is likely to be the definitive text of Diogenes until—or unless—an excavation in Oenoanda and its environs reveals the rest of Diogenes' inscription.

---

21. *The Epicurean Inscription.* For technical and aesthetic reasons, I have not included all of the signs and symbols that Smith prints in his Greek text. I have omitted, for example, Smith's signs for imperfectly preserved letters, as well as his notes on the occasional blank spaces left by the stonecutter. I also begin several of my quotations of the Greek text at the point where the surviving Greek text actually begins, rather than including Smith's suggested restorations.

22. *Diogenes Oenoandensis Fragmenta* (Leipzig, 1967).

CHAPTER 1

A Philosopher among the Sophists

τῶν ῥητορικῶν ἀποκάμψεις λόγων ὅπως ἀκούσῃς τι τῶν ἡμεῖν ἀρεσ-
κόντων. ἔνθεν σε καὶ κατελπίζομεν τὴν ταχίστην τὰς φιλοσοφίας
κρούσειν θύ[ρας.

[You will veer away from the speeches of the rhetoricians in order to
listen to some of our doctrines. And from then on it is our firm hope that
you will come as quickly as you can to knock at the doors of philosophy.]
—Diogenes of Oenoanda fr. 127 = NF 24

Cultural Archaism: Re-creating the Greek Past

The salient feature of social and intellectual life in Diogenes' era was the
cultivation of ancient learning. Greek-speaking peoples had been looking back
to classical Greece for inspiration for over half a millennium, but interest in the
Hellenic past reached a new intensity in the Second Sophistic. The extant literary papyri and quotations in Lucian, Plutarch, Dio Chrysostom, and others suggest that Homer and the historians, philosophers, and poets of classical Greece
had more readers in the second century than in any other period in antiquity.[1]
Renewed interest in the classics is also reflected in the number of libraries built
throughout the empire.[2] Status and prestige were attached to one's knowledge

---

The translation of the epigraph is that of D. Clay, "The Philosophical Inscription of Diogenes
of Oenoanda: New Discoveries 1969–1983," *ANRW* II 36.4 (1990): 2542. The authorship of this
passage is disputed. See chapter 3.

1. See Wm. H. Willis, "A Census of the Literary Papyri from Egypt," *GRBS* 9 (1968):
205–41; Orsolina Montevecchi, *La Papirologia* (Turin, 1973), 337–94; and F.W. Householder, *Literary Allusion and Quotation in Lucian* (New York, 1941). But, for the argument that Lucian did
not actually read the works he quoted, see Graham Anderson, "Lucian's Classics: Some Short Cuts
to Culture," *BICS* 23 (1976): 59–68.

2. Many cities, including Timgad, Ephesus, and Comum, received libraries as benefactions.
Comum's was given by Pliny (*Ep.* 1.8.2). The first building in Athens designed solely as a library
was constructed during the reign of Trajan; the second was built during the reign of Hadrian. See
R.E. Wycherley, *The Stones of Athens* (Princeton, 1978), 86–88.

of Greek culture, and Greek literature was esteemed more than ever for its educational and moral value.[3] Emblematic of the authority and appeal of ancient tradition in this era is the frequent occurrence of such honorary titles as the "new Penelope," the "new Homer," and the "new Themistocles."[4]

While the teachings of the classical Greeks were being preserved and cultivated in the Second Sophistic,[5] they were also exerting a profound influence on contemporary thought and creativity. Erudite imitation of classical models was admired far more than originality.[6] Archaism became the rule not only in literature and the visual arts but in other realms as well, so it is not an exaggeration to speak of cultural archaism.[7]

In this era historians who wrote histories of the world ended their narrations four or five centuries before their own time.[8] Cephalion, who writes during the reign of Hadrian, begins his *Histories* with the quasi-mythological Semiramis and ends with Alexander.[9] Jason of Argos, who can also be placed in the second century on the basis of his archaizing name and the Suda's claim that he was "younger than Plutarch," ends his world history with the fall of Athens in the year 322 B.C.E.[10] The same terminus seems to have been chosen by the writers of local histories.[11] This archaizing extended also to historiographic style.

---

3. See, especially, B.P. Reardon, *Courants littéraires grecs des IIe et IIIe siècles après J.-C.,* Annales littéraires de L'Université de Nantes 3 (Paris, 1971), part 1, pp. 3–96; and C.P. Jones, *Culture and Society in Lucian* (Cambridge, Mass., 1986), 149–59.

4. See Louis Robert, "Une épigramme satirique d'Automédon et Athènes au début de L'empire", *REG* 94 (1981): 338–361; and "Deux poètes grecs a l'époque imperiale," in *Stele: Tomos eis Mnemen Nikolaou Kontoleontos* (Athens, 1977) 1–20.

5. Recent scholarship (e.g., Reardon, *Courants littéraires,* 6) credits writers of the second century with preserving classical literature for posterity. Formerly, second-century epitomizers and editors were blamed for its loss. Cf. B.E. Perry, "Literature in the Second Century," *CJ* 50 (1955): 295–98.

6. See Reardon, *Courants littéraires,* 8–9. Imitation need not imply lack of creativity or originality, however. See C.P. Jones, *Lucian,* 155–56.

7. I have taken the term *cultural archaism* from E.L. Bowie ("Greeks and Their Past in the Second Sophistic," *Past and Present* 46 [1970]: 205).

8. See Bowie "Greeks and Their Past," 174–88, 191–95. Some historians, notably Appian and Cassius Dio, took a different approach and changed world history into Roman history; Bowie (176) calls these writers "realists." Despite their Roman themes, most realists seem to have taken Herodotus as their model. See G.W. Bowersock, "Herodotus, Alexander, and Rome," *American Scholar* 58 (1989): 407–14.

9. F. Jacoby, *Die Fragmente der griechischen Historiker* (Leiden, 1926–58) 93–94; 2A:436–45.

10. Jacoby, *Die Fragmente der griechischen Historiker,* 94; 2A:445–46.

11. Bowie ("Greeks and Their Past," 184–88) records some evidence for the archaic and classical emphasis of local histories written in the second century, but (as he admits) the evidence is inconclusive. Very few works are extant, and although titles such as *On Sicily* and *On the City of Ephesus* suggest that the works were about the distant past, we cannot be sure.

Cephalion's work was divided into nine books named after the Muses and was written in Herodotean Ionic.[12] Arrian's *Anabasis* was divided into seven books and imitated Xenophon's Attic.[13] Thucydides also had his imitators, at least in Lucian's imagination.[14]

Travelers' guidebooks indicate a similar preoccupation with the distant past.[15] In his *Description of Greece,* Pausanias (who also adopts a Herodotean style)[16] records detailed information about classical and Hellenistic monuments and inscriptions but usually ignores monuments that are less than several centuries old. Homer and the archaic and classical poets appear frequently among his literary allusions and quotations, but he never mentions a contemporary Greek or Roman writer.[17] Even if Pausanias' emphasis on the classical were due to his use of antiquated written sources, as some scholars have suggested, it is clear that he wrote for contemporaries who were interested in ancient monuments rather than in the artifacts of recent history.[18]

Extreme archaism also pervades Apollodorus' mythographical *Bibliotheca.* Apollodorus refuses to contaminate Greek myths with later Roman developments and interpretations, so in the *Bibliotheca* he allows Aeneas to fade back into his Homeric role as a minor Trojan hero (5.21),[19] and does not honor Rome

---

12. Diogenes of Oenoanda seems also to have been reading Herodotus. He mentions Cleobis and Biton in fr. 136 (NF 93) and Croesus in fr. 23 (NF 19). Cf. M.F. Smith, "Fifty-Five New Fragments of Diogenes of Oenoanda," *AS* 28 (1978): 81.

13. Of course, Arrian's status as the "new Xenophon" depended on more than his writing style; see P. Stadter, *Arrian of Nicomedia* (Chapel Hill, N.C., 1980), 1, 5, 31, 54, and passim.

14. In *On Writing History* (15) Lucian has Crepereius Calpurnianus of Pompeiopolis steal Thucydides' first sentence, inserting "Parthians and Romans" instead of "Lacedaemonians and Athenians" and replacing his mentor's name with his own unpronounceable one.

15. Periegetic literature was not written for actual travelers only. Pausanias, whose work is our only completely extant example of this genre, included enough historical, mythological, and religious information to interest any "armchair traveler." Another second-century periegetic writer was Telephus of Pergamum. See H. Bischoff, "Perieget," *RE* 19 (1937): 725–42.

16. He writes in Attic, however. See Christian Habicht, *Pausanias' Guide to Ancient Greece* (Berkeley, 1985), 137. On Pausanias' relationship to Herodotus, see Habicht, 97–98 and nn. 7 and 9.

17. See Habicht, *Pausanias' Guide,* 133–34. Wilamowitz put it thus: "the age of the heroes was closer to him than the recent past" (*Der Glaube der Hellenen,* vol. 2 [Berlin, 1932], 501).

18. Bowie writes: "[Pausanias'] omission of the later period must have been patent to his readership, and both readers and writers must have acquiesced in the neglect. This acquiescence is only intelligible if it was taken for granted that the intervening years were of no interest to a Greek" ("Greeks and Their Past," 189). Wilamowitz claimed that Pausanias failed to treat recent monuments because he was using earlier periegetic writers, but Habicht (*Pausanias' Guide,* 165–75) demonstrates that Wilamowitz' attack on Pausanias amounted to a personal vendetta.

19. Perhaps Apollodorus is influenced unwittingly by the Roman Aeneas and his *pietas.* His last reference to Aeneas in the epitome is: "Aeneas picked up his father Anchises and fled; and the Greeks let him because of his *eusebeia.*"

itself with the slightest mention when he relates the story of Heracles crossing Italy with the cattle of Geryon (2.5.10). Apollodorus' "obstinate refusal to recognise the masters of the world"[20] has led at least one scholar to date his work to some time before the Roman Empire, although most authorities agree that he wrote in the second century.

These archaizing tendencies were not limited to the academic realm of the written word. In sculpture, the practice of copying Greek masterpieces grew in popularity, reaching its height in the Antonine period.[21] The use of mirror copies of famous sculptures, especially as symmetrical decorations for architectural facades, also came into vogue.[22] Lucian, always sensitive to the excesses of his contemporaries, lampoons the proliferation of copies in his *Philopseudes* (18). His own taste for fifth- and fourth-century art coincides with his contemporaries' tastes, however.[23] A penchant for classical styles is also reflected in the portrait statues of Hadrian and in the carved sarcophagi of the Hadrianic era.[24] In addition, the early part of the century saw a renewed interest in architectural restoration, while new construction mixed Roman and classical elements.[25] The Olympieion in Athens was completed in 131/2, seven centuries after it was begun, and Herodes Atticus undertook his restoration of the stadium in Delphi and construction of other buildings there.[26]

---

20. Sir James George Frazer, introduction to the Loeb edition of Apollodorus, *The Library* (Cambridge, Mass., 1921), xiii.

21. See Cornelius Vermeule, *Greek Sculpture and Roman Taste: The Purpose and Setting of Graeco-Roman Art in Italy and the Greek Imperial East,* Jerome Lectures Twelfth Series (Ann Arbor, 1977), 14; and Brunilde Sismondo Ridgway, *Roman Copies of Greek Sculpture: The Problem of the Originals* (Ann Arbor, 1984), 16. Hellenistic works seem to have been copied as often as classical ones (see Ridgway, 11); second-century tastes in visual arts seem to have been more eclectic than were literary tastes.

22. See Vermeule, *Sculpture and Taste,* 27.

23. See C.P. Jones, *Lucian,* 154–55. Pausanias expresses similar preferences. See Habicht, *Pausanias' Guide,* 131–32.

24. For the classicizing trend in imperial portraiture, see Margarete Bieber, *Ancient Copies: Contributions to the History of Greek and Roman Art* (New York, 1977), 207–9. For the classicism practiced by Athenian sarcophagus carvers, see Bieber, 216–19; and Vermeule, *Sculpture and Taste,* 88.

25. A.J. Spawforth and S. Walker suggest that Hadrian "may have intended a deliberate fusion of Roman, Athenian and Hellenistic Greek elements" in his Athenian building program ("The World of the Panhellenion," *JRS* 75 [1985]: 93).

26. On the Olympieion, see Dio Cassius 69.16; Pausanias 1.18.6; Philostratus *VS* 533; *Historia Augusta, Life of Hadrian* 13.6. See also R.E. Wycherley, "The Olympieion at Athens," *GRBS* 4 (1963): 157–75. On the possible connection between the dedication of the sanctuary of Olympian Zeus and Hadrian's founding of the Panhellenion, see Spawforth and Walker, "The World of the Panhellenion," 78–104. The sophist Polemo gave the oration at the ceremony Hadrian held on its completion. On restorations at Delphi, see H.W. Parke and D.E.W. Wormell, *The Delphic Oracle,* vol. 1 (Oxford, 1956), 286.

The revival of the Delphic oracle was also part of the archaizing trend.[27] The oracle's importance had decreased during Hellenistic and early imperial times, and although the Pythia was still occasionally consulted, oracular responses in verse had become rare. During the reign of Hadrian many people went back to consulting the Pythia. When the emperor himself visited Delphi, he first asked a question that interested his Greek subjects: "Where was Homer born, and who were his parents?"[28] As befitted the question, the response was delivered in hexameters. The oracle continued to answer in verse until the end of the century, when its popularity fell sharply once again.[29]

Archaism also colored the smallest details of everyday life. It influenced the diction of the educated (or at least of the pedantic), as is evident from Lucian's *A Slip of the Tongue in Salutation*.[30] It also influenced parents' selection of names for their children, as in Herodes Atticus' choice of the names Achilles, Polydeuces, and Memnon for his adopted sons.[31] Homeric names increased in popularity throughout the empire but seem to appear with special frequency in a wide area around the Troad. In Oenoanda we find the Homeric names Sarpedon and Tlepolemos, appropriate names for children born in Lycia and near Rhodes (the respective homes of those heroes). Also represented in Oenoanda are Croesus (an appropriate name in light of Oenoanda's proximity to Lydia), Simonides, Demosthenes, and, of course, Diogenes.[32] Arrian of Nicomedia extended his imitation of Xenophon's style to the naming of his own dogs, which he named after Xenophon's.[33] Similarly, many people persisted in using the ancient Greek names for such geographical areas as Lydia, Caria, and Phrygia, although under the Roman provincial administration these places were no longer politically distinct.[34] Even dreamers could not resist the tendency to atticize. In

---

27. For this revival, see Parke and Wormell, *The Delphic Oracle,* 284 ff., 373.

28. The Pythia's answer was unusual; she made Homer the son of Telemachus. See Parke and Wormell, *The Delphic Oracle,* 285.

29. See Parke and Wormell, *The Delphic Oracle,* 287.

30. This title is given to *Pro Lapsu* by C.P. Jones (*Lucian,* 88).

31. See Philostratus *VS* 558. Apollonius of Tyana was apparently hostile toward the use of Roman names: see *Letters of Apollonius* 71, 72. See also Bowie, "Greeks and Their Past," 200.

32. These names appear in the second-century Demostheneia inscription (Michael Wörrle, *Stadt und Fest im kaiserzeitlichen Kleinasien: Studien zu einer agonistischen Stiftung aus Oinoanda* [Munich, 1988]; cf. *IGR* iii 487) and in the genealogy inscribed on the early third-century mausoleum of Licinia Flavilla (*IGR* iii 500).

33. See Bowie, "Greeks and Their Past," 193.

34. See Bowie, "Greeks and Their Past," 200. Mentioning another example, Bowie writes: "A whole range of Greek writers (Strabo, Appian, Aelian, Philostratus) perversely refer to Puteoli as Dicaearcheia, although to judge from inscriptions of the period no Greek-speaking trader who called at the port would have known what that name referred to: there the transliteration *Potioloi* from the Latin *Puteoli* is normal" (201).

Sacred Tales Aelius Aristides records his nocturnal meetings with the likes of Lysias, Demosthenes, Plato, and Sophocles,[35] and an inscription in Pergamon records that the sophist Polemo set up a dedication to Demosthenes "in accordance with a dream."[36]

The coinage of local mints, especially in the East, also reflects a revived interest in the philosophers, poets, and other luminaries of the Greek past. Ephesus issued bronze coins with portraits of its native son Heracleitus, and Mytilene issued coins depicting Sappho, Alcaeus, and Pittacus.[37] Pythagoras appeared on coins minted by Samos, as did Bias on coins issued by Priene, Hippocrates on coins from Kos, and Anaxagoras on coins from Clazomenae.[38] Halikarnassos issued a coin with a portrait of Herodotus on one side and Hadrian on the other, and every town that was ever called the birthplace of Homer seems to have issued a coin with his portrait.[39] The reliefs on these coins were probably modeled after portrait statues; commemorative statues may have been erected simultaneously with the issue of the coins.[40]

In the midst of this energetic cultivation of Greek learning, Diogenes of Oenoanda revived Epicurus' teachings and commemorated the philosopher with a public monument that also paid homage to Homer, Herodotus, Aristippus, Anaxagoras, Democritus, Thales, Socrates, Plato, and Aristotle. Oenoanda was small, insignificant, and originally non-Greek, but the Greek renaissance had reached it nonetheless. Elsewhere in the Greek-speaking world, many other people also rediscovered Epicureanism: despite Epicurus' strictures against traditional learning, his teachings had become traditional themselves. There is some irony in this development, and Cicero, who loved to ridicule the Epicureans' alleged lack of erudition, would have protested it. There had always

---

35. E.g., see Aristides *Or.* 50.

36. Christian Habicht, *Die Inschriften des Asklepieions,* Altertümer von Pergamon 8.3 (Berlin, 1969). Habicht's identification of the stone as a statue base is apparently incorrect; see D.S. Potter, review in *CR* 33 (1983): 318.

37. The earliest known coin depicting Heracleitus was issued under Antoninus Pius; see S. Karweise, "Ephesos," *RE* Suppl. 12 (1970): col. 339. Three more issues from the third century are known; see G.M.A. Richter, *The Portraits of the Greeks,* vol. 1 (London, 1965), 80. See also Richter, 1:70 figs. 253–56, 259–61 (Sappho); and 81 fig. 247; 181 fig. 367 (Alcaeus and Pittacus on the same coin).

38. See Richter, *Portraits of the Greeks,* 1:79 figs. 302–3 (Pythagoras), 314 and 358 (Bias); 153 figs. 872 and 874 (Hippocrates). The portrait of Anaxagoras is not securely identified, as no name appears on the coin. See Richter, *Portraits of the Greeks,* abridged and revised by R. Smith (Ithaca, 1984), 86.

39. Halikarnassos later issued Herodotus coins with Antoninus Pius, and then Gordian III on the obverse. See Richter, *Portraits of the Greeks,* 1:147 figs. 821–24. Coins depicting Homer are known from Chios, Kyme, Kolophon, Smyrna, and Nikaia. See Richter, 55 figs. 125–27.

40. See Richter, *Portraits of the Greeks,* 1:11, 79.

been educated Epicureans—even Cicero admired the learning of his contemporaries Zeno, Philodemos, and Lucretius—but Epicurus was not one to eulogize past masters or famous men. As Cicero disparagingly comments about the Garden in his own day, "In the school of Epicurus I never heard the names of Lycurgus, Solon, Miltiades, Themistocles, or Epaminondas, who are on the lips of all the other philosophers" (*De Finibus* 2.21.67).

It should not surprise us that the century that produced historians who emulated Herodotus, Xenophon, or Thucydides and sculptors who copied Polyclitus or Phidias gave to Epicurus his first imitator, a veritable "new Epicurus."[41] Epicurus belonged to the fringe of respectable antiquity but was born safely before the crucial cutoff point, the death of Alexander.[42] Diogenes comes close to giving himself the title "new Epicurus" in his punning claim that he has provided his inscription "to protect" or "to help" (ἐπικουρεῖν) its readers.[43] In the same fragment, when Diogenes describes himself as being "at the sunset" of life and departing with a "paean of rejoicing," he imitates language variously attributed to Metrodorus and Epicurus.[44] He also displays Epicurus' *Kyriai Doxai* prominently in a continuous band across the entire inscription (adding a collection of Epicurean sayings he has apparently composed himself), and in accordance with Epicurus' practice he uses the epistolary form for his treatises. Direct imitation is found in the opening of Diogenes' *Letter to Antipater,* which echoes that of Epicurus' *Letter to Pythocles* in its acknowledgment of the young follower's request for instruction and its praise for his diligence.[45] In addition, by recording his will on stone Diogenes imitates Epicurus, who had apparently made his last testament a public document in Athens.[46] Finally, like Epicurus, who was his own epitomizer, Diogenes presents at least one of his treatises in the form of an epitome.[47] Thus, the imitation of ancient models, so

41. See D. Clay, "A Lost Epicurean Community," *GRBS* 30 (1989): 319; and Clay, "The Philosophical Inscription."

42. A remark in Lucian's *A Slip of the Tongue in Salutation* (*Pro Lapsu* 6) suggests that although he considered Epicurus a respectable Greek source he did not reckon him among the truly ancient.

43. Fr. 3 (Ch fr. 2), col. V, line 7. See G.N. Hoffman, "Diogenes of Oenoanda: A Commentary" (Ph.D. diss., University of Minnesota, 1976), 166. The pun may have had wide currency; it appears also in Athenaeus *Deipnosophistae* 7.278f.

44. See Clay, "The Philosophical Inscription," 2529–30.

45. See M.F. Smith "Eight New Fragments of Diogenes of Oenoanda," *AS* (1979): 72–73, on fr. 63 (NF 107); and Clay, "The Philosophical Inscription," 2526ff. Verbal echoes are also present: Clay compares fr. 3 (Ch fr. 2), col. II, lines 10–11 to *Sententia Vaticana* 47.

46. Diogenes' will is found in fr. 117 (Ch fr. 50); Epicurus' will is recorded in Diogenes Laertius 10.16. See D. Clay, "Epicurus in the Archives of Athens," in *Studies in Attic Epigraphy, History, and Topography Presented to Eugene Vanderpool Hesperia* Suppl. 19 (Princeton, 1982);17–26.

47. On the use of epitomes by Epicurus, see chapter 2. Diogenes also may have taken imitation to its logical extreme by composing the *Letter to Mother,* which I view (see chapter 3) as a fictional letter supposedly from the young Epicurus.

characteristic of second-century culture, is a prominent feature of Diogenes' inscription. Diogenes' desire to emulate Epicurus and to preserve and promote his writings is not, however, his only link to the Second Sophistic.

The Voice of an Era: The Sophists

The resurgence of enthusiasm for classical Hellenism was epitomized by the activities of the sophists, whose orations summed up the intellectual and political achievements of their Greek ancestors. It has often been noticed that none of the sophists' speeches mentioned in Philostratus' *Vitae Sophistarum* (Lives of the Sophists) has historical themes or allusions that deal with events occurring after the year 326 B.C.E.[48] The sophists' engagement with the past is especially evident in the sophistic form par excellence, the declamation or μελέτη.[49] In these performances, the sophists assumed the masks of historical personages. Sometimes historical debates were reenacted, but often the speakers presented hypothetical situations, invented sequels to actual events, or even reversed historical verdicts. Isaeus "the Assyrian sophist" had the Spartans debate whether or not to fortify their city.[50] Hermogenes put Herodotus' Phye on trial for disguising herself as Athena and riding into Athens with Peisistratus.[51] Lollianus of Ephesus imagined that the Athenians had decided to sell off the islands to raise funds. His declamation culminated in the prayer "O Poseidon, revoke the favor you gave Delos—Let her escape while she is up for sale!"[52] A declamation could be admired for imaginative and creative use of traditional material but could be criticized as κακόπλαστον (ill conceived) if the sophist made blatant factual errors. The favorite topics for declamation dealt with Athenian heroes and the classical age, but earlier eras were frequently treated, as in Aristides' "Embassy to Achilles," Polemo's portrayal of Solon, and the declamations on Darius and Xerxes by Scopelian of Clazomenae.[53] For sophists who wished to deal with the twilight of antiquity, Alexander the Great was a worthy subject (see Philostratus *VS* 620; Alexander is also mentioned by Diogenes in fr. 51 [Ch fr. 122]).

---

48. See Bowie, "Greeks and Their Past," 171.

49. On declamation, see George Kennedy, "The Sophists as Declaimers," *Approaches to the Second Sophistic* ed. G.W. Bowersock (University Park, Pa.; 1974), 17–22; and D.A. Russell *Greek Declamation* (Cambridge, 1983).

50. Philostratus *VS* 514. Aristides treated this topic also; see *VS* 584.

51. (Pseudo?)-Hermogenes *Progymnasmata* 104.16; cf. Herodotus 1.60.

52. Philostratus *VS* 527. This prayer is typical of sophistic exhibition in that it requires that the audience remember that Delos was a wandering island until it was anchored by Poseidon.

53. Aristides' declamation (*Or.* 16) is extant. Polemo's is known from the title "Solon Demands that His Laws Be Rescinded after Peisistratus Has Obtained a Bodyguard," cited by Philostratus (*VS* 542). Scopelian's Persian declamations are also mentioned by Philostratus (*VS* 519).

Style, pronunciation, and word choice were of utmost importance. Some sophists aimed for an authentic sound by avoiding all Latinisms, or even all vocabulary and constructions that postdated Aeschines or Demosthenes.[54] Scopelian consciously imitated Gorgias; Herodes Atticus followed Critias. The bold claimed the right to be less strict, at least in their everyday speech: when a student of Herodes asked the sophist Philagrus in which classic source one might find a particular word that Philagrus had uttered in anger, he retorted, "In Philagrus" (Philostratus *VS* 579).

From Philostratus one receives the impression that the sophists were constantly followed by huge crowds of admirers and that their performances were everywhere attended by the wealthiest and most important people in the empire. He relates, for example, that one sophist from Cilicia arrived in Athens to find that all the young men who would have comprised his audience had followed Herodes Atticus out to Marathon (*VS* 571). Philostratus' account also frequently locates the philhellenic emperors in the sophists' audiences. As Bowersock has demonstrated, inscriptional and other external evidence generally confirms Philostratus' presentation. Orators were nothing new, but the sophists of the Second Sophistic had attained an "immense worldly success" that distinguished them from their predecessors.[55] This success also distinguished them from philosophers and rhetors, although those professions (or avocations, as the case may be) had many adherents.

Professional Rivalry

In an era that granted special Muses to the sophists and elevated Demosthenes above Homer, the philosopher's life must have been less than ideal.[56] Rather than withdrawing from the realm of popular oratory, however, many second-century philosophers entered into direct rivalry with the rhetors and sophists.

---

54. See Aristides *Rhetoric* 2.6. Lucian enjoyed lampooning this practice in, for example, *Lexiphanes* and *Rhetorum Praeceptor*. It is an oversimplification, however, to equate Atticism with sophistic style. See G.W. Bowersock, *Greek Sophists in the Roman Empire* (Oxford, 1969); E. Norden, *Die antike Kunstprosa*, 2d ed. (Leipzig, 1909) 351–92; and Wilamowitz, "Asianismus und Atticismus," *Hermes* 35 (1900): 1–52.

55. G.W. Bowersock, "Philostratus and the Second Sophistic," in *Cambridge History of Classical Literature*, vol. 1, *Greek Literature*, ed. P.E. Easterling and B.M. Knox (Cambridge, 1985), p. 655. Although Bowersock (in *Sophists*) may have overemphasized the *political* strength of the sophists, the evidence he collected supports his claims for their social success.

56. On rating Demosthenes over Homer, see Ian Rutherford, "Inverting the Canon: Hermogenes on Literature," *HSCP* 94 (1992): 355–78, who cites the Lucianic *Encomium of Demosthenes* in addition to Hermogenes' *On Ideas*. Philostratus mentions the "Muses of the Sophists" in *VS* 613.

Despite his Epicurean beliefs, Diogenes of Oenoanda was one of those who chose to compete with his more vocal contemporaries.

The distinctions between the titles *philosophos, rhetor,* and *sophistes* were often blurred among Diogenes' contemporaries; not even the broadest definitions were universally accepted.[57] Most of our literary sources offer no definitions but simply make clear which occupation the writer respected or despised the most.[58] Each of the three terms was a coveted honorific title, but not always in the same circles.[59] Those who aspired to the prestige of a particular title could never be sure which label they would receive from their peers. Many would certainly be offended by the recent study that characterizes the sophists as showmen who had "broken into the media" while it characterizes the philosophers and rhetors as "conscientious and austere professionals."[60]

To Philostratus "sophist" was a glorious title, but some of the men he honored with that appellation are called "philosopher" or "rhetor" elsewhere.[61] Several inscriptions combine two of the titles and bestow them on a single person. For example, one calls a poet "rhetor and philosopher"; one praises a man as a "rhetor in speech but a philosopher in thought"; and another commemorates a man who was both "rhetor and sophist."[62] I do not find the titles "philosopher" and "sophist" paired in any inscription, but the two are linked by

---

57. On Philostratus' overlapping categories of rhetor, sophist, and philosopher, see Bowersock, *Sophists,* 10–15; C.P. Jones, "The Reliability of Philostratus," in *Approaches to the Second Sophistic,* ed. G.W. Bowersock (University Park, Pa.: 1974), 11–14; E.L. Bowie, "The Importance of Sophists," *YCS* 27 (1982): 39; and Graham Anderson, *Philostratus: Biography and Belles Lettres in the Third Century a.d.* (London, Sydney, Dover, N.H., 1986), 8ff. and 20 n. 59. The distinctions drawn between sophist and philosopher in several ancient authors, including Plutarch, Dio Chrysostom, and Epictetus, are discussed in G.R. Stanton, "Sophists and Philosophers: Problems of Classification," *AJP* 94 (1973): 350–64. For an interesting discussion of the distinctions between philosophers and sophists depicted in portrait busts, see R.R.R. Smith, "Late Roman Philosopher Portraits from Aphrodisias," *JRS* 80 (1990): 127–55 (especially 148–50).

58. See Aelius Aristides' attack on philosophers in *Oration on the Four.* Lucian even calls Jesus of Nazareth a "sophist" (*The Passing of Peregrinus* 13).

59. Anderson notes: "The more philosophical a writer's sympathies, the less likely he will be to use the term sophist in a complimentary manner" (Philostratus, 9)

60. Anderson, *Philostratus,* 10. Anderson has recently reconfigured the relationship between philosophy and sophistic in "Cookery and Confection: Sophistic Philosophy, Philosophic Sophistry," chapter 6 of *The Second Sophistic.*

61. See C.P. Jones, "The Reliability of Philostratus," 12: Isocrates calls himself a philosopher and scorns sophists, Hermocrates of Phocaea is called a philosopher in an inscription at Pergamum, and (if Bowersock is right) the sophist Secundus of Athens is the same person as Secundus the Silent Philosopher.

62. All three inscriptions mentioned here are discussed in Bowersock, *Sophists,* 11–12. The rhetor with philosophic thoughts is the Hadrianic sophist Dionysius of Miletus, who is honored by an inscription published in J. Keil, "Vertreter der zweiten Sophistik in Ephesus," *JOAI* 40 (1953): 6.

Philostratus, and Athenaeus includes a philosopher—an Epicurean philosopher—in his *Deipnosophistai* (*Dons at Dinner*).[63]

Philostratus (*VS* 479–92) also provides for a special category of "philosophers who seemed to be sophists"—that is, philosophers who used oratorical skills to present their theories. Unfortunately, Philostratus does not explain in detail how oratory served philosophy, and of his eight examples of sophistic philosophers only two (Dio Chrysostom and Favorinus) belong to the second century. Diogenes Laertius also mentions an enigmatic category of Epicureans "to whom the genuine Epicureans give the name 'sophists'" (10.26). A recent study has suggested that Laertius may have had in mind such figures as Timocrates of Heraclea, who was a teacher of the sophist Polemo.[64] If correct this suggestion would further illustrate the subjectivity of such titles—Philostratus writes of Timocrates with great admiration but refers to him as an eloquent philosopher, not as a philosophical sophist. As we shall see, a category that links sophist with philosopher would be quite appropriate for Diogenes of Oenoanda. He would resent our associating him with the sophists at all, however. He views himself as a pure philosopher;[65] for him both "sophistry" and "rhetoric" are vices.

In fragment 34 (Ch fr. 28), for example, although the damaged text makes it difficult to see exactly what Diogenes is discussing, it is clear that he interrupts his argument to say:

col. II   ἐνταῦθα
            δὲ ἐκτρέπεσθαι δεῖ τοὺς
            σοφιστικοὺς λόγους
            τούτους ὡς ἐπιβούλους
    10   καὶ προπηλακιστὰς καὶ
            ἐξ ὀνομάτων κοινό-
            τητος μεμηχανημέ-
            νους ἐπὶ τῇ τῶν ταλαι-
            πώρων ἀνθρώπων. . . .

---

63. Bowersock (*Sophists,* 11–12) writes that the professions of sophist and philosopher are conjoined on inscriptions, but the example he cites seems to be found only in the *Suda* (for Hippias of Elis). Bowie gives Athenaeus' work the pleasing title *Dons at Dinner* in "Greeks and Their Past," 180.

64. See Clay, "A Lost Epicurean Community," 314 n. 3. In an earlier era, Philodemus was also concerned about some unnamed Epicurean sophists, who have been identified variously as Epicureans like the Amafinius whom Cicero denounces (*Tusculan Disputations* 2.7–8 and 4.6–7) or Cicero's own teacher Phaedrus. See Elizabeth Asmis, "Philodemus' Epicureanism," *ANRW* II 36.4 (1990): 2378–79 nn. 27 and 29, 2400–2403.

65. See fr. 29 (Ch fr. 24), col. I, line 1; fr. 30 (Ch fr. 25), col. I, line 7.

[But here it is necessary to deflect those sophistic speeches since they are treacherous and abusive and are designed from the vagueness of terms [to confuse] wretched people. . . .][66]

For Epictetus and Marcus Aurelius the words "sophistic" and "sophist" have similar derogatory connotations. Such is often the case for Dio Chrysostom and Plutarch.[67] Dio, for example, thus explains why "the tribe of sophists" have acquired fame.

When a lot of young men with nothing to do go leaping about a man with cries of admiration, as the Bacchants leap about Dionysus, inevitably that man after no great lapse of time will gain a reputation with many others for talking sensibly. Why, that is very much the way in which parents teach their children how to talk, expressing keen delight over anything the children may utter. . . . The sophists also can't help adopting the thought of their listeners, whatever it happens to be; but the majority of these are pretty much simpletons, victims of an unkind fate.[68]

Like Diogenes, Dio Chrysostom often contrasted sophistry with serious philosophy. Not just philosophers wished to disassociate themselves from sophists, however. Even Aristides, who detests philosophers, sometimes uses the word *sophist* as a term of derision.[69] He apparently would prefer, in some settings at least, to be called a rhetor.[70]

Diogenes, however, had no respect for rhetors. Two fragments of the inscription contrast rhetoric with Epicureanism or with philosophy in general.

---

66. Translations are mine unless otherwise noted. For my translations I am heavily indebted to the translations of Chilton, Casanova, and Smith. A. Casanova, *I Frammenti di Diogene d'Enoanda,* Studi e Testi (Florence, 1984); C.W. Chilton, *Diogenes of Oenoanda: The Fragments* (Oxford, 1971); and M.F. Smith, *The Epicurean Inscription.*

67. See Epictetus 1.27.6 and 3.8.1.; Marcus Aurelius 1.16.4 and 6.30.3 (where Antoninus Pius is praised for not being a sophist); and Dio Chrysostom 8.33, 32.68, and 55.7. Plutarch writes that philosophy should be clear and "free from sophistry" (76a, 78e–f, 580b). As C.P. Jones points out, it is indicative of Plutarch's (or Pseudo-Plutarch's) understanding of the word that "he considers it a mark of Herodotus' malice to call certain of the Seven Wise Men 'sophists'" ("The Reliability of Philostratus," 12). For other examples, see Stanton, "Sophists and Philosophers," 357.

68. *Or.* 35.8, trans. H.L. Crosby, *Dio Chrysostom* (Cambridge, Mass., 1940).

69. Occurrences are listed by C.A. Behr, *Aelius Aristides and the Sacred Tales* (Amsterdam, 1968) p. 106–7 n. 39. But note the criticism of A.J. Festugière, "Sur les Discours sacrés d'Aelius Aristide," *REG* 82 (1969): 148, who finds that in many of those instances the word *sophist* is used in a sympathetic or neutral way.

70. This would be in keeping with his rejection of extempore speaking. See Anderson, *Philostratus,* 9.

First, one of Diogenes' "Various Maxims" associates the troubles of a rhetor's work with the harsh life of a soldier and implies that no rhetor can attain the Epicurean goal of *ataraxia:*

> Τὸ κεφάλαιον τῆς εὐ-
> δαιμονίας ἡ διάθε-
> σις, ἧς ἡμεῖς κύριοι.
> χαλεπὸν στρατεία
> 5 κἂν ἑτέρων ἀρχῇ·
> τὸ ῥητορεύειν σφυγμοῦ
> καὶ ταραχῆς γέμον,
> εἰ πεῖσαι δύναται· τί οὖν
> μεταδιώκομεν πρᾶ-
> 10 γμα τοιοῦτον, οὗ τὴν
> [ἐ]ξουσίαν ἔχουσιν ἄλλοι;[71]

[The main point for happiness is our disposition, over which we have control. Military service is rough, even if you are in command of others. Being a rhetor is full of feverish lust and turmoil over whether one can be persuasive. Why, then, do we pursue such a thing, in which others have the power?]

Then, in fragment 127 (NF 24), once assigned to the *Letter to Mother,* the addressee is told:

> col. I
>   τῶν ῥητορικῶν ἀπο-
> 5 κάμψεις λόγων ὅπως
>   ἀκούσῃς τι τῶν ἡμεῖν
>   ἀρεσκόντων. ν ἔνθεν
>   σε καὶ κατελπίζομεν
>   τὴν ταχίστην τὰς φι-
> 10 λοσοφίας κρούσειν θύ-
>
> col. II [ρας. . . .

---

71. Fr. 112 (Ch fr. 41). This and other passages from "Various Maxims" have been attributed variously to Epicurus, Diogenes, and other Epicureans. The mannered word order (of the same type Diogenes uses elsewhere) and the neat parallel construction of this maxim make it likely that Diogenes wrote it.

[You will veer away from the speeches of the rhetoricians in order to listen to some of our doctrines. And from then on it is our firm hope that you will come as quickly as you can to knock at the doors of philosophy. . . .][72]

The tendency in scholarship on Diogenes is to attribute to Epicurus or his immediate followers any passages that lack obvious references to Oenoanda or to stone carving, and some readers may doubt that these three texts can be attributed with certainty to Diogenes himself. The opposition of philosophy and rhetoric is of course not new, and disagreements among Epicureans as to the merits of epideictic and practical oratory had already troubled Philodemus in the first century. If Diogenes himself is not the author of these texts, that he had them inscribed in Oenoanda indicates at least that he agreed with their contents and also that he found them relevant to his second-century world. The first (fr. 34) condemns the sophists' style of speaking, the second (fr. 112) criticizes the profession of rhetor, and the third (fr. 127) advises us to denounce rhetoric in favor of philosophy. Thus, according to Diogenes' inscription, "sophistry" and "rhetoric" are not only inferior to philosophy but also constitute a hindrance to its pursuit. Diogenes' usage also agrees with other imperial sources that suggest that sophists were generally considered to be a special type of rhetor. It would appear from Philodemus' "On Rhetoric," however, that Diogenes is more hostile toward oratory than were Epicurus and his immediate followers. When certain first-century Epicureans in Cos and Rhodes taught that all rhetoric was lacking in *techne,* Philodemus warned them that their radical stance was akin to parricide: Epicurus, Metrodorus, and Hermarchus had acknowledged that sophistic oratory is an art.[73] Diogenes may have received his view from the Rhodian school; I suspect, however, that his stance was due more to the current professional rivalry between philosophers and orators than to an internal Epicurean debate.

---

72. I follow the translation of Clay, "The Philosophical Inscription," 2542. M.F. Smith originally assigned this fragment to the *Letter to Mother* because they have the same physical characteristics: "a height of 0.38–0.41 m., a column or columns of 10 lines, letters averaging about 2.4 cm., and little or no margin above or below" (*Thirteen New Fragments of Diogenes of Oenoanda* Denkschriften der österreichische Akademie der Wissenschaften, Philologisch-Historische Klasse, 117 [Vienna, 1974], 31). Smith stood by his judgment when he published a revised edition of the letter in "Diogenes of Oenoanda: New Fragment 24," *AJP* 99 (1979): 329–31, but he later decided that this fragment probably should not be added to *Letter to Mother.* See Smith, *The Epicurean Inscription,* 559–60. See also D. Clay, review of Smith, *Thirteen New Fragments, AJP* 97 (1976): 309; and Marcello Gigante, *Scetticismo e Epicureismo* (Naples, 1981), 186. In chapter 3 I mention the possibility that fr. 127 may belong to the *Letter to Mother* after all.

73. *P. Herc.* 1427, col. 7.18–29. This passage is discussed by David Sedley, "Philosophical Allegiance in the Greco-Roman World," in *Philosophia Togata: Essays on Philosophy and Roman Society* (Oxford, 1989), 97–119; and by Asmis, "Philodemus' Epicureanism," 2401.

A further contrast between philosophy, on the one hand, and rhetoric and sophistry, on the other, is implicit elsewhere in the inscription. In a fragment from the introduction to the *Ethics* (fr. 29 = Ch fr. 24), Diogenes writes:

col. I   . . . τὸ φιλο
            [σο]φεῖν μεταδιώκου-
            [σ]ιν ὡς ἤτοι παρ' ἰδι-
            ωτῶν ποριούμενοι
      5   ταῦτα ἢ βασιλέων, οἷς
            μέγα τι καὶ τείμιον
            κτῆμα φιλοσοφία
            πεπίστευται. οὐχ ἵ-
            να οὖν τι τῶν εἰρη-
      10   μένων καὶ ἡμεῖν γέ-
            νηται, πρὸς τὴν αὐ-
            τὴν ὡρμήσαμεν πρᾶ-
            ξιν, ἀλλ' ὅπως εὐδαι-
            μονήσωμεν τὸ ἐπι-

col. II   ζητούμενον ὑπὸ τῆς
            φύσεως κτησάμενοι
            τέλος. τί δ' ἐστὶ τοῦ-
            το, ὅτι τε μήτε πλοῦ-
      5   τος αὐτὸ δύναται
            παρασχεῖν μήτε δό-
            ξα πολειτική, μήτε
            βασιλεία μήθ' ἁβρο-
            δίαιτος βίος καὶ τρα-
      10   πεζῶν πολυτέλεια
            μήτ' ἀφροδεισίων
            ἐγλελεγμένων ἡδο-
            ναί, μήτ' ἄλλο μη-
            δέν, φιλοσοφία δὲ

col. III   περιπο[ιεῖν δύναται],
            ἡμεῖς [νῦν ἀποδείξο]-
            μεν ὅλ[ον προθέντες τὸ]
            πρόβλη[μα ὑμεῖν.]

[Many people] pursue philosophy for the sake of [wealth and glory], thinking they will obtain these things from private individuals or kings

who have decided that philosophy is some great and expensive posses-
sion. Not in pursuit of those things mentioned above have we hastened
toward that same study, but rather so that we might find happiness,
having achieved the object of life sought by nature. What this object is—
and that neither wealth can obtain it, nor political reputation, nor king-
ship, nor a life of luxury, nor a rich table, nor the pleasures of exotic
sexual activity, nor anything else, but that [only] philosophy can procure
it—this we now shall explain, putting the whole matter before you.]

Here too, in Diogenes' announcement that his dedication to philosophy is not
motivated by desire for money or glory, we find a manifestation of the rivalry
between sophists and philosophers.[74] Not all sources agree that the sophists' acceptance of payment for instruction and performance distinguished them from
philosophers, but this seems to have been the popular conception.[75] Even in the
fourth century C.E. Themistius could claim that by Platonic definition he was
not a sophist, because he never accepted fees.[76] Popular opinion seems also to
have held that all philosophers, regardless of their creed, must scorn wealth and
glory. The philosopher's rejection of money (especially large sums offered by
kings) was also a favorite theme for fictitious letters,[77] and the issue is often
raised by Diogenes Laertius, who records many illustrations of philosophers'
contempt for wealth[78] and frequently cites Onetor's essay "Whether a Wise
Man Will Make Money."

The controversy was fueled by charges that many sophists, beginning with
the "old sophists" of the "first" Sophistic of the fifth and fourth centuries, were
excessively mercenary.[79] In the second century, Lucian refers to his earlier
speaking career as a time when he "numbered among the highly paid sophists"
and received "a very large public payment for *rhetorike*" (*Apol.* 15). The ex-
travagant pay earned by sophists is often mentioned by Philostratus, who in-
forms us that Herodes Atticus gave the sophist Polemo an honorarium of one

---

74. Cf. fr. 154 (NF 49).

75. R. Jeuckens, *Plutarch von Chaeronea und die Rhetorik* (Strassburg, 1907), 47–54, argues
that sophists were by definition paid teachers or professors, but Aristides (*Defense of Rhetoric* 431)
implies that only base "hirelings" work for pay.

76. See Themistius *Or.* 21.26.260c, 345c. See also Wilmer Cave France, *The Emperor Julian's
Relation to the New Sophistic and Neo-Platonism* (London, 1896), 18.

77. See chapter 3.

78. See Hope, *The Book of Diogenes Laertius: Its Spirit and Its Method* (New York, 1930),
158.

79. Some sources seem not to make a distinction between "old" and "new" sophists. For example, Cynic epistles from the Second Sophistic make use of earlier Cynic criticism of classical
sophists. See K. Funk, "Untersuchungen über die lucianische Vita Demonactis," *Philologus* Suppl.
B 10 (1905–7): 590.

hundred fifty thousand drachmas for three declamations delivered in Athens (*VS* 538). Polemo was not satisfied with that sum and ultimately received instead two hundred fifty thousand drachmas, a sum equal to the annual salary of five hundred Roman legionnaires.[80]

Philostratus knows that the subject is touchy. He takes care both to defend the sophists' practice of accepting fees and to assert that his favorites were not overly greedy. According to Philostratus' account Scopelian charged entrance fees for his lectures on a sliding scale and championed endangered defendants gratis if they had no money (*VS* 519). Philostratus also reports that the sophist Lollianus had his students pay for a shipment of grain when the city was unable to cover the cost. He then repaid his students by giving back the fees for his lectures (*VS* 526–27). Philostratus' own teacher, Proclus of Naucratis, charged one hundred drachmas for each course but generously allowed his students to use his library (*VS* 604). Philostratus' apologetic purpose is especially evident when he reports that Protagoras was the first to charge fees for lectures, a practice Philostratus says is "not despicable, for we prize things we have to pay for more than things we get for free"(*VS* 495).

A Philosophical Voice

As befits such a vocal era, Diogenes' inscription is peppered with vocatives, some of which are addressed to Diogenes himself. This loquacious style may owe something to the influence of contemporary sophists, but in certain instances Diogenes deliberately affects a philosophical tone. In the *Letter to Antipater,* for example, when Diogenes shares with his friend the gist of a conversation he has had with a fellow Epicurean named Theodoridas of Lindos, he puts on display his own participation in a philosophical dialogue. Diogenes' self-conscious adoption of this philosophical style is apparent in his opening: "This is the sort of beginning our discourse had. . . ." (fr. 63, col. IV, lines 7–9 = Ch fr. 16, col. III, lines 7–9). Then the philosopher follows this introduction with: "'Diogenes,' Theodoridas said, 'that [sc. the doctrine] of Epicurus on the innumerability of the worlds is true . . ." [ὦ Διόγενες, ὁ Θεοδωρίδας εἶπεν, ὅτι μὲν ἀληθές ἐστιν τὸ Ἐπικούρῳ περὶ ἀπειρίας κόσμων . . .]. Other sections of the inscription contain passages in full dialogue form. Diogenes' treatise *On Old Age* (frr. 137–79 = Ch frr. 55–71 and various New Fragments), which is in extremely poor condition, clearly takes the form of a dialogue between an old man (Diogenes himself) and a group of young men. Another

---

80. Philostratus *VS* 538. See Habicht, *Pausanias' Guide,* 129 n. 53.

very small fragment (fr. 154 = NF 49) also records this scrap of dialogue: "If you yourself say, 'If then, Diogenes, not even in wealth is happiness ever found . . .'"[81]

The popularity of Plato during the second century ensured that Diogenes' contemporaries would consider the dialogue a philosophical genre, and the form was widely used for philosophical prose (by writers such as Dio Chrysostom) and for mock-philosophical works (by Lucian).[82] Diogenes' inscription also displays his competence in other philosophical styles: the epistle, the maxim, the epitome, and the philosopher's will. Although Diogenes' selection of these popular genres is worlds away from Lucretius' evocation of Empedocles and Parmenides, the choice is in some ways analogous: both Epicurean writers are claiming a place for the Garden in the realm of esteemed philosophical traditions. By adopting the contemporary genres popularly understood as "philosophical," Diogenes also draws an even clearer boundary line between himself and the sophists.

Diogenes' mentor Epicurus may have been the first Greek philosopher to write treatises in epistolary form, but in Diogenes' era letters in circulation included those ascribed to "Socrates," "Diogenes the Cynic," and "Pythagoras."[83] Readers who were aware that such letters were unauthentic seem to have been unperturbed, and the letter was chosen as a medium by many of Diogenes' philosophical contemporaries. Thus in good philosophical style, Diogenes records his *Letter to Antipater* (frr. 62–67 = Ch frr. 15–20),[84] *Letter to Friends* (fr. 122 = Ch fr. 51), and *Letter to Mother* (frr. 125–26 = Ch frr. 52–53). More fragmentary letters are also found in fragments 68 and 128 (NF 58 and 110). The *Letter to Antipater* is particularly telling because Diogenes not only imitates Epicurus and Greek philosophers in general by using the epistolary form but also makes repeated references to other letters that have been passed around his circle of Epicureans.

The Epicurean *Kyriai Doxai* are so prominent in the extant Epicurean corpus that we sometimes forget that the sayings of many philosophers were in

---

81. See Smith, *The Epicurean Inscription,* 421.

82. The two books Dio is said to have carried with him when he was exiled were Demosthenes' *On the False Embassy* and Plato's *Phaedo* (Philostratus *VS* 488)—an eclectic selection indicative of the taste of the era. On Plato's readers, see De Lacy, "Plato and the Intellectual Life of the Second Century A.D.," and M.B. Trapp, "Plato's *Phaedrus* in Second-Century Greek Literature," both in *Antonine Literature,* ed. D.A. Russell (Oxford, 1990), 141–74; and see J. Whittaker, "Platonic Philosophy in the Early Centuries of the Empire," *ANRW* II 36.1 (1987): 81–123. On the sophists' reaction to Plato's condemnation of classical "sophists," see De Lacy, 9–10.

83. See chapter 3.

84. Chilton also includes two more very small fragments in this text (frr. 21–22).

circulation in antiquity. Diogenes Laertius, for example, includes such sayings in his accounts of each philosopher's life and works and often refers to the problem that some sayings had been attributed to more than one man. He found that μηδὲν ἄγαν, for example, was ascribed to several of the Seven Sages.[85] Other biographers sometimes used collections of sayings as the backbone of a philosopher's biography, but maxims were also transmitted in collections that offered no accompanying narrative.[86] One such collection was the *Sayings of Pythagoras,* which Galen claims to have read and recited aloud twice a day.[87] In keeping with current philosophical convention and recognized Epicurean practice, Diogenes of Oenoanda preserves a collection of Epicurus' *Kyriai Doxai* and another collection of aphorisms that Diogenes himself composed.[88]

Two other significant genres used by Diogenes are the epitome and the philosopher's will. Epitomes had always been used by Epicureans but had come to be used by other schools as well. One second-century example is the epitome of Hierocles the Stoic; many others are cited by Diogenes Laertius.[89] Although the epitome was not an exclusively philosophical form (some works from all literary forms were reduced to epitomes in the second century), Diogenes seems to be imitating Epicurus when he entitles one of his works "Diogenes of Oenoanda, on Feelings and Actions . . . an Epitome" (fr. 28 = Ch fr. 23). Epicurus himself refers to the *Letter to Herodotus* as an "epitome" and apparently compiled epitomes of his own, *Against the Physicists* and another work his followers called "The Great Epitome."

---

85. 1.41. Elsewhere he mentions sayings that were attributed to two philosophers: for example, one saying was attributed to Aristippus and Diogenes (1.78), another to Aristippus and Plato (1.82), and another to Aristotle and Diogenes (5.18).

86. Lucian parades the former type of biography in his *Demonax,* which includes fifty-five sayings of Demonax. The *Gnomologium Vaticanum,* ed. L. Sternbach (reprint, Berlin, 1963) provides an example of maxims preserved without a narrative. See also H. Chadwick, "Florilegium," *Reallexikon für Antike und Christentum* 7 (1969): 1131–60. For the combination of maxims and biographical sketch, see F. Wehrli, "Gnome, Anekdote und Biographie," *MusHelv* 30 (1973): 193–208.

87. See Galen *On the Passions and Errors of the Soul* 6. For the Pythagorean sayings, see H. Chadwick, *The Sentences of Sextus* (Cambridge, 1959).

88. The *Kyriai Doxai* are written in large letters in one continuous line, but the "Various Maxims" are written in columns. One recently discovered maxim in the latter collection (fr. 116 = NF 81) ends with the words "we turned so many writings to stone for you," which shows that the collection must be Diogenes' own. See Smith, "Fifty-Five New Fragments," 69–71.

89. On the epitomizing trend in the second century, see B.E. Perry, "Literature in the Second Century," *CJ* 50 (1955): 298. B.P. Reardon notes: "The second century is the age of extracts, of collections, of florilegia; the culture of the drugstore paperback" ("The Second Sophistic and the Novel," in *Approaches to the Second Sophistic* ed. G.W. Bowersock [University Park, Pa., 1974], 28).

Also indicative of Diogenes' desire to portray himself as a philosopher is his publication of his own will, the opening segment of which has survived as fragment 117 (Ch fr. 50).[90] We know from Diogenes Laertius that many philosophers' wills (including that of Epicurus) were of interest to ancient readers; Laertius uses such wills to conclude some of his biographical sketches. While it is quite possible that some wills in circulation may have been fictional, the wills Laertius records have been generally accepted as authentic documents, because they contain neither significant amounts of philosophical posturing nor material that can be associated with the surviving anecdotal traditions. Although it is not known how or why so many wills were preserved, it is possible that they were saved by the individual philosophical schools and only later became of interest to the doxographers. Since Diogenes' will is so fragmentary, it is difficult to know whether he had it inscribed primarily to conform (prematurely) to a pattern that his readers would understand as "philosophical" or whether the will also contained information that would be especially relevant to its readers at the stoa in Oenoanda.

Since imitation of ancient Greek traditions was so important in his age, Diogenes of Oenoanda's self-conscious use of contemporary philosophical genres reveals both his desire to emulate a Greek philosopher and his attempts at self-definition. Even his choice of vocabulary and morphology may be relevant here: unlike many of the sophists, he does not atticize.[91] In this regard Diogenes may have again taken Epicurus as his particular model. Epicurus himself did not use the "pure" Attic dialect so esteemed in the second century. Throughout the inscription, Diogenes does not imitate Epicurus only, nor does he simply deliver Epicurean wisdom: by using letters, maxims, dialogues, epitomes, and his will, he also succeeds in developing a voice that his audience would identify as "philosophical." Thus, Diogenes displays all the trappings of a philosopher in such a way that one suspects that the man himself was also equipped with the proverbial beard and walking stick.[92]

This is not to say that the superficial markings of a philosopher were Diogenes' main concern in his self-presentation. To the contrary, Diogenes

---

90. Departing from the practice of Diogenes' previous editors, who have all regarded this fragment as a will, Smith simply titles the fragment "Directions to Family and Friends" (*The Epicurean Inscription,* 546).

91. See Hoffman, "Diogenes of Oenoanda," 66. Hoffman identifies Diogenes' prose with Norden's Asianic "pretty style" (*die zierliche Stilart*). See E. Norden, *Die antike Kunstprosa,* 5th ed. (Stuttgart, 1958), 134. Since the sophists did not all try to affect an Attic dialect, however, Diogenes' Asiatic rhythms and word order do not necessarily set him apart.

92. See Lucian *The Eunuch* 9 and *Demonax* 13. See also D. Clay, "Lucian of Samosata: Four Philosophical Lives (Nigrinus, Demonas, Peregrinus, Alexander Pseudomantis)," *ANRW* II 36.5 (1992): 3414–15.

aspires throughout the inscription to present his whole life as a model philosophical existence. This is entirely in keeping with the popular conception of
what it meant to be a philosopher in Diogenes' era. Diogenes was convinced of
the truth of the teachings of the Garden, but his readers' judgment of his philosophical credentials was more likely to be based on their understanding of his
actual behavior than on the quality of his presentation of Epicurean doctrine. In
the second-century world a true philosopher would be recognized not by his ad-
vocacy of a particular philosophical system but by his lifestyle. The main cre-
dential was an austere manner of life that involved the rejection of wealth,
fame, and power; also necessary was the philosophers' willingness and ability
to deliver frank criticism whenever society needed correction.[93]

We have already seen that Diogenes embodied the philosophers' rejection
of worldly riches and fame (see fr. 29 = Ch fr. 24), thus fulfilling his contemporaries' expectations of good philosophical deportment while also proving
himself to be an exemplary Epicurean. We shall also see that Diogenes names
his contemporaries' need for frank instruction (which he describes as Epicurean
medicine for their ills) as the impetus behind his creation of the inscription (see
frr. 2–3 = Ch frr. 1–2). Diogenes presents himself, moreover, as quite willing to
offer his advice on a personal basis in his daily life (see fr. 3 [Ch fr. 4], cols. III
and IV) or to shout it out to the world at large (see fr. 32 [Ch fr. 54], col. II, line
13). Having met these general "philosophical" requirements, Diogenes also
demonstrates that he is more than an expounder of Epicureanism; he is the embodiment of an Epicurean life.

An important aspect of his life as a true Epicurean is the affection Diogenes
expresses toward his friends and companions in philosophy: Theodoridas,
Antipater, Menneas, Dionysius, Carus and his "other friends" in Athens, Chalcis, and Thebes (see fr. 62 = Ch 15), as well as in Rhodes (see fr. 122 =
Ch 51).[94] These friends (including an unnamed woman in Rhodes who took him
in when he was ill) reciprocate by showing compassion and concern for Diogenes. Even his readers at the stoa in Oenoanda are addressed as dear friends
(e.g., as ὦ φίλοι at fr. 21 [NF 40], col. III, line 14 and as ὦ φίλτατοι at fr. 119
[NF 18], col. I, line 7). Perhaps the most important emblem of Diogenes' practice of Epicureanism, however, is his attitude toward his own illness and (possibly impending) death. Being full of faith in Epicurus' teaching that extreme

93. See Clay, "Lucian of Samosata," 3411–14; and J. Hahn, *Der Philosoph und die Gesellschaft: Selbstverständnis, öffentliches Auftreten und populäre Erwartungen in der hohen Kaiserzeit*
(Stuttgart, 1989).

94. Clay ("Lucian of Samosata," 3441) describes how Lucian portrays the Epicurean Celsus in
Alexander the False Prophet as "the perfect Epicurean."

pain cannot last long, Diogenes is able to maintain a calm and untroubled attitude toward his illness (see frr. 121 [NF 23] and 122 [Ch fr. 51]), and having no fear of "Tityuses and Tantaluses," Diogenes is able to laugh at death itself (see fr. 73 = Ch fr. 14). As a final proof of his philosophical life, Diogenes even uses his own will as an opportunity to deliver Epicurean wisdom about the proper attitude toward illness and death: "If I survive, I shall accept with pleasure the life granted to me, but if I do not survive [death is nothing to me]" (fr. 117).[95]

Diogenes' inscription also projects this personal and daily embodiment of the philosophical life back on the life of Epicurus himself. The most salient example of this second-century representation of a conventionally "philosophical" Epicurus appears in the *Letter to Mother* (frr. 125–26 = Ch frr. 52–53), which is discussed in chapter 3 of this study. A more recently discovered fragment that affords us another example of Diogenes' interweaving of the biographical and the philosophical is fragment 72 (NF 7), which describes in vivid detail Epicurus' travails during a shipwreck. Although he was "lacerated through having fallen upon sea-gnawed rocks," and although he lay on the shore for two days, "spent by hunger and his wounds," Epicurus managed to survive.[96] The philosophical disposition on display here in the text as we have it is Epicurus' attitude toward chance (τύχη): as this example from the life of Epicurus demonstrates, chance can "but rarely" harm a wise person; for chance "seldom impedes the wise person" whose life is directed not by τύχη but by reason (fr. 71 = NF 8).[97]

A Cosmopolitan Age

μία πάντων πατρίς ἐστιν ἡ πᾶσα γῆ καὶ εἶς ὁ κόσμος οἶκος.
—Diogenes of Oenoanda fr. 30 = Ch fr. 25

Truly re-creating the past was of course impossible in the second century: despite this celebration of Hellenism the emperor remained Roman and the Hellenized towns and cities of Asia Minor still belonged to Roman provinces. In addition to the Roman administrative structure, signs of Roman culture

---

95. Smith (*The Epicurean Inscription*, 547) cites the *Letter to Menoeceus* (125–26) as a parallel for Diogenes' statement here. Diogenes' inclusion of this message, "which is unlikely to have formed the preamble to his actual will," causes Smith to reject the idea that fr. 117 is meant to be a will at all.

96. Smith, *The Epicurean Inscription*, 402. On the history of interpretation of this fragment, see Smith, 519.

97. Cf. *Principal Doctrine* 16 as recorded by Diogenes Laertius. Diogenes of Oenoanda quotes a version of that doctrine in this fragment.

inevitably appeared. Even Oenoanda had gladiatorial shows, Roman baths, and citizens who proudly displayed Roman names.[98] Rather than hindering the Greek renaissance, however, Roman domination of the Greek-speaking world seems to have contributed to its growth. Faced with Roman control, Rome's Greek-speaking subjects felt compelled to protect their Hellenic identity: their response to the Roman political empire was to create a Greek cultural empire.[99] Diogenes' promulgation of Epicureanism (and the growth of Epicureanism in the second century in general) is an important element of this wider pattern of resistance to Roman culture. Of all the Greek philosophies, the Romans had embraced Stoicism and made it their own, and in the early and high empire Stoicism sat very comfortably with Roman imperialism.[100] It is against the Stoics that much of the Epicurean polemic in Diogenes' inscription is directed.

The Greek renaissance itself did not necessarily represent militant opposition to Rome.[101] Anti-Roman sentiment is discernible in some sources, and open dissidence was especially prevalent in Greek centers like Alexandria, but many second-century classicists expressed wholehearted approval of Rome. Aelius Aristides, for example, honored Cyzicus, Corinth, Athens, Rhodes, and Smyrna with panegyrics but wrote one of his finest for Rome (though it was exclusively *Hellenic* and contained not a single Roman name). To some extent the cities even used Greek cultural offerings to attract the emperors and court their favor.[102] Rome often responded favorably; the philhellenic Hadrian was perhaps the greatest supporter of the Greek renaissance.

---

98. When Licinius Longus (second century C.E.) was elected Lyciarch he presented gladiatorical spectacles to Oenoanda; see D. Magie, *Roman Rule in Asia Minor,* 2 vols. (Princeton, 1950), 534. Licinius Longus seems to have been a relative of Diogenes; see Shelagh Jameson, "Two Lycian Families," *AS* 16 (1966): 125–37.

99. Aelius Aristides' panegyric of Athens describes this well. See Anderson's remarks on the era's "self-confident Hellenism" (*Philostratus,* 8).

100. On Stoicism and the philhellenic emperors, see P.A. Brunt, "Stoicism and the Principate," *Papers of the British School at Rome* 43 (1975): 7–35. On the Stoics as Lucian's "favorite butts," see C.P. Jones, *Lucian,* 28–29. Lucian has the Stoic Hermotimus say that he chose Stoicism because he saw "most people" choosing it, so he decided it must be the best (*Hermotimus* 16). On Stoicism's gradual shift toward acceptance and even promotion of Roman imperialism, see A. Erskine, *The Hellenistic Stoa: Political Thought and Action* (Ithaca, N.Y., 1990).

101. This subject has provoked much disagreement. See the preceding note and R. MacMullen, *Enemies of the Roman Order* (Cambridge, Mass., 1966), 189, 244; C.P. Jones, *Plutarch and Rome* (Oxford, 1971), 126–30; and B. Frischer, *The Sculpted Word* (Berkeley, 1982), 186–92.

On Pausanias' animosity toward Rome, see Habicht, *Pausanias' Guide,* 119–25. On Greek "martyrs" and anti-Roman pamphlets in Alexandria, see C.P. Jones, *The Roman World of Dio Chrysostom* (Cambridge, 1978), 38 and 125.

102. During the second century, the emperor was sometimes so mobile that he was becoming "a sort of moving capital of the empire in himself" (F. Millar, *The Emperor in the Roman World* [London, 1977], 3). Cities visited by the emperor were likely to obtain benefits from him, although

Citizenship in the Greek cultural empire seems to have been open to anyone well-read enough to desire it. The Greek revival was promoted by real Athenians, such as Herodes Atticus, but was embraced with equal enthusiasm by people with dubious or tenuous claims to Greekness, such as Lucian, who tells us he was Syrian (his mother tongue may have been Aramaic). People on the fringes of the Greek world seem to have been especially energetic in their cultivation of Greek literature and values.[103] Dio Chrysostom reports of the people of Borysthenes in Pontus: "Although they no longer speak Greek clearly because they live among Barbarians, they all know at least the *Iliad* by heart" (*Or.* 36.9). Often such peoples took care to establish legitimate links to the Greek world through foundation legends. Tarsus, for example, downplayed its eastern connections, traced its descent from Heracles (or Perseus), and claimed to have been founded by Argives.[104] Less creativity was required of towns that could discover ready-made ancestors in Homer. This brings us back to Lycia, where cities with Semitic origins named their demes after Bellerophon and Sarpedon.[105] The Oenoandans—situated on the edge of Lycia, at the crossroads between Pisidia, Phrygia, Lydia, and Caria—could find no Homeric connection, but the family to which Diogenes seems to have belonged traced its ancestry back to Sparta.[106] The city as a whole also claimed Apollo as its ancestral god.[107]

While many were eager to establish Greek lineage or to locate their ancestors in Greek texts, being ethnically Hellenic seems not to have been a prerequisite. Non-Greeks were meant to be denied official membership in Hadrian's Panhellenion, but even there ingenuity counted: ethnically diverse Cibyra (a city to the north of Oenoanda) was admitted even though it was not

---

sometimes the cities and towns seem to have spent more on the emperor than they received. See also Millar, 28–40.

103. C.P. Jones writes on Tarsus: "For a city like Tarsus the craving for Hellenic credentials was made all the keener by its proximity to the Orient" (*Roman World,* 75). See also F. Millar's comments on Heliodorus the "Arab" sophist in "P. Herennius Dexippus: The Greek World and the Third-Century Invasions," *JRS* 59 (1969): 12–13.

104. See C.P. Jones, *Roman World,* 72; and Louis Robert, "Documents d'Asie Mineure," *BCH* 101 (1977): 88–132. On Nicaea's "discovery" of Hellenic origins, see Jones, 89.

105. See A.H.M. Jones, *The Greek City* (Oxford, 1940), 49. Even the name *Lycia* was Greek. See also A.H.M. Jones, *The Cities of the Eastern Roman Provinces* (Oxford, 1971), 96.

106. Spartan ancestry is claimed in the early third-century inscription of Licinia Flavilla (*IGR* iii 500); Cleander, the Spartan mentioned in the inscription, was also the alleged founder of nearby Kibyra. See Hall, "Who Was Diogenes of Oenoanda?" *JHS* 99 (1979): 160–63. Pedigrees were frequently traced back to the classical age even in Attica itself; Herodes Atticus claimed Miltiades as his ancestor. See Habicht, *Pausanias' Guide,* 127.

107. See the frequent mentions of Apollo in the inscription published by Wörrle in *Stadt und Fest.*

until the second or third century that it became "a colony of the Lacedaemonians and related to the Athenians," a claim that was recorded on stone in Oenoanda.[108] Aristides alluded to these open borders in the opening of his *Panathenaic Oration* when he reminded the Athenians that they were regarded as "foster parents" to anyone who could "somehow be classified as Greek." In general, the enthusiasm for Hellenism seems not to have engendered xenophobia; the cities of the Greek East were remarkably open and hospitable to foreigners.[109] Philostratus, in his praise of Smyrna, says about the ideal city:

> A city which is much frequented by foreigners, especially if they are lovers of learning, will be prudent and moderate in its councils, and prudent and moderate in its citizen assemblies, because it will be on its guard against being convicted of wrongdoing in the presence of so many eminent persons; and it will take good care of its temples, gymnasia, fountains and porticoes, so that it may appear to meet the needs of that multitude.[110]

According to Philostratus, many foreign visitors poured into the cities to hear the sophists. Heracleides the Lycian, for example, attracted to Smyrna the youth not only of mainland Greece, Ionia, Lydia, Phrygia, and Caria but also of the East and Egypt. "Thus he filled Smyrna with a brilliant throng, and he benefited the city in several other ways too" (*VS* 613).

Diogenes espoused the cosmopolitanism of his contemporaries and thus promoted an openness unprecedented in the history of Epicureanism. In fragment 3 (Ch fr. 2) Diogenes says that it is "philanthropic" to give Epicurean teachings to "strangers"; and in fragment 32 (Ch fr. 26), where Diogenes announces that pleasure is "the great end of the best way of life," he shouts his message to "all Greeks and barbarians" (col. II, lines 11–12). Then, in fragment 30 (Ch fr. 25), where Diogenes announces that the Oenoanda inscription is intended also for those whom some would call *foreigners,* it becomes clear that by "foreigners" he means not only people beyond the borders of Oenoanda, Lycia, or the Greek-speaking world but strangers throughout the globe.

---

108. *IGR* iii, 500. See Spawforth and Walker, "The World of the Panhellenion," 82. According to Strabo (13.4.17), Greek was only one of four languages spoken at Cibyra; many of its inhabitants spoke Pisidian, Solymian, or Lydian.

109. A xenophobic backlash against the more prevalent second-century attitudes appears in the proem to Diogenes Laertius' *Lives and Opinions of Eminent Philosophers,* which contains a polemic against writers who trace the origins of Greek philosophy to Egypt and the East. See Pamela Gordon, "On *Black Athena:* Ancient Critiques of the 'Ancient Model' of Greek History," *Classical World* 87 (1993): 71–72.

110. *VS* 613; trans. W.C. Wright, *Philostratus* (Cambridge, Mass., 1921).

col. I
12   . . . οὐ ⟨χ⟩ ἥκιστα δέ
      [δὴ ἐπ]ράττομεν
      [ταυτε]ῖι διὰ τοὺς

col. II   καλουμένους μὲν
          ξένους, οὐ μήν γε ὄν-
          τας. καθ’ ἑκάστην
          μὲν γάρ ἀποτομὴν
5   τῆς γῆς ἄλλων ἄλλη
          πατρίς ἐστιν, κατὰ δὲ
          τὴν ὅλην περιοχὴν
          τοῦδε τοῦ κόσμου μί-
          α πάντων πατρίς ἐσ-
10   τιν ἡ πᾶσα γῆ καὶ εἷς
          ὁ κόσμος οἶκος.

[. . . and not least we did [this] for those who are called foreigners, though they are not really so. For, while the various segments of the earth give different people a different country, the whole compass of this world gives all people a single country, the entire earth, and a single home, the world.][111]

This "warm supranationalism"[112] may be attributable to Stoic influence (as some have suggested), but it accords well with the cosmopolitan values expressed in contemporary nonphilosophical sources. Epicurus, however, would not have approved: according to Clement of Alexandria, Epicurus claimed that only the Greeks are capable of philosophy.[113] A bit of Epicurus' Hellenocentric outlook may be discernible, however, when Diogenes announces that his message is for "all Greeks and foreigners" (βάρβαροι). One wonders whether Rome was excluded or was cast among the unnamed barbarians.

An Epicurean Benefaction

To welcome "the world," the cities depended on the lavish gifts of private individuals. In his narration of anecdotes and colorful data about the sophists' lives,

---

111. Trans. Smith, *The Epicurean Inscription,* 381.

112. J. Ferguson, "Epicureanism under the Roman Empire," *ANRW* II 36.4 (1990): 2292.

113. *Strom.* 1.15. Clement contrasts Epicurus' contemptuous attitude toward "barbarians" with Plato's admiration for Egyptian wisdom. The conviction that Greek was the only language capable of intellectual precision seems to have led Philodemus (*De Dis* 3.4.4–6, p. 37 Diels) to claim that

Philostratus frequently portrays them as the donors of great benefactions.[114] Their gifts ranged from emergency earthquake relief and grain to aqueducts, libraries, theaters, and endowments for festivals. In Ephesus the sophist Damianus supported the poor, restored public buildings, and built a stoa that stretched from town to the temple of Artemis so that worshipers would not be hindered by the rain.[115] In Smyrna, the city that "sacrificed to the Muses of the sophists" more than did any other city (*VS* 613), the sophist Nicetes built a structure connecting the town center with the city gates, and the sophist Heracleides of Lycia donated a golden-roofed oil fountain for the gymnasium of Asclepius (see *VS* 511, 613). The most spectacular benefactions in Greece and Asia Minor were made by the sophist Herodes Atticus.[116] Often such benefactions were made while the sophist served as local magistrate or priest, but even some sophists who held no office gave generously. Their gifts enhanced their own prestige and that of their cities.[117] Some sophists resisted the role of benefactor, however. Philostratus and Cassius Dio relate how the sophist Favorinus petitioned Hadrian for immunity from serving as high priest, and in his own *Sacred Tales* Aelius Aristides describes his perennial efforts to avoid holding office and undertaking the financial obligations that accompanied most posts.

Philostratus writes as though it were common knowledge that the most important private benefactors were sophists. Following Philostratus' lead, recent scholarship has also connected benefactions with this particular group.[118] If the granting of benefactions could indeed be identified as an activity peculiar to the sophists, we would have clear evidence that Diogenes engaged in an activity more characteristic of a sophist than of a philosopher. It appears that Philostratus has misled us, however.[119] When inscriptional evidence is taken into account the picture changes: the sophists, being only one species "of the genus

---

Greek was the language of the gods. Epicurus' labeling of the Cyzicenes as "enemies of Greece" may also be evidence of his chauvinism, if it is true, as some have suggested, that Epicurus objected to their interest in Babylonian astronomy. See David Sedley, "Epicurus and His Professional Rivals," in *Etudes sur l'Epicurisme antique,* ed. Jean Bollack and André Laks (Lille, 1976), 139.

114. E.g., see *VS* 511, 568, 613. On benefactions in the empire in general, see A.H.M. Jones, *The Greek City,* 247–250; and Paul Veyne, *Le pain et le cirque: Sociologie historique d'un pluralisme politique* (Paris, 1976) 539–730. On legal aspects of benefaction, see D. Johnston, "Munificence and *Municipia:* Bequests to Towns in Classical Roman Law," *JRS* 65 (1985): 105–25.

115. See Philostratus *VS* 605. Philodemus calls the structure a stoa; we may think of it as a colonnaded street.

116. See P. Graindor, *Un milliardaire antique, Herode Atticus et sa famille* (Cairo, 1930).

117. On the social function of benefactions, see Peter Brown, *The Making of Late Antiquity* (Cambridge, Mass., 1978), especially 36.

118. See Bowersock, *Sophists,* 26–28.

119. On Philostratus' credibility in general, see C.P. Jones, "The Reliability of Philostratus," 11–16.

Greek aristocrat," are outnumbered by benefactors who do not appear to have been sophists.[120] We can imagine, however, that the sophists were the loudest, most visible benefactors. Philostratus was not the first to publicize their generosity; the sophists' touting of their own construction projects must have spurred the wealthy in their audiences to compete. Most important, even when Philostratus' zeal to glorify his sophists is taken into account the chronological link remains: Diogenes' era saw a revival both of Greek culture and of the Greek city. Much of the necessary construction was carried out through private funds, and Diogenes' stoa was presumably no exception.

When Diogenes presents his stoa to Oenoanda his self-proclaimed aim is to help people through the teachings of Epicurus. Diogenes distinguishes his from the ordinary benefactions routinely made by priests and magistrates by asserting that he offers the inscribed teachings in good Epicurean manner "while not engaging in politics" (οὐ πολειτευόμενος [fr. 3 (Ch fr. 2), col. I, lines 4–5]). In the poorly preserved third column of fragment 2 (Ch fr. 3), he also suggests that his gift is a salutary alternative to the more lavish offerings of his contemporaries.

col. III

```
         τὸν [μὲν κενὸν φό-]
5    βον ἐκ θ[ανάτου τὸν δ' ἐκ]
     τῶν θε[ῶν φημὶ πολλοὺς]
     ἡμῶν κα[τέχειν, τὸ δὲ ποιη]-
     τικὸν τῆ[ς τῷ ὄντι τει]-
     μίας χαρᾶ[ς οὐκ εἶναι θέα]-
10   τρα καὶ ν[—— καὶ]
     βαλανεῖα [καὶ μύρα]
     καὶ ἀλείμ[ματα, ἃ δὴ κα]-
     ταλελοίπ[αμεν τοῖς]
     πλήθεσιν, ἀ[λλὰ τὴν | φυσιολογίαν]. . . .
```

[I declare that the [vain] fear of [death and that] of the [gods grip many] of us, [and that] joy [of real value is generated not by theatres] and [. . . and] baths [and perfumes] and ointments, [which we] have left to [the] masses, [but by natural science. . . .][121]

Since Diogenes mentions baths (apparently among other luxuries), it is tempting to imagine that Diogenes envisioned himself as a rival to Opramoas of Rhodiapolis, the benefactor who gave (among many other gifts) an especially

120. See Bowie, "The Importance of Sophists," 53 and 30.
121. This is Smith's translation of the restored text (*The Epicurean Inscription,* 367).

large and impressive bath building to Oenoanda after the destructive earthquake of 141 C.E.[122]

Diogenes' role as a benefactor should not be viewed in this eccentric Epicurean sense only. An unusual architectural feature of the inscription demonstrates
that the stoa was designed for the inscription; thus, the building itself was part
of Diogenes' gift.[123] As an example of civic architecture, Diogenes' stoa fits the
well-established pattern of benefactions made for a city's enrichment and beau-
tification. Stoas were considered to be especially appropriate benefactions.
For centuries they had provided space for activities ranging from philosophical discussions to the sale of market goods and the posting of decrees.[124] In
second-century Asia Minor the city was the center of cultural life, and even the
smallest cities strove to provide an urban center conducive to intellectual and
social interaction.[125] A stoa of monumental proportions, offering protection
from rain and sun, was indispensable. Moreover, the stoa was particularly appropriate for a philhellenic context because it was a quintessentially Greek
building.[126]

A Philosopher in a Sophists' World

The preeminence of the second-century sophists helps explain why Diogenes
chose to display the tenets of Epicureanism on the walls of a stoa in Oenoanda.

122. See Clay, "A Lost Epicurean Community," 320. While this date is later than the Hadrianic
date recently suggested for Diogenes (see my introduction), it is not necessarily incompatible with
the approximate dating suggested by the similarity between the lettering of the Demostheneia inscription and Diogenes' inscription. The baths were built over fifteen years after the Demostheneia
was established, but it seems plausible that a stonecutter who was active in 124 would still be working in 141.

123. See Clay, "The Philosophical Inscription," 2463, for this unusual feature (a scored margin
that projects from the stoa wall and separates the treatise *On Old Age* from the rest of the inscription). That Diogenes presented the building itself and not just the inscription seems more likely
than Chilton's first conjecture that Diogenes "must . . . have had to obtain permission from the
magistrates and town council to carve his message on the wall" (*Diogenes of Oenoanda: The
Fragments* [Oxford, 1971], xxi). For other benefactions in Oenoanda, cf. the complex with the
enigmatic name of *boukonisterion* that was dedicated "to Septimius Severus in place of the office
of *elaiothesia*" by another Diogenes; and the festival established by M. Aurelius Artemon and his
wife Polykleia. See J.J. Coulton, "Oinoanda: The Agora," *AS* 34 (1986): 80, 88. For the *philotimia*
of C. Iulius Demosthenes in Oenoanda, see Wörrle, *Stadt und Fest.*

124. On the multiple uses of stoas, the frequent mentions of stoas in lists of a city's amenities,
and the naming of stoas after the benefactor, see J.J. Coulton, *The Architectural Development of the
Greek Stoa* (Oxford, 1976), 8–13. For stoas as benefactions, see C.P. Jones, *Roman World,* 110–14.

125. A city with the proper amenities could also hope to attract tourists or perhaps an imperial
visit. See Millar, *Emperor,* 375 ff.

126. Coulton writes: "Indeed the stoa became something of a hallmark of the Greek way of life"
(*Architectural Development,* 1).

Perhaps deliberate competition with the sophists was his goal. But it is more likely that he was responding to a convention set by the sophists: intellectual activity was meant to be a public event. The doctor Galen understood this; he adopted the sophists' style and attracted huge crowds for his disquisitions on anatomy.[127] A society in which people enjoyed gathering in theaters to hear sophists argue about fifth-century Athenian imperialism or the crossing of the Hellespont also provided a social context for the public (and monumental) display of a philosophical handbook. Furthermore, if silent reading was truly such a rarity in antiquity, visitors to Diogenes' stoa would have participated in a performance of its own kind.

The sophistic style of speaking is also discernible in Diogenes' inscription. Some sections are written as though they were orations: the limestone blocks address an assembled crowd (ὦ ἄνδρες, ὦ φίλοι, ἄνθρωπε, etc.)[128] and exhort it to take up philosophy. Diogenes may even have presented some passages orally before they were copied onto papyrus rolls and inscribed on the stoa wall. Since he wrote in an era when sophists could not be avoided and when rhetoric dominated the educational system, it was natural for him to adopt the style of a public speaker.

Closer affinities with the sophistic mode of performance are especially clear in Diogenes' introduction to the entire inscription (frr. 2–3 = Ch frr. 1–2)[129] and in his introduction to *On Ethics* (frr. 29–30 = Ch frr. 24–25). It was usual for a sophist to preface a performance with an ostensibly informal and conversational proem called a *proagon* or *prolalia*.[130] Although few sophistic introductions are extant, the casual tone and relaxed pace of the *prolaliai* are clear from references to the fact that many sophists gave these preliminary speeches while sitting down and then rose to deliver their formal orations.[131] The informality was a rhetorical ploy designed to disarm the audience; the sophist did not actually relax his vigilance.

These introductions, which Philostratus considers essential to any good oration, preceded most formal speeches, including declamations and encomiums. They gave the celebrity a chance not only to warm up the audience but to indulge in some elaborate self-presentation. Achieving the right combination of

---

127. See Bowersock, *Sophists,* 71–72, 74, and (on the professional title *iatrosophistes*) 67.

128. The vocatives quoted appear as follows: ἄνθρωπε in fr. 3 (Ch fr. 2), col. III, line 9; ὦ ἄνδρες in fr. 32 (Ch fr. 26) col. I, line 6, ὦ φίλοι in fr. 21 (NF 40), col. III, line 14 through col. IV, line 1.

129. For full quotation, see chapter 2.

130. See Graham Anderson, *The Second Sophistic: A Cultural Phenomenon in the Roman Empire* (London and New York, 1993), 53–55; D.A. Russell, *Greek Declamation* (Cambridge, 1983), 77–79; and H.G. Nesselrath, "Lucian's Introductions," in *Antonine Literature,* ed. D.A. Russell (Oxford, 1990), 111–40. Philostratus usually calls these introductions *dialexeis* or simply *prooimia*.

131. See Aristides *Or.* 51.33. See also Russell, *Greek Declamation,* 77.

personal promotion and respectful homage to the audience seems to have been especially challenging for foreign sophists visiting Athens. Philostratus writes with approval of Polemo's proem to his oration at the dedication ceremony for the Olympieion—the theme of Polemo's introduction was the divine inspiration of his own speech (see *VS* 533). He also admires a suave introductory speech by Alexander of Cilicia that combined an apology for so long delaying his first visit to Athens with an introductory performance that was "like an epitome of a Panathenaic oration" (*VS* 572). Philostratus disapproves, however, of a proem of Philagrus of Cilicia ("the most volatile and hot-tempered of the sophists" [*VS* 579]) that was considered disjointed and childish because the sophist inserted a eulogy for his own wife into his praise of Athens (see *VS* 579). According to Philostratus, Herodes Atticus had warned Philagrus that the purpose of the proem was to win the goodwill of the audience, but Philagrus either did not understand or chose to ignore that advice (see *VS* 579). By the time he launched into his formal oration his audience had become hostile and vindictive.

Many of the orations of Dio Chrysostom (one of the few "philosophers who seemed to be sophists" that Philostratus treats) also possess long, rambling proems.[132] In the *Alexandrian,* for example, Dio's preface is almost one-third the length of the entire speech.[133] In it he tries to win the audience's favor and prepare them for the stern advice he will offer. His *Olympian,* a "heavyweight synthesis of philosophy and rhetoric" that was probably delivered at the games in 97 C.E., also has a distended preface.[134] By talking about his own experiences Dio arouses his audience's curiosity and sympathy. Only after he has discussed his recent journey from the Danube does he propose that he address them on humanity's notions of the divine.

When viewed in the light of the sophists' proems, Diogenes' long-winded, casual, and decidedly nonlapidary introductions become more explicable: he was influenced by the sophistic style of his contemporaries. Diogenes' conversational tone in his main introduction (frr. 2–3 = Ch frr. 1–2) is probably an affectation, but it is possible that he delivered this *prolalia* aloud (and while sitting down), while scribes recorded it. Wealthy sophists had secretaries who transcribed their orations; perhaps Diogenes did also. The pace also seems to

---

132. For C.P. Jones the speeches of Dio that "by their joining of earnestness and display" best reveal Philostratus' category of sophistic philosopher are the *Rhodian, Alexandrian,* and *Trojan.* In the *Olympian* and others, "the display is still present, though outweighed by the earnestness" (*Roman World,* 35).

133. Twenty-nine paragraphs make up the preface; the entire speech contains only one hundred one paragraphs.

134. Bowersock, "Philostratus and the Second Sophistic," 670.

reflect the influence of extemporaneous speaking. Some sophists avoided the challenge, but many declaimed *ex tempore* on subjects chosen by their audience.[135] Since scribes were often on hand to record such performances, orations must have circulated with sentences similar to the following one from Diogenes' introduction (fr. 3 = Ch fr. 2).

col. III

5   εἰ μὲν
οὖν εἷς μόνον ἢ δύ᾽ ἢ
τρεῖς ἢ τέτταρες ἢ
πέντε ἢ ἓξ ἢ ὅσους,
ἄνθρωπε, βούλει τῶν
10   τοσούτων εἶναι πλείονας, μὴ πάνυ δὲ πολ-
λούς, διέκειντο κα-
κῶς, κἂν καθ᾽ ἕ[να————]
[κ]αλούμενος [πάν]-

col. IV   τα παρ᾽ ἐμαυτὸν ἔπρατ-
τον εἰς συμβουλίαν
τὴν ἀρίστην.

[Now if only one person, or two, or three or four, or five or six, or, sir, as many more than that as you wish, but not too many, were in an evil condition, calling on them even one by one, I would do what I could to give them my best advice.]

Diogenes tells us in the next column that since the large number of the people in need of Epicurean advice prevented him from calling on them "one by one" he decided that an inscription was the best way to reach them.

Like Dio's preface to the *Alexandrian,* Diogenes' preface to his inscription introduces the main points of the address and asserts that its purpose is extremely serious.[136] Diogenes asks his spectators to give the inscription serious attention again in his preface to the *Ethics* (fr. 30 = Ch fr. 25).

---

135. Reardon (*Courants littéraires,* 112) compares their extempore speaking to jazz improvisation.

136. Diogenes stresses his seriousness in fr. 3 (Ch fr. 2), col. II. Dio asks his audience to be serious in the opening line of his oration.

col. III
5   ἔν]

μόνον δ' ἀξιῶ [ὡς καὶ ἔ-]
ναυχος, ὑμᾶς μ[ὴ τῶν πα-]
ροδευόντων τ[ρόπον],
μηδ' ἄν τι ἀκηδ[είας]
10   καὶ ἄλυος [ἦ ἐφισ]-
τάναι τοῖς γεγρ[αμμέ]-
νοις, ποικίλως [ἐπ' αὐ]-
τῶν ἕκαστον ἐ[πιστρέ]-
φοντας καὶ πα[ραβαί]νοντας. . . .

[One thing only I ask, as I did just now, that you do not look at what is
written after the fashion of passers-by, or in a spirit of carelessness and
boredom, paying only fickle attention to one section after another and
passing on. . . .][137]

These requests for a serious audience are also symptomatic of an age when
audiences were accustomed to being entertained by the sophists' declamations.
Although the hotheaded Philagrus was rumored to have roused drowsy listeners with a slap in the face (see *VS* 578), and though his Cilician compatriot
Alexander allegedly reprimanded the emperor for his inattention (see *VS*
570–71), a sophist usually praised and flattered his audience and only rarely
reproached it.[138]

   Like the sophists, Diogenes also adopted the lifestyle of an itinerant intellectual. To meet with other Epicureans he sailed to nearby Rhodes as well as to
Thebes, Chalcis, and Athens, and at least one Epicurean seems to have come
from Lindos to work with Diogenes at Oenoanda.[139] This time-consuming and
expensive travel is common to both Diogenes and the sophists, as is the geographical name-dropping that preserved for us Diogenes' itinerary.[140] The popu-

---

   137. Trans. Chilton, *Diogenes of Oenoanda,* 11. I have also followed Chilton's edition for the
emended text of the last line of this fragment.
   138. See Nesselrath, "Lucian's Introductions," 129.
   139. See fr. 62 (Ch fr. 15), col. II, lines 3–4. Theodoridas the Lindian is named in fr. 63 (Ch fr.
16), cols. II–IV.
   140. For tourism in the Roman Empire, see L. Friedländer, *Sittengeschichte Roms,* 8th ed.
(Leipzig, 1910), vol. 2. On name-dropping, Anderson writes: "it is noteworthy how often the obses-
sion for tossing round the landmarks of Greece provides a starting-point for a sophist's magnilo-
quence" (*Philostratus,* 30). It has also been argued recently that travel was essential for the more
radical second-century philosophers because they were more able to speak frankly as outsiders.
See, especially, chapter 15 of J. Hahn, *Der Philosoph und die Gesellschaft: Selbstverständnis,
öffentliches Auftreten und populäre Erwartungen in der höhen Kaiserzeit* (Stuttgart, 1989).

larity of travel also explains why the inscription mentions so many foreign visitors to Oenoanda.[141] The short-lived inscription probably outlasted the era of open travel, however. As Bowersock wrote of the sophists' itineraries: "These extensive travels, with numerous friends in diverse cities, illustrate a coherence of the Roman empire that had been long in the making and was not to exist again."[142]

"A Sophist in Speech but a Philosopher in Thought"

When Diogenes of Oenoanda is viewed as a contemporary of the sophists his desire to give a public exposition of Epicureanism emerges as part of a wider second-century phenomenon. In the process Diogenes may begin to appear less eccentric than he is usually thought to be, though his limestone philosophical handbook remains unique in both form and content. In fact, Diogenes' eccentricities and his idiosyncratic way of asserting his own personality are characteristic of the Second Sophistic. Despite the fact that a single movement, the revival of Greek culture, was so widely received in the second century, this was not an age of conformity. There were many rebels, many *rarae aves,* and plenty of material for Lucian's satire.[143]

Scholars studying of the second century tend to single out one character as a personal favorite, either as the exception to the rule of second-century mediocrity or as the lone intelligent observer of the strange goings-on of the Second Sophistic. For many that one character is "the inimitable Lucian."[144] For others the one who stands head and shoulders above all others is Galen. Aristides also has his supporters, as do Marcus Aurelius, Dio Chrysostom, Plutarch, and Aulus Gellius.[145] One recent book champions Pausanias and, after surveying

---

141. Ξένοι are mentioned in fr. 3 (Ch fr. 2), col. V, line 7 and fr. 119, col. III, line 2 (Ch fr. 49, line 2); βάρβαροι in fr. 32 (Ch fr. 26), col. II, line 12.

142. *Sophists,* 1.

143. Philostratus mentions numerous unusual individuals, from the hermaphrodite sophist Favorinus, to the sophist who barked at other performers (see *VS* 587). On diversity in the Second Sophistic, see B. Baldwin, *Studies in Lucian* (Toronto, 1973), 20. On clashes between flamboyant personalities, see Bowersock's chapter "Professional Quarrels," in *Sophists,* 89–100.

144. Gibbon writes: "But if we except the inimitable Lucian, this age of indolence passed away without having produced a single writer of original genius or who excelled in the arts of elegant composition" (*Decline and Fall of the Roman Empire* [New York, 1932], 51). See also C.P. Jones, *Lucian,* 1–5.

145. B.A. van Gronigen lists Marcus Aurelius and Dio Chrysostom as exceptions to his view of the "sham" world of the second century ("General Literary Tendencies in the Second Century A.D.," *Mnemosyne* 18 [1965]: 55). He also concedes that Plutarch, Galen, Arrian, and Lucian are "more or less independent personalities" (56). Plutarch is "the greatest Greek writer of the early empire" for G. Kennedy (*The Art of Rhetoric in the Roman World* [Princeton, 1972], 554). In accor-

the practices of the sophists, protests rhetorically: "How could *Pausanias* be stuck among these?"[146] The present study, though viewing Diogenes as very appropriately on display among the sophists, gives him the honorary title "new Epicurus" and hands him the palm for combining the virtues of adaptability and originality and becoming "a sophist in speech but a philosopher in thought."[147]

---

dance Bowersock writes: "In his friends, in his erudition, in his style Plutarch is a man of his time. But in his literary aspirations and his personality he stands apart" ("Philostratus and the Second Sophistic," 669). C.P. Jones cites Burckhardt and Mommsen as two of Dio Chrysostom's admirers (*Roman World,* v). Among Gellius' new admirers is L. Holford-Strevens, *Aulus Gellius* (London, 1988).

146. Christian Habicht, *Pausanias' Guide,* 139. The emphasis, which is not meant to ridicule an excellent book, is mine. Habicht concludes his discussion of Pausanias' contemporaries with: "Thank God his work has lasted rather than the mass of the sophists' speeches!" (140).

147. The phrase in quotes is a paraphrase of Werner Peek, *Griechische Versinschriften aus Kleinasien* (Vienna, 1980), 588, modified to suit Diogenes of Oenoanda.

CHAPTER 2

Diogenes of Oenoanda and Second-Century Epicureanism

Apud istos quicquid Hermarchus dixit, quicquid Metrodorus, ad unum refertur.

[Among those people whatever Hermarchus said, whatever Metrodorus said, is attributed to one man.]

—Seneca *Epistles* 33.4

My goal in chapter 1 was to demonstrate that the Oenoanda philosophical inscription owes its formal presentation and even its very existence to the Greek cultural revival of the Roman Empire. Once that link between Diogenes of Oenoanda and the cultural archaism of the second century is established, the question that arises is, Was Diogenes' revival of Epicureanism a purely academic exercise, or was it a serious response to contemporary issues? Put another way the question is, What relation did Diogenes' Epicureanism have to the real world of the second century? This question is relevant to all Second Sophistic figures who exhibit a predilection for the past.[1]

Over a quarter of a century ago a study of second-century literature claimed that the culture of the Second Sophistic was so detached from reality that its motto might have been *non vitae sed scholae*.[2] Recently, however, many schol-

---

1. F. Millar raises similar questions in "P. Herennius Dexippus: The Greek World and the Third-Century Invasions," *JRS* 59 (1969): 12: "What was the relationship between the all-pervasive literary culture . . . with its obsessive and apparently sterile fascination with the classical past, and men's conduct in the world? . . . Was constant reference to the classical past predominantly a neutral intellectual exercise, or a means of flight from an oppressive and inglorious present; or had it a real function in providing a frame of reference or a channel of communication?" Millar identifies his first question as "the most crucial question" about that culture and society (12) but concludes that it is unanswerable. In the case of Diogenes of Oenoanda, we have enough information to answer the question at least in outline.

2. B.A. van Groningen, "General Literary Tendencies in the Second Century A.D.," *Mnemosyne* 18 (1965): 50. Similarly, E.L. Bowie writes that second-century archaizing "in its extreme

ars have found that the Greek renaissance was fully engaged with the world at large. Thus, Peter Brown has aptly linked this age of cultural archaism with an "Age of Idealization," when the solutions to the serious problems of the day were sought not in innovation but in paradigmatic, classical behavior.[3] Style and substance were inextricably intertwined: while orators imitated Demosthenes, philosophers emulated Pythagoras, emperors modeled themselves after Augustus, and doctors (with the help of Asclepius) emulated Hippocrates. Recent studies of individual authors have begun to explore the complex and sometimes subtle interplay between present reality and ancient tradition. Lucian, for example, has been portrayed by some as a classicizing academic who worked *in vacuo*[4] but by others as an important social satirist.[5] Several recent studies have placed Lucian between the two extremes and have shown how he combined classical erudition with mordant criticism of his contemporaries.[6] In the following chapters I argue that Diogenes, like Lucian (and like some other second-century classicists), operated in two realms. He participated in the fashionable revival of ancient Hellenic culture, but he also brought the teachings of the past to bear on the concerns and anxieties of his contemporaries.

The precise contents of Diogenes' teachings were not simply resurrected from old books. Diogenes and other Epicureans updated Epicurus' philosophy to suit the needs of their contemporaries. Such an interpretation is more com-

---

forms seems to be an attempt to pretend that the past is still present" ("Greeks and Their Past in the Second Sophistic," *Past and Present* 46 [1970]: 204).

3. Brown offers the label "Age of Idealisation" as an alternative to Dodd's "Age of Anxiety"; see Brown, *A Social Context to the Religious Crisis of the Third Century a.d.,* Center for Hermeneutical Studies Colloquy 14 (Berkeley, 1975): 3. See also Brown, "The Saint as Exemplar in Late Antiquity," *Representations* 1.2 (1983): 1–25.

4. See J. Bompaire, *Lucien écrivain: Imitation et création,* Bibliothèque des Ecoles Françaises d'Athènes et de Rome 190 (Paris, 1958).

5. See A. Peretti, *Luciano: Un intellettuale greco contro Roma* (Florence, 1946); and Barry Baldwin, "Lucian as Social Satirist," CQ 11 (1961): 199–208. The clearest exposition of external evidence that shows Lucian to be concerned with his own era is in the research of Louis Robert; see "Lucian en son temps," in *A travers l'Asie Mineure: Poètes et prosateurs, monnaies greques, voyageurs et géographie,* Bibliothèque des Ecoles Françaises d'Athènes et de Rome 239 (Paris, 1980). See also Graham Anderson, "Lucian: Tradition versus Reality," *ANRW* II 34.2 (1994): 1422–47.

6. In *Studies in Lucian* (Toronto, 1973), Barry Baldwin tempered his earlier interpretation and acknowledged that Lucian was shaped by both his personal experience and his classical education (see, especially, 107). See also Jennifer A. Hall, *Lucian's Satire* (New York, 1981); C.P. Jones, *Culture and Society in Lucian* (Cambridge, Mass., 1986); and R. Bracht Branham, *Unruly Eloquence: Lucian and the Comedy of Traditions* (Cambridge, Mass., 1989). Branham points out that for Lucian the cultural past was "not only a means of escape . . . but . . . also a means of criticizing the present" (220 n. 6), and that Lucian even used traditional devices to lampoon his contemporaries' infatuation with tradition (1–8 and passim).

plex than one might expect; the possibility that the inscription could represent a second-century version of Epicureanism has not been generally recognized.

Diogenes and the Alleged Conservatism of Epicureanism

Throughout its short history, scholarship on Diogenes of Oenoanda has focused on recovery of the lost writings and doctrines of Epicurus.[7] The hope has been that Diogenes' treatises and his quotations of Epicurus would fill significant gaps in our knowledge of Epicureanism. An additional source for Epicurus would certainly be welcome; only a few original texts are extant, and most are in poor condition.[8] The text of Diogenes Laertius' *Lives and Opinions of Eminent Philosophers* preserves three epistles of Epicurus and the collection of forty sayings known as the *Kyriai Doxai,* or *Principal Doctrines.* From Herculaneum we have carbonized fragments of Epicurus' work *On Nature* and some short fragments of other works.[9] To this list may be added some quotations of Epicurus found in various authors and in the collection known as the *Sententiae Vaticanae.*[10] These texts are but a small fraction of Epicurus' writings, as the catalog of works recorded by Diogenes Laertius (10.27–28) makes clear. For our understanding of many aspects of Epicureanism we depend on Lucretius and on shorter discussions and references in the works of Cicero, Philodemus, Plutarch, Sextus Empiricus, Porphyry, and Simplicius.[11]

Scholars generally agree that Oenoanda's contribution to our small corpus of genuine works of Epicurus is meager; few of the known fragments actually quote Epicurus. The only direct quotations whose attribution to Epicurus is not debated are thirteen maxims recorded in a single continuous line of sayings that apparently extended across the entire width of the inscription. These thirteen maxims are not completely new. Excepting some minor differences, they are

---

7. A notable exception to this approach may be found in the work of Diskin Clay, such as his article "An Epicurean Interpretation of Dreams," *AJP* 101 (1980): 342–65, which emphasizes Diogenes' eccentricities and innovations.

8. On the poor condition of the text of Diogenes Laertius, see Eduard Schwartz, "Diogenes Laertius," *RE* 5.1 (1905): cols. 739, 740, 748.

9. The texts from the tenth book of Diogenes Laertius and the papyri as well as fragments culled from literary sources are collected in the edition of G. Arrighetti, *Opere,* 2d ed. (Turin, 1973), under the headings *Deperditorum librorum reliquiae, Epistularum fragmenta,* and *In certae sedis fragmenta.*

10. These quotations are also included in Arrighetti's edition (cited in the preceding note). The nature of the *Sententiae Vaticanae* is discussed later in this chapter.

11. The works of Philodemus will grow in importance as better texts are made available. The works of Diogenianus, Polystratus, Aetius, and Erotianus, can be included in this list of sources. The more important sources are now conveniently collected in A.A. Long and D.N. Sedley, The *Hellenistic Philosophers* (Cambridge, 1987).

similar to maxims recorded by Diogenes Laertius in the *Kyriai Doxai.* In addition to the familiar maxims, at least eight others are recorded in this line. Whether these additional eight sayings should be attributed directly to Epicurus is discussed later in this chapter.

According to most editors, at least two other works inscribed on the wall(s) should also be regarded as genuine texts of Epicurus.[12] Both texts are fragmentary letters. Neither of them is attested elsewhere, and their contents suggest that they are not fragments of works of Epicurus for which titles have survived. The longer letter is the *Letter to Mother,* which I discuss as a pseudepigraphical work in chapter 3. The other (fr. 128 [= NF 110]) is extremely fragmentary, but it has been suggested that it is a letter of consolation written by Epicurus and otherwise known only from a description in Plutarch's *Moralia.*[13]

Despite the low yield of original texts of Epicurus, most scholarship on Diogenes still maintains that the inscription is a good source for the original doctrines of Epicurus. The assumption (often stated explicitly) is that Diogenes' second-century handbook represents an account of Hellenistic Epicureanism, orthodox in every detail.[14] Such an approach is in accord with the traditional interpretation of Epicureanism, which is thought to have been so conservative that it never developed beyond Epicurus' original ideas.[15] One essay thus characterizes traditional scholarship on Lucretius: "Epicurus had found the full truth. For his followers, then, there was not much to do. Theirs was but to keep the right doctrine and deliver it unblemished to new gen-

---

12. D. Clay ("The Philosophical Inscription of Diogenes of Oenoanda: New Discoveries 1969–1983" ANRW II 36.4 [1990]: 2541–42) argues that an additional letter or letters are represented by frr. 130 (NF 3) and 127 (NF 24). Smith originally assigned these fragments to the *Letter to Mother.* A. Barigazzi, in "Una nuova lettera di Epicuro in Diogene d'Oenoanda?" Prometheus 1 (1975): 99–116, argues that fr. 10 (Ch fr. 7), cols. I–III is a direct quotation from a letter of Epicurus. I find this unlikely because the Stoics are named.

13. See M.F. Smith, "Eight New Fragments of Diogenes of Oenoanda," AS 29 (1979): 79–81. The letter to which Plutarch refers (Mor. 1101) was written to Dositheus and Pyrson on the death of Hegesianax; NF 110 seems to record at least the first three letters of Dositheus' name.

14. Chilton writes: "Diogenes is not an original thinker, but Epicureans never were; their sole aim was to pass on the teachings of the Master" (*Diogenes of Oenoanda The Fragments* [Oxford, 1971], xlv). M.F. Smith writes: "Epicureans were well known for their loyalty to their master's doctrines, and Diogenes is no exception" ("More New Fragments of Diogenes of Oenoanda," in *Etudes sur l'Epicurisme antique,* ed. J. Bollack and A. Laks [Lille, 1976], 282). G.N. Hoffman writes: "Diogenes is almost perfectly faithful to the teachings and the spirit of Epicurus and his school" ("Diogenes of Oenoanda: A Commentary" [Ph.D. diss., University of Minnesota, 1976], 50).

15. Welcome signs that old assumptions are now being questioned include the papers (published in *GRBS* 30 [1989]) delivered at a conference called "Tradition and Innovation in Epicureanism," held at Duke University in 1989.

erations."[16] An unprejudiced reading of Diogenes of Oenoanda suggests, however, that the establishment of the "right doctrine" was sometimes an open issue. By the first century B.C.E. this was already apparent to Epicureans and detractors alike. In the *De Finibus* Cicero exposed disagreements among Epicureans on a variety of ethical issues, and Philodemus wrote an attack on dissident Epicureans and tried to urge his contemporaries to return to the founder's teachings.[17] Epicureanism may have been conservative, but it did not remain completely static throughout its long history.

Diogenes of Oenoanda presents some arguments that were clearly developed in response to Stoic ideas. The centuries-old rivalry between Stoics and Epicureans cannot be traced back to Epicurus' lifetime: although Zeno and Epicurus were contemporaries, we have no evidence for hostilities between the two philosophers, and Epicurus obviously never confronted the views of Chrysippos, who was a small child when Epicurus died. Plutarch (1086e–f and 1108b) does not include any Stoics in his list of philosophers attacked by the early Epicurean Colotes (fl. c. 310–260 B.C.E.).[18] The extant sources suggest that early Epicurean criticism of opposing views was instead directed against the Academy, pre-Socratics, and others.[19] Animosity between Stoics and Epicureans seems to have crystallized in republican Rome, where Epicureanism was viewed as the antithesis of Roman Stoicism. On this point DeWitt puts the blame on Cicero, "who matches Epicureans and Stoics as if rival schools of gladiators."[20]

Previous work on the question of whether Lucretius was concerned with the contemporary controversy has exposed aspects of later Epicureanism relevant to

---

16. Knut Kleve, "The Philosophical Polemics in Lucretius," in *Entretiens sur L'antiquité Classique,* vol. 24, *Lucrèce* (Geneva, 1977), 47. Departing from the tradition he thus characterizes, Kleve then describes how Epicureans constantly revised and updated their polemics.

17. Philodemus' *On Rhetoric* exposed unorthodox Epicurean teachings. Elizabeth Asmis characterizes *P. Herc.* 1005, the remains of an essay whose title is debated, as an attack on "dissident Epicureans" ("Philodemus' Epicureanism," *ANRW* II 36.4 [1990]: 2379).

18. On the lack of disagreement between early Stoics and Epicurus, see Phillip De Lacy, "Lucretius and the History of Epicureanism," *TAPA* 79 (1948): 12–23; and E. Bignone, *L'Aristotele Perduto e la Formazione Filosofica de Epicuro* (Florence, 1936), 2:532–33.

19. Polystratus, the third head of the Epicurean school, wrote *Against Those Who Unreasonably Despise Popular Beliefs,* which has survived in fragments at Herculaneum. Most of his attack seems to be directed against Academic skeptics. We know from Plutarch that Colotes' polemic was also directed against skeptics. See David Sedley's review of *Polistrato,* by G. Indelli *CR* 33 (1983): 335–36.

20. N. DeWitt, *Epicurus and His Philosophy* (Minneapolis, 1954), 11. DeWitt argues that Epicurus himself formulated many of his ideas as a refutation of Platonism; others stress instead Epicurus' opposition to Aristotle. On the popularity of Stoicism in Rome, see P. Boyancé, "Le stoicism à Rome," in *Actes du VIIe congrès,* Association Guillaume Budé (Paris, 1964): 218–55.

Diogenes of Oenoanda. Lucretius never names the Stoics, but several studies have demonstrated that certain Lucretian polemics are directed against specific Stoic ideas that developed after Epicurus' lifetime.[21] Some scholars resist the idea that Lucretius had the Stoics in mind,[22] but all must acknowledge the anti-Stoic stance of Diogenes of Oenoanda, because he names the Stoics explicitly;[23] his decision to house the inscription in a stoa (Diogenes' name for the building in fr. 3 [Ch fr. 2]) may even have been a whimsical anti-Stoic gesture.[24] Many Lucretian proclamations that sound suspiciously anti-Stoic also find precise parallels in Diogenes' inscription, where the latter author names his enemy.[25]

Similar issues are beginning to emerge in reference to the Epicurean refutation of skepticism. Although the only antiskeptical statement in the extant texts of Epicurus is directed against Democriteans, the common assumption is that Epicurus himself formulated a full-fledged refutation of Pyrrho and/or Arcesilaus. A recent article suggests, however, that Epicurean antiskeptical arguments, including Diogenes of Oenoanda's account of Aristotle as a Heracleitan skeptic in fragment 5 (Ch fr. 4) were later developments.[26] Although antiskeptic polemic can be traced back to Epicurus' disciple Colotes, each generation seems to have developed the refutation according to present need.

Late Epicurean texts (including parts of the Oenoanda inscription) frequently seem to agree very closely with traditional conceptions of Epicurus' own philosophy. I suggest that often this apparent agreement is due not to Epicurean conservatism but to the nature of our sources. A survey of the sources reveals that most of them are far removed (both temporally and geographically) from Epicurus.[27] This is obvious in the case of the Roman poet Lucretius and

21. See De Lacy, "Lucretius and the History of Epicureanism," 12–23; Kleve, "Philosophical Polemics," 58–71; and C. Bailey, *Titi Lucreti Cari De Rerum Natura,* 3 vols. (Oxford, 1947), 708–712 and passim.

22. See David J. Furley, "Lucretius and the Stoics," BICS 13 (1966): 13–33; Furley is countered by J. Schmidt, *Lukrez und die Stoiker: Quellenuntersuchungen zu De Rerum Natura* (Ph.D. diss., University of Marburg, 1975).

23. See fr. 6 (Ch fr. 5), col. II, lines 7–8; fr. 10 (Ch fr. 7), col. I, line 8; fr. 10 (NF 1), col. III, lines 8–10; fr. 22 (NF 54); fr. 38 (NF 61); and possibly also fr. 39, col. III, line 13 (Ch fr. 35, col. I, line 13). Frr. 20 (NF 39) and 21 (NF 40) also seem to be directed against the Stoics, although they are not named in known surviving stones.

24. See M.F. Smith, "Two New Fragments of Diogenes of Oenoanda," *JHS* 92 (1972): 155.

25. For example, fr. 6 (Ch fr. 5), where the Stoics are attacked, is paralleled by *De Rerum Natura* 1.635–920. Both Diogenes and Lucretius begin their polemics by attacking Heracleitus, who was revered by the Stoics. Frr. 20 and 21 (NF 39 and NF 40), which ridicule the Stoic belief that the earth was created by god for humanity, are paralleled by *De Rerum Natura* 5.156–234.

26. Paul A. Vander Waerdt, "Colotes and the Epicurean Refutation of Skepticism," *GRBS* 30 (1989): 225–67.

27. In *Epicurus' Scientific Method* (Ithaca, N.Y., 1984), Elizabeth Asmis recognizes that the "wide chronological range" of these authors "poses a serious problem" (10), so she attempts to

his contemporaries Cicero and Philodemus.[28] There is an even greater distance between Epicurus, on the one hand, and Diogenes, Plutarch, and Sextus Empiricus, on the other.[29] Discussions of the conservatism of Epicurean ideas expressed in these writers involve a certain amount of circular argumentation. If Sextus Empiricus, for example, presents an idea that also appears in the text of Diogenes of Oenoanda, it does not necessarily follow that both have derived their arguments from Epicurus himself. Both texts could represent developments that emerged during the second century or during the five centuries that had passed since the life of Epicurus.

If we set aside Lucretius' and the other late Epicurean texts, we are left with the *Principal Doctrines, Letter to Herodotus, Letter to Pythocles* (which some authorities consider inauthentic), *Letter to Menoeceus,* the fragments of *On Nature,* and the other fragmentary texts from Herculaneum. This would seem to be a fair number of texts with which to compare later Epicurean sources. The problem is that, with the exception of the fragments of *On Nature* and the other fragments accidentally saved by Vesuvius, all of these texts are preserved only in the work of Diogenes Laertius. Thus, these texts, like the writings of Lucretius, Plutarch, and Sextus Empiricus, also represent later records of Epicurean thought. Most of the texts in Diogenes Laertius may contain Epicurus' exact words, and they were probably chosen because they seemed to be most representative of Epicureanism. They were chosen, however, by a writer with late second-century sensibilities. His choice of texts, which reflects contemporary concerns, controls our interpretation.

Diogenes Laertius seems to have lived at the height of the Second Sophistic, possibly in a region near Lycia.[30] Like many of his contemporaries (some of

---

place later Epicurean texts in their historical contexts. She usually concludes that later sources are trustworthy, however. See Brad Inwood's review of *Epicurus' Scientific Method,* CP (1986): 353.

28. Lucretius lived between c. 99 and c. 55 B.C.E., Cicero between 106 and 43 B.C.E. The Roman cultural context of *De Rerum Natura* has been a neglected topic, but a recent essay stresses that in contrast to Greek Epicureanism, the context of Lucretius' poem is "Roman, oligarchic, and literary, not Greek, scholastic, and philosophical" (J.D. Minyard, *Lucretius and the Late Republic: An Essay in Roman Intellectual History* [Leiden, 1985], 35). D. Clay's *Lucretius and Epicurus* (Ithaca, N.Y., 1983) also stresses the Roman and uniquely Lucretian aspects of *De Rerum Natura.* This is a welcome change from the tendency to treat Lucretius as though he were a translator of Epicurus. See, especially, Clay, 54–56.

29. Epicurus wrote between 341 and 271 B.C.E. If Diogenes of Oenoanda was an old man under Hadrian, he was a contemporary of Plutarch (46–c. 120 C.E.). Porphyry (third century C.E.) and Plutarch afford us access to some earlier material: Porphyry (*On Abstinence* 1) discusses the writings of Hermarchus, who succeeded Epicurus as head of the school in 271 B.C.E., and Plutarch (*Adversus Colotem*) refutes the Epicurean Colotes (fl. c. 310–260 B.C.E.).

30. Diogenes Laertius is traditionally placed in the early third century C.E. (see Schwartz, "Diogenes Laertius," col. 761), but that dating depends on the date of Sextus Empiricus (whom Laer-

whom I discussed in chapter 1), he ignores whatever is recent or Roman. His antiquarian interests are evident throughout the work, especially when he comments upon the survival of ancient Greek monuments, customs, and books.[31] His philological bent—he often expresses curiosity about ancient Greek words—is typical of the era.[32] Also characteristic of second-century literature is Laertius' *quasisavant* tone and his manifest desire to entertain his readers.[33] No other era would produce a history of philosophy in which the author included his own poems (fifty-two in number) about the philosophers. In format, purpose, and scale his book is the philosophical counterpart to Philostratus' *Lives of the Sophists,* and his blending of philosophy, sayings, and biographies may also be compared to Philostratus' *Life of Apollonius of Tyana.*

Laertius' favorite sources were the *Memorabilia* and *Omnigena Historia* of the sophist Favorinus; he quotes them so often that it was once alleged that his book was merely an epitome of the sophist's work.[34] Like so many second-century writers, Laertius idealizes his Greek forebears; one of his tasks was to argue that philosophy itself was something uniquely Greek. For example, in response to claims that philosophy was invented by Babylonians, Egyptians, or other non-Greeks, he asserts in his proem that "the achievements which they attribute to the barbarians belong to the Greeks, with whom not merely philosophy but the human race itself began."[35] His desire to commemorate the great Greek thinkers was conceived in an extreme version of the same spirit that inspired many of the second-century texts I discussed in chapter 1.

---

tius cites), which is also insecure. See Arnaldo Momigliano, *On Pagans, Jews, and Christians* (Middletown, Conn., 1987), 169–71. J. Mejer (*Diogenes Laertius and His Hellenistic Background* [Wiesbaden, 1978], 57–58) and F. Kudlien ("Die Datierung des Sextus Empiricus und des Diogenes Laertius," *RhM* 106 [1963]: 251–54) would move Laertius back into the second century. Some have thought that his name was neither Roman nor Homeric (*pace* Wilamowitz, "Epistola ad Maassium," *Philologische Untersuchungen* 3 [1880]: 163) but was derived from the name of the village Laerte in Caria (see Richard Hope, *The Book of Diogenes Laertius: Its Spirit and Its Method* [New York, 1930], 7).

31. See Mejer, *Hellenistic Background,* 53–54. On Laertius' neglect of recent history, which used to be treated as proof that his book was merely an epitome of an earlier work, see Mejer, 56–57.

32. See Mejer, *Hellenistic Background,* 54.

33. B.P. Reardon writes that Philostratus, Diogenes Laertius, and Plutarch's *Lives* exhibit "les tendances littéraires quasisavantes" of the era (*Courants littéraires grecs des IIe et IIIe siècles après J.-C.,* Annales littéraires de L'Université de Nantes 3 [Paris, 1971], 33).

34. He quotes Favorinus' works at least fifty times, more than any other source. See Mejer, *Hellenistic Background,* 30. The theory that his book was actually an epitome of Favorinus was argued by Ernst Maass, *de biographis Graecis quaestiones selectae, Philologische Untersuchungen* 3 (Berlin, 1880).

35. *Lives* 1.3; trans. R.D. Hicks, *Diogenes Laertius: Lives of Eminent Philosophers,* vol. 1 (Cambridge, Mass., 1972), 5.

Diogenes Laertius was also an Epicurean of sorts.[36] Epicurus and Plato, who receive lengthier treatments than any other philosophers in the work, are the only philosophers for whom he expresses particular admiration.[37] The favorable account of Plato seems to have been written in honor of the woman to whom Diogenes Laertius dedicates his work—as Diogenes tells us, she was a Platonist. Significantly, Diogenes addresses this unnamed Platonist directly in only two places: first, in the Life of Plato (3.47); second, in the Life of Epicurus (10.29), where Laertius seems eager to convince his reader that Epicurus is as worthy of her serious attention as is Plato. Laertius' own allegiance seems to have been to Epicurus, whom he praises explicitly (10.9, 26, and 138). He preserves more quotations of Epicurus than of any other philosopher, and he places Epicurus at the end of his book, as though Epicureanism were the last and greatest achievement of philosophy. Diogenes' partiality to Epicurus also caused him to depart from his usual practice of recording mostly anecdotal material about the philosophers. As Diogenes Laertius himself admits, most anecdotes in circulation about Epicurus were extremely negative. Instead of recording and refuting them all, Laertius abandons his anecdotal style and allows Epicurus to speak for himself, enabling the reader "to study the man on all sides and know how to judge him" (10.29). His selection of Epicurean texts was of course far from random; his sympathies led him to choose only those texts which would (according to his own tastes) present Epicurus in a favorable light.

Thus, like Diogenes of Oenoanda, Diogenes Laertius was influenced by the intellectual currents of the Second Sophistic. He seems also to have subscribed to Epicurean beliefs and was probably in contact with other Epicureans in Asia Minor, as Diogenes of Oenoanda certainly was.[38] Consequently, similarities between the Epicureanism of Diogenes of Oenoanda and the Epicureanism of Diogenes Laertius do not prove that both accounts are absolutely true to the original; they suggest instead that both writers attest to the shape of Epicureanism in second-century Asia Minor. If we are interested in determining whether

---

36. Most scholarship that has dealt with the issue of Diogenes Laertius' philosophical preferences has acknowledged his partiality for Epicurus, although some has also stressed his admiration for Plato. See Richard Hope, *Diogenes Laertius,* 140–43. More recently, Mejer has written that the issue of Laertius' convictions is not settled (*Hellenistic Background,* 46 n. 95), but he acknowledges that Laertius' quotations of Epicurus "may be an indication of his close relations to the Epicureans" (8 n. 16). Momigliano suggests that Laertius was a skeptic (*On Pagans, Jews, and Christians,* 173).

37. See Ulrich von Wilamowitz, "Lesefrüchte," *Hermes* 34 (1899): 633.

38. Diogenes of Oenoanda mentions his meetings with otherwise unknown Epicureans, such as Theoridas of Lindos.

the inscription contains any late developments, we must recognize that Diogenes Laertius is not a good source against which to contrast Diogenes of Oenoanda.

The problem is compounded by the fact that Diogenes Laertius is not a particularly reliable source for philosophical thought in general. Today, no competent study of Aristotle, for example, would be based on Laertius' simplified and incomplete account, which seems to have been derived from a Stoic source.[39] For studies of Epicurus, however, Diogenes Laertius is used heavily, for want of other intact sources in Greek.

Laertius does not explicitly state the purpose of his book, but it is clear that he is more interested in the characters and lives of the philosophers than in philosophy per se. This too is characteristic of the approach to classical antiquity during the Second Sophistic. About half of Diogenes Laertius' biographies of philosophers (not including the sages in book 1) include no account at all of their doctrines, and when doxographical accounts are included they are much shorter than the biographical sections.[40] Laertius' rare comments on his own methods confirm the impression that he includes doxographical accounts only when he thinks the biographies would be deficient otherwise. For example, before giving an account of Plato's dialogues and an outline of his inductive procedure, Laertius writes that he is including this information "in order that the facts I have collected respecting his life may not suffer by the omission of his doctrines."[41] Concerning Aristotle, Laertius writes: "His writings are very numerous and, considering the man's excellence in all subjects, I deemed it incumbent on me to catalog them" (5.21). Laertius finds it would take too long to discuss all of Aristotle's ideas, however (5.34).

That Diogenes Laertius' concern for philosophy is secondary to his interest in philosophers' lives is also evident from the fact that although he often names and criticizes the sources for his accounts of philosophers' lives, he seldom cites his sources for his descriptions of their doctrines.[42] Thus, in his chapters on Aristotle he cites Hermippus, Timaeus, Demetrius of Magnesia, Aristippus,

---

39. See P. Moraux, "L'exposé de la philosophie d'Aristote chez Diogène Laerce 5.28–34," *Revue Philosophique de Louvain* 47 (1949): 5–43.

40. See Hope, *The Book of Diogenes Laertius,* 198; and Mejer, *Hellenistic Background,* 4.

41. 3.47. Laertius' brevity in the case of Plato can be explained; in the sentence that follows he adds that if he were to explain Platonism in detail it would be like taking "owls to Athens," since the woman to whom he dedicates his work is already an enthusiastic Platonist.

42. The major exception is his Stoic doxography in 7.38–157. This is one of the few passages for which credence can be given to the view that the work of Laertius is merely an epitome of someone else's book. See Mejer, *Hellenistic Background,* 5–7. Mejer lists Laertius' other references to sources for doxographical matters (7–8 n. 16).

Favorinus, Eumelus, Apollodorus, and others as sources for Aristotle's biography (5.1–9), but he does not name a single source for his outline of Aristotle's philosophical ideas (5.28–34). In the case of Epicurus he cites Timocrates' exposé on Epicurus' personal life and the scandalous letters of Diotimus the Stoic, but he names very few sources for his survey of Epicureanism. There are a few references to Epicurus' own writings in that survey, but they are interspersed with references to Diogenes of Tarsus, which suggests that the citations of Epicurus' writings come directly from the secondary source.[43] Furthermore, Laertius does not tell us what source has supplied the *Principal Doctrines* or the three epistles he records. Because Diogenes Laertius is more interested in the lives and characters of the great philosophers than in their ideas, he is also not concerned to record evidence for innovations and developments within a particular philosophy or any differences of opinions between disciples.[44] Although Laertius' presentation of philosophical schools as monolithic structures has not affected scholarship on philosophical schools for which we have many additional sources, it has exerted a heavy influence on modern descriptions of Epicureanism.

Thus, there is a serious methodological problem confronting anyone who maintains that Epicureanism traveled from early Hellenistic Athens to second-century Oenoanda without changing: while late Epicureanism is well documented, resources for reconstructing the original thought of Epicurus are scarce.[45] Moreover, our later sources come primarily from only two eras and locations: first-century B.C.E. Italy, and second-century C.E. Greece and Asia Minor. Unfortunately, one result of the recognition of the methodological stricture imposed here is quite negative: we admit that we know less about Epicurus than we thought. But there are positive results also. Epicureanism has sometimes been treated as though it were not a serious philosophical system. If we recognize that many of our sources present either simplified or merely rudimentary versions of Epicurus' doctrine,[46] it becomes apparent that our earlier evidence (the better witnesses to Epicurus' own teachings) reflects an

---

43. The Epicurean epitome of Diogenes of Tarsus and some writings of Epicurus are mentioned in 10.118 and 136. On Diogenes of Tarsus, who lived in the second century B.C.E., see Hans von Arnim, "Diogenes" no. 46, *RE* 5.1 (1905); cols. 776–77.

44. Mejer (*Hellenistic Background,* 6, 51) cites a few exceptions: 7.84, 1.86, and 7.160–67.

45. In a review of D. Clay's *Lucretius and Epicurus,* D.P. and P.G. Fowler remark: "The study of Lucretius' *De Rerum Natura* is in important respects similar to that of Roman comedy: in both we are concerned with the relationship of a Latin text to a Greek background, and in both we are in the illogical position of having to reconstruct that background from the Latin text" (*CR* 35 [1985]: 275).

46. We must also recognize that anti-Epicurean polemic articulated by Cicero, Plutarch, early Christians, and others has influenced modern views of Epicureanism. See DeWitt, *Epicurus,* 3–6.

Epicurean system that was more subtle, more sophisticated, and less doctrinaire than Diogenes Laertius makes it out to be.[47] The later texts do not always do Epicurus justice.

The Fluidity of Epicurean Texts

A recent study of recruitment among Epicureans argues that Epicurus and his successors deliberately confined circulation of his writings to members of the Epicurean community.[48] The study argues that to attract new followers, Epicureans relied not on written texts but on a system of passive recruitment: they set up statues of Epicurus in strategic positions throughout the cities. The visual impact of these fascinating and "magnetic" statues of the seated Epicurus was such that they attracted adherents to the school.

Although this theory is too extreme[49]—there is little evidence that the statues could have played such a role, and there is undeniable evidence that Epicureans did circulate written texts—it is clear that Epicurus' treatises were indeed written for a limited, familiar audience. Epicurus acknowledged as much himself; Seneca quotes a letter in which Epicurus writes to a follower: "haec ego non multis, sed tibi; satis enim magnum alter alteri theatrum sumus" (*Ep.* 7.11). The language of the so-called esoteric works is especially idiosyncratic,[50] but even the exoteric writings, such as the *Letter to Menoeceus,* are difficult and seem to have been written with a small community in mind.[51] It appears that most of the extant writings of Epicurus were written for Epicureans already acquainted with the essentials of the philosophy.[52] Furthermore, testimonials to Epicurus'

---

47. On the traditional sources for Epicureanism, A.A. Long observes: "Such evidence could, and often did, give an impression that the system itself was lacking in philosophical sophistication. Study of the Herculaneum texts has gone a long way toward refuting this assessment of Epicurus" ("Epicurus and Philodemus," *Cambridge History of Classical Literature,* vol 1, *Greek Literature,* ed. P.E. Easterling and B.M. Knox [Cambridge, 1985], 627).

48. Bernard Frischer, *The Sculpted Word: Epicureanism and Philosophical Recruitment in Ancient Greece* (Berkeley, 1982). The thesis I describe here is argued throughout Frischer's book, in particular in chapter 2, "A Reconstruction of the Epicurean Policy on Recruitment and Conversion" (67–86).

49. See D. Clay's review of *The Sculpted Word,* by Bernard Frischer, *AJP* 105 (1984): 484–89.

50. H. Usener contrasts the esoteric with the exoteric writings in *Epicurea* (Leipzig, 1887; reprint Rome, 1963), xlii.

51. Clay writes: "His language bears the marks of an isolated and esoteric philosophical dialect that was current in Epicurus' garden early in the third century B.C. and understood and spoken only there and then, but appears to have lacked any connection with Greek as it was used and spoken outside Epicurus' garden" (*Lucretius and Epicurus,* 57). See also Clay, 297 nn. 4 and 5.

52. Arrighetti calls *On Nature* a "text for initiates": "Veramente un testo da iniziati" (*Opere,* 626).

writings are rare in the generation after his death, and we have none at all in sources contemporary with him.[53] This was not due to any interdiction by Epicurus against the dissemination of Epicurean documents;[54] rather it seems to be due to the difficult style and specialized nature of Epicurus' writings.

The generations following Epicurus' lifetime produced Epicureans who wrote for a wider public. Although the texts themselves are not extant, we have evidence for the industrious production of epitomes of Epicurean theory, especially in the third, second, and first centuries B.C.E.[55] It is widely believed that the composition of epitomes had begun with Epicurus himself, who wrote several condensed outlines (including the extant *Letter to Herodotus*) "for those who are unable to work in detail through all that I have written about nature or to peruse the larger books which I have composed."[56] Because the epitomes written by Epicurus' followers have not survived, it is impossible to know whether the epitomes attempted to present the philosophy to newcomers.[57] But our extant treatments of Epicureanism were clearly meant to do so.

Lucretius, Diogenes Laertius, and Diogenes of Oenoanda popularized Epicureanism and made it accessible (in very different ways) to a broad audience. Some of the works of Philodemus may also be regarded as popularizing texts, although they may not have been intended for general circulation.[58] Lucretius was unusual in his selection of didactic poetry as a medium for the promulgation of Epicureanism, but there were many prose handbooks of Epicureanism, as is clear from the nonextant sources cited by Laertius.[59] The authors of later handbooks made frequent use of anecdotes, poems, and rhetorical flourishes,

---

53. See Usener, *Epicurea*, 34, 68–70, 85–90, 342–43.

54. D. Clay argues that Epicurus actually went so far as to ensure public access to his writings by depositing them in the Metroon or State Archives of Athens (*Epicurus in the Archives of Athens, Hesperia* Suppl. 14 (Princeton, 1982), 17–26. Such a measure would be extraordinary (as Clay acknowledges), and the evidence for it is inconclusive.

55. One epitomizer cited by Diogenes Laertius (10.118) is Diogenes of Tarsus; evidence for others is collected by A. Angeli, "Compendi, Eklogai, Tetrapharmakos: Due Capitoli di Dissenso nell' Epicureismo," *Chronache Ercolanesi* 16 (1986): 54–55.

56. This is Bailey's translation (*Epicurus: The Extant Remains* [Oxford, 1926], 19) of the beginning of the *Letter to Herodotus* (Diogenes Laertius 10.35).

57. Epitomizers and Hellenistic doxographers are discussed by Mejer (*Hellenistic Background*, 81–89), who laments that we know "deplorably little" (86) about works on dogmas for which only titles have survived.

58. De Lacy ("Lucretius and the History of Epicureanism," 21), points out the characteristics Philodemus' writings have in common with popular philosophical essays. Since Philodemus' Epicurean works are known only from Herculaneum and are not cited by any ancient sources, it can be argued that they were written for a limited circle only. See Long, "Epicurus and Philodemus," 629.

59. 10.1–13. Some of these sources (e.g., the *Life of Epicurus* by Apollodorus the Epicurean) were biographies that included explanations of philosophical positions. *P. Oxy.* 215 is a fragment of what was possibly another introduction to Epicurean doctrine for outsiders. See Dirk Obbink,

and their books were unlike anything produced by Epicurus.[60] The purpose of these later works was quite different also: we have no remains of works of Epicurus that were written with the express purpose of attracting converts,[61] but Diogenes of Oenoanda, with his desire to broadcast the "remedies that bring salvation" (Fr. 3 [Ch fr. 2], col. III) was obviously a proselytizer.

Epicureans also kept some of Epicurus' own works in circulation, to the extent that Diogenes' contemporary Plutarch viewed Epicurus' writings as a contradiction of the Epicurean adage "Live unknown" (λάθε βιώσας).[62] Thus, Plutarch protests (as if to Epicurus):

> Do not write letters to your friends in Asia, nor enlist recruits from Egypt, nor escort the youth of Lampsacus as if under armed guard, nor send off books to every man and woman, to make a display of your wisdom.[63]

Plutarch had access to genuine writings of Epicurus, but many who wished to study Epicurus in the original apparently had difficulty procuring the desired titles. This is the subject of a papyrus letter from early second-century C.E. Alexandria in which the writer promises to send upriver a selection of Epicurean books.[64] We also have evidence that Epicurean writings other than those of Diogenes of Oenoanda were available in the second century, but there is very little evidence for the continued circulation of Epicurus' own esoteric writings. A census of Egyptian papyri reveals no texts of Epicurus at all, although there are several papyrus fragments of first- and second-century tracts or essays on Epicureanism.[65] By the fourth century the emperor Julian could praise the gods for not allowing most of Epicurus' books to survive.[66]

"P. Oxy. 215 and Epicurean Religious *Theoria*," in *Atti del xvii Congresso internazionale di papirologia* (Naples, 1983–84), 607–19.

60. Diogenes Laertius included in his work epitaphs he had written himself for the philosophers.

61. We do have a title possibly indicative of such a work: *Protreptikos* (Diogenes Laertius 10.28).

62. The adage (Usener *Epicurea,* 551) is known only from Plutarch's quotation.

63. *Live Unknown* 1129a. I read an element of censure in Plutarch's reference to *female* as well as male readers of Epicurean texts (πᾶσι καὶ πάσαις); the inclusion of women in the sect was (to Plutarch and others) proof of Epicurean debauchery. See my discussion in chapter 3.

64. See J.G. Keenan, "A Papyrus Letter about Epicurean Philosophy Books," *Getty Museum Journal* 5 (1977): 91–94.

65. See W.H. Willis, "A Census of the Literary Papyri from Egypt," *GRBS* 9 (1968): 205–41. Willis believes that a summary of papyri can tell us what people were reading, but E. Turner questions the value of the statistics because of "the extent to which caprice governs the survival and discovery of papyri" (*Greek Papyri, An Introduction* [Princeton, 1968], 97–98).

66. Julian 301c. The emperor is also content with the loss of the works of Pyrrho.

Not all Epicureans were content with the popular texts. Philodemus, for example, was quite familiar with the original works of Epicurus; the surviving remnants of Epicurus' *On Nature* probably belonged to his own library.[67] More often, however, later Epicureans seem to have produced epitomes and contemporary handbooks of Epicureanism as substitutes for the original writings of Epicurus.[68] The writers of these popular works on Epicureanism, including Diogenes of Oenoanda, sometimes needed to condense or simplify the specifics of Epicurean doctrine; in other instances they sought to illustrate and elaborate them. These are interpretive endeavors; they entail changes and innovation in the received tradition. Unintentional changes were especially likely to creep in when the authors relied not on Epicurus but on other handbooks and epitomes, as Diogenes Laertius often did. Although he is not specific about his sources for particular doctrines, Laertius cites a gamut of works in his treatment of Epicurus, including Diogenes of Tarsus' *Epitome of Epicurus' Ethical Opinions,* Demetrius of Magnesia's *On Poets and Writers of the Same Name,* Aristippus' *On the Luxury of the Ancients,* and Theopompus' *Marvels.*

The authors of popular texts were not concerned only with making difficult texts accessible. They also had to update Epicurus' campaign against fear and ignorance so that it responded to contemporary needs. New arguments were needed to answer new challenges, and old polemics were dropped as they became unnecessary. This dynamic operated on an academic level, as in the passages where Diogenes of Oenoanda refutes Stoic doctrine, and also on an evangelical level, as in Diogenes' arguments against the second-century belief in oracular prophecy. Since every Epicurean propagandist's goal was to rescue people from pain and fear (especially fear of death and fear of the gods), every successful missionary had to update Epicurus' teachings so that they responded to the specific misapprehensions of his contemporaries.[69]

Moreover, later Epicurean writers had to contend with the extremely negative conception of Epicurus held by many of their contemporaries. Because Epicurus was often popularly portrayed as an atheist, a greedy egoist, or a debauched sensualist,[70] Diogenes of Oenoanda and other handbook writers had to

---

67. See Long, "Epicurus and Philodemus," 629.

68. Other philosophical schools also produced handbooks and introductory studies, as is also clear from Diogenes Laertius' texts.

69. T.P. Wiseman contrasts Rome's "gentlemen" Epicureans with the propagandists, noting that the latter "set out to rescue men from fear, of the gods and of death, and it was the man in the street who needed—and accepted—their reassurance," and that Lucretius belonged to the gentlemen's world and the propagandists' (*Cinna the Poet and Other Roman Essays* [Leicester, 1974], 27.

70. Cicero exploited this situation when he composed *In Pisonem.* In Diogenes' era Plutarch exploited popular opinion in *Non Posse,* and Lucian says that Alexander the False Prophet did the

devote great energies to his defense. Diogenes Laertius first summarizes the types of rumors spread by Epicurus' calumniators and then begins his defense with the statement "But they are out of their minds" (10.9). In his defense, Laertius writes that the real Epicurus lived a simple life and was content with bread and water (10.11). He also cites Epicurus' gratitude toward his parents, his generosity toward his brothers, and his gentleness toward his servants. As for Epicurus' reverence toward the gods and his love for his country, Laertius says they were so great that "it is impossible to express them" (10.10).

Diogenes of Oenoanda took a similar approach, although he does not (in the known fragments) catalog the rumors perpetrated by Epicurus' detractors. An implied defense of Epicurus may be latent in his introduction to the inscription (frr. 2–3 = Ch frr. 1–2), where he states explicitly that his purpose is philanthropic. Another gentle but persuasive defense of the founder is contained in the *Letter to Mother* (discussion of which is reserved for chapter 3), where Epicurus' filial piety is given full expression. In response to the charge of atheism Diogenes resorts in fragment 16 (Ch fr. 11) to pinning the accusation on other philosophers (namely, Protagoras, Diagoras, and Anaxagoras).[71]

The scarcity of genuine texts, and the difficult style of the authentic texts that were available, sometimes inspired the production of pseudepigraphical "Epicurean" texts. The *Letter to Pythocles* may be such a text, although even if the text as a whole is inauthentic, some passages may represent Epicurus' own words. Usener believed that the whole letter, except for the epistolary ornamentation and the introduction, was a compilation of excerpts from Epicurus' *On Nature*,[72] and he judged the resulting text to be poorly assembled and quite "unworthy" of Epicurus.[73] In my reading, the *Letter to Mother* found in our inscription is clearly pseudepigraphical but seems to be an entirely new creation rather than a pastiche. Epicureanism was not the only philosophy or sect to produce

---

same when he lumped together "Christians, atheists, and Epicureans" (*Alexander* 25). See Adelaide D. Simpson, "Epicureans, Christians, Atheists in the Second Century," *TAPA* 72 (1941): 372–81. See also Hella Adam, *Plutarchs Schrift non posse suaviter vivi secundum Epicurum* (Amsterdam, 1974), 20–39. Lactantius expresses a view typical of both ancient and modern readers when he writes: "dicit Epicurus neminem esse qui alterum diligat nisi sua causa" (*Institutiones Divinae* 3.17.42.) See also Dirk Obbink, "The Atheism of Epicurus," *GRBS* 30 (1989): 187 ff.

71. See Chilton's discussion in his commentary (*Diogenes of Oenoanda*, 55–56) and in "An Epicurean View of Protagoras: A Note on Diogenes of Oenoanda Fragment XII (W)," *Phronesis* 7 (1962): 105–9.

72. Philodemus' suspicions confirm the impressions of Usener, who writes: "his causis olim mihi persuaseram epistulam ad Pythoclem non esse scriptam ab Epicuro sed conpilatam, ex Epicuri libris, fictam a sectatore quodam. nunc Philodemi testimonio constat iam inter ipsos Epicureos dubitatum esse rectene ea magistri nomen prae se ferret" (*Epicurea*, xxxix).

73. *Epicurea*, xxvii–xli.

such letters; there is abundant evidence for the composition of inauthentic letters from other "ancient" philosophers, especially in the second century. The *Letter to Pythocles* is much older, however: Philodemus knew of it and wrote that he suspected that it, along with some other nonextant letters, was not genuine.[74]

Pseudepigraphical letters were an ideal medium for the publication of innovative ideas. Because they used the authoritative voice of the chosen philosopher, these letters had the advantage that their teachings would be incorporated into the "original" teachings of the philosopher. Regardless of the intentions of the authors of pseudepigraphical letters, the scarcity of genuine texts guaranteed that letters purporting to be written by philosophers would find many readers. Some of the forces that led to the production of pseudepigraphical letters could also cause certain letters to be struck from the the canon. David Sedley has suggested recently that Philodemus (or his teacher Zeno) may have questioned the authenticity of the *Letter to Pythocles* simply because it was "out of step" with some other (now lost) astronomical work in the Epicurean canon.[75] Ironically, the very desire to promote orthodox Epicurean teachings may sometimes have led later interpreters of Epicurus to brand authentic texts as apocryphal.

Another type of extremely fluid Epicurean text is the aphorism. Like pseudepigraphical letters, aphorisms bore the authority of the ancient philosopher but could contain new ideas. Diogenes of Oenoanda used a set of Epicurean maxims as the foundation and anchor of his inscription—inscribed in large letters in a single continuous line, they apparently ran across the entire length of the stoa. This set of Epicurean maxims represents only one version of the *Kyriai Doxai;* several of the maxims appear to be almost identical to the set with which Diogenes Laertius ends his tenth, and last, book, but some of the maxims are different. Laertius gives his series of forty aphorisms the following introduction.

Καὶ φέρε οὖν δὴ νῦν τὸν κολοφῶνα, ὡς ἄν εἴποι τις, ἐπιθῶμεν καὶ τοῦ παντὸς συγγράμματος καὶ τοῦ βίου τοῦ φιλοσόφου, τὰς Κυρίας αὐτοῦ δόξας παραθέμενοι καὶ ταύταις τὸ πᾶν σύγγραμμα κατακλείσαντες, τέλει χρησάμενοι τῇ τῆς εὐδαιμονίας ἀρχῇ.

---

74. *Epicurea,* 34.
75. "Philosophical Allegiance in the Greco-Roman World," in *Philosophia Togata: Essays on Philosophy and Roman Society* (Oxford, 1989), 106.

[Come, then, let us put the crown, as it were, to the whole work and to the life of our philosopher, in setting out his *Principal Doctrines* and closing the whole work with them, thus using as our conclusion the starting-point of happiness.][76]

The title *Kyriai Doxai* is mentioned by Philodemus, Cicero, Plutarch, Diodorus, and Lucian. In Latin, Lucretius calls the sayings *patria praecepta* and *aurea dicta,*[77] and Cicero calls them *sententiae selectae* and *quasi ratae selectae.*[78] Cicero also refers to them ironically as "oracles of wisdom, as it were" [*quasi oracula sapientiae*] (*De Finibus* 2.7.20). In English these maxims have been called *Principal Doctrines, Peculiar Propositions, Established Beliefs, Fundamental Tenets, Cardinal Principles, Sovran Maxims, Authentic Doctrines, Master Thoughts, Principal Sayings,* and *Articles of Faith.*[79] They are often quoted, and they were well known in antiquity even among non-Epicureans; Seneca quotes the first *doxa* when he denies apotheosis to the emperor Claudius: "He can't become an Epicurean god, for this god 'is neither troubled himself nor causes trouble for others'" (*Apocolocyntosis* 8). According to Lucian a copy of the *Kyriai Doxai* was publicly burned by Alexander of Abonouteichus (*Alexander* 47). Both Diogenes Laertius and Cicero refer to the Epicurean practice of memorizing the sayings.[80]

That ancient sources were familiar with the *Kyriai Doxai* does not signify that a single collection was written by Epicurus and survived intact until it was preserved in the manuscripts of Diogenes Laertius. Given Epicurus' apparent practice of writing epitomes of his own works, it is not inconceivable that he took that practice to its logical extreme and presented some of his ideas in the

---

76. 10.138; trans. Bailey, *Epicurus,* 171. Elsewhere Bailey paraphrases "the crown of all Epicurus' writings and of the philosophic life" (344).

77. *De Rerum Natura* 3.9–13:

tu pater es, rerum inventor, tu patria nobis
suppeditas praecepta, tuisque ex, inclute, chartis,
floriferis ut apes in saltibus omnia libant,
omnia nos itidem depascimur aurea dicta,
aurea, perpetua semper dignissima vita.

It is possible that *aurea dicta* refers to all of Epicurus' writings, not only the *Kyriai Doxai.*

78. *De Finibus,* 2.7.20: "Epicuri *Kyrias Doxas,* id est quasi maxime ratas"; *De Natura Deorum* 1.30.85: "in illis selectis eius brevibusque sententiis, quas appellatis *Kyrias Doxas.*"

79. All of these appellations are recorded by DeWitt, *Epicurus,* 111, except for *Master Thoughts,* which is Clay's recent suggestion (*Lucretius and Epicurus,* 73).

80. Laertius (10.12) writes that Diocles of Magnesia claimed that Epicureans memorized Epicurus' writings. Cicero refers twice to the memorization of the *Kyriai Doxai* in particular, at *De Finibus* 2.7.20 and *De Natura Deorum* 1.40.113.

form of aphorisms. It seems improbable, however, that the entire collection of *Kyriai Doxai* was written as a forty-point creed to be memorized.

Nineteenth-century scholarship (mostly in German) rejected the ancient conception of the nature of the *Kyriai Doxai*.[81] Usener formulated four main arguments against the contention that Epicurus wrote the forty sayings and published them as a distinct collection.[82] First, if Epicurus had wanted to distribute forty "doctrines" he would have included all of his important ideas instead of omitting (as does the collection) references to the Canon and to physical theory. Second, the sayings are not preserved in any logical order, as would be expected if Epicurus had composed them as a series to be memorized.[83] Third, some of the maxims (*Principal Doctrines* 10, 20, and 24) appear to be excerpts from personal letters rather than succinctly formulated philosophical tenets. Fourth, there is repetition and duplication of sayings within the collection.[84]

These arguments are compelling, particularly the last two, which are based not on expectations of what Epicurus would have done but on analysis of the sayings themselves. The logical conclusion is that the *Kyriai Doxai* as they appear in the manuscripts of Diogenes Laertius represent a collection that developed around a nucleus of a few sayings of Epicurus. Perhaps the original nucleus is represented by the first four sayings, which by the first century B.C.E. were called the *tetrapharmakos*.[85] Many of the additions may be extracts from the writings of Epicurus himself (or perhaps from those of Metrodorus, Polyaenus, or Hermarchus). Others represent variants that developed in the process of transmission; by the time Diogenes Laertius (or his source) obtained them, the variations on several sayings differed enough to warrant preserving more than one version in the same collection.

Despite the objections outlined by Usener, English-language scholarship generally postulates that Epicurus himself formulated and distributed a collection of *Kyriai Doxai* like that in Laertius' text.[86] Diskin Clay, for example, endorses that approach in his recent book on Lucretius and Epicurus, although he

81. An early proponent of the theory that the collection is a florilegium is Pierre Gassendi, *Animadversiones in decimum librum Diogenes Laertii* (Paris, 1649), which I have not seen.

82. *Epicurea*, xliii.

83. As a result of the lack of an intelligible order, transpositions have been suggested by, for example, Gassendi and Giussani. See Bailey, *Epicurus,* 346.

84. *Principal Doctrine 3* is repeated by 18; 11 and 12 by 13; and 32 by 33.

85. There are problems with this view, as I will show. The name *tetrapharmakos* ("fourfold remedy") cannot be traced back any further than Cicero and Philodemos. See Anna Angeli, "Compendi, Eklogai, Tetrapharmakos," 65.

86. Bailey (*Epicurus,* 344–88) is representative. A recent survey of Epicurus by Long subscribes to this view. On the contrast between the obscurities in Epicurus' writing and the clarity of

does allow for some important subtleties.[87] Clay acknowledges that the collection of *Kyriai Doxai* (or *Master Thoughts,* as he calls them) may have been
somewhat shorter originally, and he demonstrates how some of the sayings were
altered by the process of oral transmission during the centuries after Epicurus.
He also acknowledges that the *Letter to Menoeceus* may have been the source
for some of the *Kyriai Doxai* and that some of the "prehistory" of the sayings can
be found in Epicurus' *On Nature.*[88] In general he affirms, however, that the sayings we find in the text of Diogenes Laertius represent a book that was published
by Epicurus.[89] He emphasizes the occurrence in the title of the word *kyriai,*
which is shown to mean "crucial." He also emphasizes the fact that in antiquity
the *Kyriai Doxai* were considered to be the authoritative sayings of Epicurus.[90]

The issue ought to have been settled a century ago, when Diogenes' inscription and the *Voice of Epicurus* were discovered. The *Voice of Epicurus* (Ἐπικούρου Προσφώνησις, also known as the *Sententiae Vaticanae*) is yet another
collection of Epicurean aphorisms that was found in a manuscript in the Vatican. Both Diogenes of Oenoanda and the Vatican text preserve some of the Epicurean sayings (with variations) that appear in Diogenes Laertius, along with
many previously unknown sayings. When the *Kyriai Doxai* of Diogenes Laertius are compared with the *doxai* of Diogenes of Oenoanda and the *Voice of
Epicurus,* it becomes apparent that the three texts represent three rather different sets of *Kyriai Doxai.* It is impossible to say which of these three versions
bears the closest resemblance to the text that Alexander sent up in flames
(whether the burning took place in history or only in fiction).

The Vatican manuscript contains eighty aphorisms. The first two are equivalent to the first two maxims recorded by Laertius.[91] *Kyria Doxa* 3 is not preserved in it at all, and after *Kyriai Doxai* 4 and 5 (*Sententiae Vaticanae* 3 and 5)
are recorded with minor changes (usually in word order), the texts diverge.

Principal Doctrines 2 and 17, Long comments: "As these passages show, Epicurus was quite capable of writing in a pithy, aphoristic style, and there can be little doubt that such statements were
intended for learning by heart" ("Epicurus and Philodemus," 628).

87. *Lucretius and Epicurus,* 72–81. His argument has met with approval; see the review by
D.P. and P.G. Fowler in *CR* 35 (1985): 275–79, in which they write that "there should be no doubt
that the collection stems from Epicurus' own hand" (276). As other reviewers have recognized,
Clay's book makes an important contribution to our understanding not only of Lucretius but of the
Epicurean attitude toward the texts of Epicurus.

88. *Lucretius and Epicurus,* 72. Clay describes how the oral transmission of the *Kyriai Doxai*
caused them to change (176–85).

89. *Lucretius and Epicurus,* 72.

90. *Lucretius and Epicurus,* 72–74.

91. The eighty aphorisms known as the *Sententiae Vaticanae* were discovered in 1888 in a
Vatican manuscript (cod. gr. 1950) and are published by C. Wotke in *Wiener Studien* 10 (1888):

Only thirteen of Diogenes Laertius' *Kyriai Doxai* appear among the eighty *Sententiae Vaticanae,* and except for the first four just mentioned, they do not appear in the familiar order.[92]

The text of the *Kyriai Doxai* inscribed by Diogenes of Oenoanda is in very poor condition, but the fragments of thirteen of his maxims have been identified with thirteen of the maxims in Laertius' text. Ironically, this poor state of preservation at Oenoanda is due largely to the high status accorded to the *doxai* by Diogenes. Because the maxims were originally displayed in large letters in one continuous line, a single maxim could extend across several stones. When the stoa was dismantled contiguous stones became separated, and for this reason the *doxai* are in worse condition than the rest of the passages, which were inscribed in narrow columns. Several years ago it was claimed that the fragments of the *Kyriai Doxai* in Oenoanda could help us calculate the original length of the whole inscription. Since the sayings were written in one unbroken line across its length, one could simply count the number of letters in Epicurus' *doxai* (i.e., in the version recorded by Diogenes Laertius) and multiply that by the number of centimeters each letter would require.[93] Such a method will not work: the recognizable maxims among the Oenoanda *doxai* are only roughly equivalent to Laertius' text, and the remains of most of them are so exiguous that exact correspondence cannot be argued with certainty.[94] Furthermore, one of the maxims of Diogenes of Oenoanda corresponds not to a text quoted by Laertius but to one of the *Sententiae Vaticanae;* and eight of Diogenes' maxims are not known from any other source.[95]

In the case of one maxim preserved by Diogenes, scholars of Epicurus and Diogenes seem to agree that Diogenes of Oenoanda preserves a text superior to

---

175 ff. The manuscript is dated to the fourteenth century and also contains some Xenophon, Marcus Aurelius, and Epictetus.

92. In the Vatican manuscript, saying 1 = *Kyria Doxa* 1, 2 = *KD* 2, 3 = *KD* 4, 5 = *KD* 5, 6 = *KD* 35, 8 = *KD* 15, 12 = *KD* 17, 13 = *KD* 27, 20 = *KD* 29, 22 = *KD* 19, 49 = *KD* 12, 50 = *KD* 8, and 72 = *KD* 13.

93. See Chilton, *Diogenes of Oenoanda,* xliv; Smith, *Thirteen New Fragments of Diogenes of Oenoanda,* Denkschriften der österreichische Akademie der Wissenschaften, Philologisch-Historische Klasse, 117 (Vienna, 1974), 48; and Smith, "Fifty-Five New Fragments of Diogenes of Oenoanda,"*AS* 28 (1978): 44.

94. The pairs of rough equivalents are as follows: *Kyria Doxa* 1 and fr. 29; *KD* 2 and fr. 30; *KD* 3 and fr. 34; *KD* 4 and fr. 44; *KD* 5 and fr. 37; *KD* 6, 8(?) and fr. 26; *KD* 6 and NF 42; *KD* 10 and fr. 33; *KD* 13 and fr. 35; *KD* 16 and fr. 49; *KD* 25 and fr. 40; *KD* 29 and fr. 39; *KD* 32 and fr. 43; *KD* 37 and fr. 66. All of these fragments belong to the treatise *Ethics;* it is the fifteenth line of each column that records the maxims.

95. Fr. 47 (NF 14), cols. III–IV is similar to *Sententiae Vaticanae* 33. The otherwise unknown sayings occur in the lower margin of frr. 39, 42, 47, 48, 54, 55, and 56 (Ch frr. 32, 34, 36, 39, and NF 14, NF 17, and NF 21).

Epicurus in Lycia

that of Diogenes Laertius.[96] The maxim concerned is a version of *Kyria Doxa* 5, which is preserved in the fifteenth line of fragment 37. In the text preserved by Laertius (which appears also in the *Sententiae Vaticanae*),[97] Epicurus says: "It is not possible to live pleasantly without living prudently and honorably and justly" [Οὐκ ἔστιν ἡδέως ζῆν ἄνευ τοῦ φρονίμως καὶ καλῶς καὶ δικαίως].[98] Following that statement, Laertius' text adds the phrase "without (living) pleasantly" [ἄνευ τοῦ ἡδέως]. That last phrase is obviously missing something, and it was recognized long ago that Cicero's translation of the maxim provides the missing phrase: "non posse iucunde vivi, nisi sapienter, honeste, iusteque vivatur, nec sapienter, honeste, iuste, nisi iucunde."[99] In the seventeenth century Gassendi saw that if one translated Cicero's version into Greek, one could add the reciprocal qualification (as stated in Cicero's last six words) to Laertius' text, so that the conclusion to the maxim would read: *"nor is it possible to live prudently and honorably and justly* without living pleasantly"[100] [οὐδὲ φρονίμως καὶ καλῶς καὶ δικαίως ἄνευ τοῦ ἡδέως].

Diogenes of Oenoanda's text of the maxim, discovered more than two hundred years after Gassendi pointed to Cicero, has nine words intact: ". . . and honorably and justly, nor prudently and honorably and (justly) . . ." [[. . .]ως καὶ καλῶς καὶ δικαίως, οὐδὲ φρονίμως καὶ καλῶς καὶ δικα[. . .]].[101] This fits Cicero's translation extremely well, and Diogenes' version is now used to supplement the text preserved by Laertius. Thus, Diogenes of Oenoanda preserves a version of the fifth maxim that contains the essential statement known also by Cicero, but which is missing from both Laertius' text and the manuscript of the *Sententiae Vaticanae*.

The variations among the three collections of Epicurus' sayings are precisely what we would expect to find if the *Kyriai Doxai* were an organic, expandable collection of Epicurean wisdom that was sometimes transmitted orally. The three extant collections must represent three different stages in development; no doubt there were other collections. The collection of *doxai* known by Lucretius probably represents yet another one. Lucretius seems to translate four *doxai* known from Diogenes Laertius, but only two of them correspond to the first four that Philodemus called the *tetrapharmakos,* and the other two are rather differ-

96. See Chilton, *Diogenes of Oenoanda,* 94; and Bailey, *Epicurus,* 351.
97. The printed editions of the *Sententiae Vaticanae* do not print this maxim; they simply record that *Sententiae Vaticanae* 5 equals *Kyria Doxa* 5. See Arrighetti, *Opere,* 141.
98. Trans. Bailey, *Epicurus,* 95.
99. *De Finibus* 1.18.57.
100. See Bailey, *Epicurus,* 351.
101. J. William, *Diogenis Oenoandensis Fragmenta* (Leipzig, 1907), 67.

ent from our Greek text.[102] That Lucretius does not include the whole *tetrapharmakos* suggests that he was not familiar with that tradition. Philodemus' collection was also different from that of Diogenes Laertius. When he lists the "fourfold remedy" the sayings correspond to the first four *doxai* of Diogenes Laertius, but they are far shorter.[103] It is difficult to say whether Philodemus condensed them or whether Diogenes Laertius expanded them.

Diogenes of Oenoanda's modern editors have noticed the differences between Diogenes' versions and Laertius' versions of the *Kyriai Doxai,* but they tend to view Diogenes' versions as mistakes or lapses of memory.[104] This tendency is inappropriate, especially since Diogenes of Oenoanda's collection was probably inscribed during or close to the reign of Hadrian and would thus antedate Diogenes Laertius' collection. Because the *Kyriai Doxai* from Oenoanda are so poorly preserved (or rather because so few have been discovered), it is difficult to discern any patterns in the variations. Complete texts for some of the maxims will surely be found if and when the site is excavated. Only then will we be able to discuss differences in outlook or emphasis between our three collections of Epicurean sayings. For now, it is clear that Diogenes used a collection of the *Kyriai Doxai* as the foundation of his inscription, above which he inscribed his own writings. The *doxai* were meant to represent the authoritative utterances of Epicurus, but they were open to change.

Thus, the inscription of Diogenes of Oenoanda illustrates several ways in which Epicureanism was able to change, even as it maintained the appearance of orthodoxy. The evidence is in the texts themselves; the handbooks, pseudepigraphical epistles, and maxims through which Epicureanism was transmitted were particularly capable of accommodating development. The scarcity of early Epicurean texts will always make the development of Epicureanism difficult to trace, but the longevity of the school and the diversity of its adherents assured the Garden a varied history. In Chapters 3 and 4 I examine a few texts that more clearly represent the specifically second-century outlook of Diogenes of Oenoanda.

---

102. *Kyria Doxa* 1 is translated in Lucretius 1.44–49 and is cited again in 2.646–51 and 5.82. *Kyria Doxa* 2 is expanded in 3.830–46. It is never safe to assume that Lucretius means to translate Epicurus literally, but 1.690–700 gives a version of *Kyria Doxa* 23; and 5.1151–60 gives a version of *Kyria Doxa* 35.

103. *Adversas [Sophistas]* 4.6–18 Sbordone.

104. Clay writes: "where Diogenes' text differs from that of Diogenes Laertius it appears that his memory has played tricks on Epicurus' Greek" (*Lucretius and Epicurus,* 78). Elsewhere, however, Clay argues that in several instances Diogenes of Oenoanda "has preserved on stone language of Epicurus which has been lost in the ms. tradition of Diogenes Laertius" ("The Philosophical Inscription," 2539).

CHAPTER 3

Defending Epicurus: The *Letter to Mother*

ἀλλὰ γράφειν ὡς . . . ἡ δὲ μήτηρ ἀτόμους ἔσχεν ἐν αὐτῇ τοιαύτας,
οἷαι συνελθοῦσαι σοφὸν ἂν ἐγέννησαν;

[Did not he [s.c. Epicurus] even write that . . . his mother had in her atoms
of such a sort that their conjunction must produce a sage?]
—Plutarch *Non Posse* 1100a–b

Current editions of Epicurus include fragments of an epistle from Diogenes' inscription that editors have dubbed the *Letter to Mother*.[1] No identifying heading
has been found, and the text as we have it is incomplete, but the letter appears
to be a faithful son's response to a message from his mother, who has been
troubled by nightmares about him. In fragment 125 (Ch fr. 52) the son offers as
consolation an Epicurean explanation of illusion and reassures his mother that,
contrary to her fears, he is attaining a state not inferior to that of "the indestructible and blessed nature" (cf. *Principal Doctrine* 1).

col. II   εἰσι τοιαῦται καὶ μὴ
           παρόντων οἷαι καὶ πα-
           ρόντων· ἁπταὶ γὰρ οὐ-
           κ οὖσαι, διανοηταὶ δέ,
      5   τὴν αὐτήν, ὅσον ἐφ' ἑαυ-
           τα[ῖ]ς, ἔχουσι δύναμιν
           πρὸς τοὺς παρόντας
           τῇ ὅτε καὶ παρόντων
           ἐκείνων ὑφειστήκε-
     10   σαν. πρὸς οὖν ταῦτα,

---

1. See G. Arrighetti, *Opere,* 2d ed. (Turin, 1973), 437–41. The letter is frr. 125–26 in Smith's
edition (Ch frr. 52–53).

col. III ὦ μῆτηρ [θάρρει· μ]ὴ
γὰρ ἐπιλ[ογίσῃ τ]ὰ φά-
ζματα ἡμ[ῶν κακά]. τί-
θει δ᾽ αὐτ[ὰ ὁρῶσα] κα-

5 θ᾽ ἡμέρα[ν ἀγαθ]όν τι
ἡμᾶς π[ροσκ]τωμέ-
νους εἰς [τὸ μακρ]οτέ-
ρω τῆς ε[ὐδαιμ]‹ο›νίας
προβαίν[ειν. ο]ὐ γὰρ μει-

10 κρὰ οὐδέ[ν τ᾽ ἀνύ]τοντα

col. IV περιγείνεται ἡ[μ]εῖν
τάδ᾽ οἷα τὴν διάθεσιν
ἡμῶν ἰσόθεον ποιεῖ
καὶ οὐδὲ διὰ τὴν θνη-

5 τότητα τῆς ἀφθάρτου
καὶ μακαρίας φύσεως
λειπομένους ἡμᾶς
δείκνυσιν. ὅτε μὲν
γὰρ ζῶμεν, ὁμοίως

10 τοῖς θεοῖς χαίρομεν

[. . . [Images] of the absent are the same as those of the present. For being not tangible, but intelligible, they have in themselves the same capacity towards those present (that is, to those who experience them) as when they arose, when their subjects were present also. So in view of these things, Mother, take heart. You must not assume that visions of me are sinister. Instead, consider that I am daily acquiring something good and am advancing to a higher level of happiness. For not slight or of no avail are the advantages that accrue to me, such that they make my condition godlike and show that not even mortality can make me inferior to the indestructible and blessed nature. For as long as I live I rejoice even as do the gods. . . .][2]

2. I have used the translations of C.W. Chilton, A. Casanova, M.F. Smith, and D. Clay (C.W. Chilton, ed., *Diogenes of Oenoanda: The Fragments* [Oxford, 1971]; A. Casanova, ed., *I frammenti di Diogene d'Enoanda,* Studi e testi 6 [Florence, 1984]; M.F. Smith, ed., *Diogenes of Oenoanda: The Epicurean Inscription* [Naples, 1993]; D. Clay, "An Epicurean Interpretation of Dreams," *AJP* 101 [1980]: 353). I have omitted the first column because the text is too defective to allow for interpretation. J. William's restoration in *Diogenis Oenoandensis Fragmenta* (Leipzig, 1907), based on Lucretius 4.26 ff. and 722 ff., is widely accepted. For an explanation of the theory of dreams revealed here, see chapter 4.

After a gap in which the writer seems to have explained that "death is nothing to us" (cf. *Principal Doctrine* 2), our text resumes in fragment 126 (Ch fr. 53) with his apparent assertion that the happiness he has gained cannot be taken away even by death.

col. I   ... τὴν ἴσ[ην, ἂν]
           [γ'] ἀντιλάβηται τῆς
           ἐλαττώσεως· ἂν μὴ
           αἰσθάνηται δέ, πῶς
      5   ἐλαττοῦται; μετὰ
           δὴ τοιούτων ἡμᾶς ἀ-
           γαθῶν προσδόκα, μῆ-
           τερ, χαίροντας αἰεὶ καὶ
           ἔπαιρε σεαυτὴν ἐφ' οἷς
     10   πράττομεν.

[... the same, if one suffers diminishing; but if one is not conscious, how is one diminished? Surrounded by such good things, then, think of me, mother, as rejoicing always and have confidence in how I am faring.]

Before the text breaks off again two columns later, the son brings up the topic of finances.

col. I 10   τῶν

col. II   μέ[ν]τοι χορηγιῶν
            φείδου πρὸς Διός
            ὧν συνεχῶς ἡμεῖν
            ἀποστέλλεις. οὐ
      5   γὰρ σοί τι βούλομαι
            λείπειν, ἵν' ἐμοὶ περιτ-
            τεύῃ, λείπειν δ' ἐ-
            μοί μᾶλλον, ἵνα μὴ
            σοί, καίτοι γε ἀφθ[ό]-
     10   νως κἀμοῦ διάγ[ον-]

col. III   τος ἐν πᾶσιν, διὰ [τὸ τοὺς]
            φίλους καὶ τὸ συνεχῶ[ς]
            τὸν πατέρα ἡμεῖν πέμ-
            πειν ἀργύριον, προσφά-

5   τως δὲ δὴ καὶ διὰ τοῦ Κλέ-
     ωνος τὰς ἐννέα μνᾶς
     ἀπεσταλκότος. οὔκουν
     ἑκάτερον ὑμῶν ἰδίᾳ δεῖ
     βαρεῖσθαι[3] δι' ἡμᾶς, συν-
10   χρῆσθαι δὲ τῷ ἑτέρῳ τ[ὸ]ν [ἕτερον. . . .

[But by Zeus, be sparing with the supplies you are constantly sending me. I do not wish you to be in need so that I may have abundance—I would rather suffer need so that you should not; and yet I am living in plenty in every respect thanks to friends and father continually sending me money; and only recently through Cleon who has sent me the nine minas. So none of you should be individually burdened by me, but one should make use of the other. . . .]

Beginning with Cousin's first publication of the fragments in 1892, almost all scholarship on Diogenes has rejected the possibility that this text should be grouped with Diogenes' other epistles and has welcomed it instead as a genuine document from the correspondence of Epicurus.[4] Cousin himself believed that the language of the letter was simpler and clearer than the rest of the inscription.[5] But most of the arguments of Cousin and of subsequent editors are based on the content of the letter. First, the letter-writer's financial situation does not accord with anything we know about Diogenes but does seem to fit the biographical tradition of Epicurus preserved by Diogenes Laertius, who records several anecdotes about the poverty of Epicurus' parents.[6] Second, the story that Epicurus' mother Chaerestrata used to travel around reading purification charms (καθαρμούς) in strangers' cottages (a story Laertius himself dismisses as anti-Epicurean propaganda) has seemed especially relevant because the

---

3. On the financial meaning of βαρεῖσθαι, cf. 1 Thess. 2:7, 1 Thess. 2:9, and 2 Cor. 11:9 (parallels suggested to me by Professor Abraham Malherbe). Cf. also Lucian *De Mercede Conductis* 20 and 27, and other examples cited by Ronald F. Hock, *The Social Context of Paul's Ministry* (Philadelphia, 1980), 80 n. 44.

4. G. Cousin, "Inscriptions d'Oenoanda," *BCH* 16 (1892): 1–70. In "Die philosophische Inschrift von Oinoanda," *BCH* 21 (1897): 346–443, R. Heberdey and E. Kalinka refer to the *Letter to Mother* as *Epikurbrief,* without comment (e.g., see 430, 431, 432, 438, 442). The history of scholarship of the *Letter to Mother* is surveyed by Chilton, *Diogenes of Oenoanda: The Fragments* (Oxford, 1971), 106 ff. See also Arrighetti, *Opere,* 675. A decade ago a report on research on Diogenes stated that the attribution to Epicurus was a settled issue: A. Casanova, "Diogene d'Enoanda oggi," *Prometheus* 9 (1983): 132. Smith's *The Epicurean Inscription* now presents the possibility that the letter may be pseudepigraphical (555–60).

5. "Inscriptions d'Oenoanda," 69.

6. See R. Phillippson, "Diogenes von Oinoanda," *PW* Suppl. 5 (1931): cols. 153–70.

mother in both anecdote and letter appears to be superstitious.[7] And third, it has been argued that the Cleon who sends the nine minas must be the Cleon who delivers a letter to Epicurus in the *Letter to Pythocles* (84).[8] Also significant is the currency named: other inscriptions in Oenoanda mention Roman denarii rather than Greek minas.

The main voice of dissent to the theory that the letter was written by Epicurus is that of J. William, the editor of the 1907 Teubner text, who argues that the *Letter to Mother* is a piece of correspondence from Diogenes of Oenoanda to his own mother.[9] William bases his judgment primarily on the fact that the *Letter to Mother,* like most of Diogenes' inscription, seems to contain more elements of Koine than Epicurus' known writings. The word θνητότης (fr. 52, col. IV, lines 4–5), for example, which appears in texts by several later authors, such as J. Chrysostom and scholiasts to Lucian and Philostratus, seems not to be attested before Diogenes' use. It appears again, moreover, in another fragment of the inscription. William also points out that the name *Cleon,* being very common, may not be significant evidence.[10] William's discussion does not treat the rhetorical style of the *Letter to Mother,* but he could have adduced the letter's Gorgianic balance and repetition as evidence that the language of the letter is very unlike that of Epicurus. He might also have noted that the vocabulary of the letter-writer seems to have been influenced (anachronistically) by Chrysippus: the word φάζμα (vision, dream image) in fragment 52, column 3, lines 2–3 is used elsewhere by Diogenes but does not seem to fit the usage of Epicurus.[11]

Despite William's appeal to linguistic evidence, most readers have judged that the content and general character of the letter support the original attribution to Epicurus. In his 1972 commentary Chilton summed up the issue as fol-

---

7. See Philippson, "Diogenes," col. 165–66. The story is recorded in the *Life of Epicurus* 10.4.

8. Cousin, "Inscriptions d'Oenoanda," 69.

9. *Diogenis Oenoandensis Fragmenta,* xx–xxx. Some reviewers of William's edition agree with his verdict, and Anthony Raubitschek attributes the letter to Diogenes in his dissertation, "Epikureische Untersuchungen" (Ph.D. diss., University of Vienna, 1935). Subsequent editors, however, including Arrighetti, Parente, and M.F. Smith ("Diogenes of Oenoanda, New Fragments 122–124," *AS* 34 [1984]: 43–57), reassert that the letter belongs to Epicurus. G.N. Hoffman recognizes that "the letter may well be a rhetorical exercise (by D. or another) written in Epicurus' name" "Diogenes of Oenoanda: A Commentary" [Ph.D. diss., University of Minnesota, 1976], 442), but he does not pursue the matter.

10. He might have added that the *Letter to Pythocles* is considered spurious by some authorities, both ancient and modern. Bailey, who accepts the *Letter to Pythocles* as authentic, suggests that the Cleon mentioned in it may be "quite imaginary" (C. Bailey, *Epicurus: The Extant Remains* [Oxford, 1926], 276).

11. Chrysippus uses the term to designate one of his categories of visual perception.

lows: "The whole tone and content of the letter is quite incompatible with the wealthy, aristocratic, and not very philosophic Diogenes, but accords perfectly with our knowledge of Epicurus."[12] The only acknowledged remaining problem is the exact dating of the letter: Grilli, for example, thinks that the parents' ability to send any money at all indicates a date before Epicurus' family was expelled from Samos in 322, while Arrighetti gives it a later date because he finds it unlikely that the teenage Epicurus could have written a letter replete with so many mature Epicurean ideas.[13]

Of all the arguments in favor of Epicurus' authorship, the point that any money mentioned in his correspondence should be on the Greek standard whereas Diogenes' should be in denarii is perhaps the most compelling.[14] The recent discovery that the letter seems to have belonged to a section of the inscription that contained other letters of Epicurus would appear to offer further support.[15] But those aspects of the letter that militate against Diogenes' authorship do not necessarily establish Epicurus as the writer, nor do its Koine vocabulary and rhetorical flourishes prove that Diogenes wrote it. Scholarship on the *Letter to Mother* has asked the wrong question. The issue should not be whether the letter was written by Diogenes or Epicurus. Rather, the question should be, Is the *Letter to Mother* an authentic work of Epicurus or is it fictional?

Is the *Letter to Mother* by Epicurus?

Those who accept the *Letter to Mother* as a genuine work of Epicurus appear to take it as a real specimen from the philosopher's personal correspondence with his mother. In other words, it is not argued that Epicurus wrote the letter as a treatise on dreams and simply framed it with epistolary formulas. This was his practice elsewhere, in, for example, the *Letter to Herodotus* and the *Letter to Menoeceus.* These are not actual letters but philosophical tracts dressed as letters.[16] The disciples to whom the letters are addressed were presumably real

---

12. *Diogenes of Oenoanda,* 108.

13. Epicurus was in Athens on military service when his parents were evicted from Samos (Diogenes Laertius 10.1). Epicurus joined them at their new home in Colophon in 321 when he was twenty years old. At some time during the next decade he went to Teos to study with Nausiphanes, and he was again separated from his parents when he began teaching in Mytiline, Lampascus, and, finally, Athens. See J.M. Rist, *Epicurus: An Introduction* (Cambridge, 1972), 3–7.

14. I say this despite Anthony Raubitschek's ingenious solution in his dissertation "Epikureische Untersuchungen." (See the section titled "What about Those Minas?" at the end of this chapter.)

15. See Clay, "The Philosophical Inscription," 2541–48.

16. Adolf Deissmann, in *Licht vom Osten* (Tübingen, 1908), pointed out the distinction by calling personal communications "letters" and calling literary letters "epistles." Sykutris, in his

people who would have received a copy, but the letters were intended primarily for a larger audience.

This type of ostensibly private communication was well suited to Epicureanism. Since Epicurus advised his followers to withdraw from public life and may even have discouraged public proselytizing, a more overtly public mode of dissemination would have been inappropriate. The format of the personal letter was appropriate for Epicurus also, because he established close personal ties with his students, who followed him "as though they were adherents to a new religion."[17] In fact, the convention of committing philosophical discourse to letter form appears to have originated with Epicurus. The letters of Isocrates and Plato may provide a precedent if some of them are authentic, but Epicurus developed this prose form and used it for exclusively didactic compositions.[18] With the exception of the *Letter to Pythocles* (which may be spurious),[19] Epicurus wrote these epistles with a minimum of epistolary ornamentation; they contain no "small talk" or personal news. Clearly the *Letter to Mother*, with its references to financial matters and news of the writer's progress, does not belong to the same category.[20] And yet, with its persistent "philosophizing," it

---

"Epistolographie," *PW* Suppl. 5 (1931): col. 210–11, uses the appellation "Brief als Einkleidungsform," a term more descriptive than Deissmann's but clumsy in English. Sykutris (col. 203) claims that such epistles are never addressed to imaginary persons.

17. Sykutris, "Epistolographie," col. 203.

18. Sykutris writes: "der Klassiker des Lehrbriefes ist Epikuros gewesen" ("Epistolographie," col. 204). Unlike the three epistles of Epicurus preserved in Diogenes Laertius, Plato's seventh epistle is not exclusively didactic. Arnaldo Momigliano, in *The Development of Greek Biography* (Cambridge, Mass., 1971), 61, discusses Plato's seventh epistle as an authentic autobiographical letter, although he admits that it could be "biography disguised as autobiography." He views Plato's seventh epistle as a model for later unauthentic letters and is "reluctant to admit that forgery preceded reality in the matter of autobiographical letters."

19. See Philodemus' remarks, printed in H. Usener, *Epicurea* (Leipzig, 1887; reprint, Rome, 1963), 34.

20. Nor does the *Letter to Mother* fit into the category of true "personal letter." The contrast between it and a papyrus fragment from Herculaneum is instructive. The fragment contains what is generally accepted as a real letter from Epicurus (or possibly his companion Polyaenus) to a child, and that the letter contains nothing overtly "Epicurean" speaks in favor of its authenticity.

> Pythocles, Hermarchus, Ctesippus and I have reached Lampsacus safe and sound. We found Themista and the rest of our friends there in good health. I hope you are well too, and your mummy, and that you are obedient to them in all things. (*P. Herc.* 176 = Usener fr. 176 = Arrighetti fr. 113; trans. J.M. Rist, *Epicurus, An Introduction* [Cambridge, 1972], 12.

The string of names of familiar Epicureans in the papyrus fragment may indicate, however, that this letter was actually part of an attempt to construct "documents" for an early biography of Epicurus. Rist thinks the letter was written "either by Epicurus himself, or, more probably, by Polyaenus"(*Epicurus,* 12). Deissmann attributes the letter to Epicurus. See also A. Vogliano, "Autour du jardin d'Epicure," *E. Pap.* 4 (1938): 1–13.

seems suspiciously too "Epicurean" in content to be an actual private letter from Epicurus to his mother.[21]

Although the *Letter to Mother* bears little resemblance to Epicurus' philosophical epistles, it has salient features in common with fictitious letters that pretend to have been written by philosophers or other historical figures. The prevalence of such letters in late antiquity has generally been recognized since Bentley's *Dissertation upon the Epistles of Phalaris*.[22] That the letter in Oenoanda is inscribed on stone should not prejudice us in favor of authenticity. In the following discussion I present for comparison several letters written in the voices of ancient philosophers in the first and second centuries C.E. and suggest a comparable context for the composition of the *Letter to Mother.* My approach, which stresses the typology of fictional letters, draws attention to stereotypical themes and an interest in biographical detail. More important, I show that the *Letter to Mother* is especially concerned with the defense of Epicurus.

How to Write a Letter from a Philosopher:
The Theme of the Refused Gift

Several fictitious letters composed in the first and second centuries C.E. depict philosophers-to-be writing home to apprise their parents of their progress and to reassure them that the wisdom they are pursuing is valuable despite the hardships involved. The thirtieth letter of "Diogenes the Cynic," for example, addressed to his father soon after "Diogenes" has arrived in Athens to study philosophy, contains an anecdotal account of a "Socratic" dialogue.[23] Socrates teaches that the two roads to happiness are like the two roads that climb the acropolis: one is long and smooth, the other steep and difficult. "Diogenes" explains to his father that with Socrates' guidance he has chosen the latter. In other letters "Diogenes" asks his father and mother not to be distressed over their son's poor clothing and Cynic lifestyle; his poverty is not disgraceful but noble. Even Odysseus, "the wisest of the Greeks," returned to Ithaca dressed like a Cynic.[24]

---

21. Momigliano (*Greek Biography,* 61) believes that the "un-Platonic" nature of Plato's seventh letter supports its authenticity.

22. Richard Bentley, *A Dissertation upon the Epistles of Phalaris, Themistokles, Socrates, Euripides, and Others and the Fables of Aesop,* 1697.

23. Rudolphus Hercher, *Epistolographi Graeci* (Paris, 1873; reprint, Amsterdam, 1965), 244–45; Abraham Malherbe, *The Cynic Epistles* (Missoula, Mont., 1977), 130–31.

24. Hercher, *Epistolographi,* 236–37, vii; Malherbe, *The Cynic Epistles,* 98; and Hercher, 248, xxxiv; Malherbe 142 ff.

The first of a series of seventeen letters attributed to "Chion of Heraclea" also encourages distressed parents not to worry about their son, who, like "Diogenes the Cynic," has decided to travel to Athens to study philosophy. "Chion's" letters are written in the voice of the tyrannicide who slew Clearchus, tyrant of Heraclea, in 353/2 B.C.E., but they seem to have been composed during (or close to) the second century C.E. Together they form an epistolary novel that presents the merits of Platonism and its practical applications.[25] The novel opens in medias res with a reference to the parents' concern: "On the third day of my sojourn here near Byzantium, Lysis arrived with your letter telling me how worried you and the whole family are."[26] "Chion" acknowledges the difficulty of the struggle he has embarked on, but he asks his parents to look forward to the ultimate happiness they will obtain when their son has acquired (and eventually utilized) the virtue he set out to obtain.

ἄμεινον δὲ ὥσπερ ἀθλοφόρῳ μείζονά μοι προθεῖναι τὰ ἆθλα, ἵνα κρείττων ἐπ' αὐτὰ ἀγωνιστὴς γένωμαι οὕτως οὖν διάκεισο, ὦ πάτερ, καὶ παραμυθοῦ τὴν μητέρα, εἴπερ ἄρα ἐκείνην μὲν ἐν τοῖς παρηγορουμένοις, σὲ δὲ ἐν τοῖς παρηγοροῦσι τετάχθαι προσήκει.

[You had better think of me as one who is taking part in an honorable contest and offer a finer prize in order that I shall fight better for it. This is the state of mind in which I would like to see you, dear father, and please console my mother, for it is fitting that she be encouraged and that you encourage her.][27]

Gifts made to great luminaries of the past (young and old) are also a common epistolary theme. In the *Letter to Mother* the writer asks his mother to stop being so generous; what he has is enough, and he does not want his mother to deprive herself on his account. Such demurrals are a well-worn theme in fictitious letters, particularly in those from philosophers. Usually the rejected money is a large sum offered by a king. The philosopher typically

25. David Konstan and Phillip Mitsis write that the letters "dramatize the harmony of a philosophical vocation and the commitment to a political life appropriate to a young aristocrat" ("Chion of Heraclea: A Philosophical Novel in Letters," *Apeiron* 22 [1990]: 258). A critical edition with translation and commentary is available in Ingemar Düring, ed., *Chion of Heraclea* (Göteborg, 1951), 57.

26. Here and in the following quotations I have used Düring's translation from *Chion of Heraclea,* with some changes for the sake of clarity.

27. Hercher, *Epistolographi,* 194; trans. Düring, *Chion of Heraclea,* 44–45.

either rejects all the money, asserting that he and his friends are not in want, or rejects most of the gift but retains a small portion for his modest living expenses.

Thus, "Euripides," in the first of a series of five letters ascribed to him, virtuously returns all the money sent to him by King Archelaus.[28] He asserts that he is acting on principle, not merely in quest of a good reputation. "Socrates," in two letters attributed to him, also rejects Archelaus' money, and because the king is persistent he must refuse the gift repeatedly. "Socrates" explains his action in detail: philosophy cannot be purchased, a wise man does not need wealth, and he considers it wrong to accept money for his teaching.[29] Likewise, and for similar reasons, "Heraclitus" rejects Darius' offer to provide for him lavishly if he comes to Persia.[30] "Diogenes the Cynic" addresses a similar refusal to Antipater, and like "Euripides" he adds that he must decline the invitation to the Macedonian court for his own reasons and that he does not do so because he seeks the admiration of the masses.[31]

Also relevant are three very short letters preserved in Diogenes Laertius' accounts of the lives of the sages Solon, Pittacus, and Anacharsis. In these letters, which are recorded separately in the individual biographies, each sage writes to Croesus to decline the king's invitation to take up residence in his palace.[32] These three simple letters may represent our earliest version of the philosopher's demurral. A date as early as the fifth or fourth century has been assigned to "Anacharsis'" letter, whereas most of the fictitious letters discussed so far in this section are creations of the first or second century C.E.[33] The topos

---

28. Hercher, *Epistolographi,* 275, i. A critical edition with commentary is now available in Hanns-Ulrich Gösswein, *Die Briefe des Euripides* (Meisenheim am Glan, 1975). Gösswein's appendix contains the Greek texts of letters I discuss here.

29. Hercher, *Epistolographi,* 609, i; 613, vi; Abraham Malherbe, *The Cynic Epistles,* 27 ff.

30. Hercher, *Epistolographi,* 280, i, ii; Malherbe, *The Cynic Epistles,* 186–88.

31. Hercher, *Epistolographi,* 236, iv; Malherbe, *The Cynic Epistles,* 94.

32. Hercher, *Epistolographi,* 637, iv; 491; 105, x.

33. Reuters thinks the letter of "Anacharis" must be earlier than the third century and could be from the fourth or fifth century B.C.E. Richard Heinze, "Anacharsis," *Philologus* 50 (1891): 465, assigns it to the fourth century. Though the three letters to Croesus are written in (approximations of) three different dialects, I suspect that all three letters are closely related; perhaps Diogenes Laertius (or more likely his source) found them together in one collection and used them as material for each of the respective sages' biographies.

Gösswein (*Die Briefe des Euripides,* 29 and passim) dates "Euripides'" letters to the first or second century C.E. Harold Attridge (*First Century Cynicism in the Epistles of Heraclitus,* Harvard Theological Studies 29 [Missoula, Mont., 1976]) dates those letters to the first century C.E. W. Obens ("Qua aetate Socratis et Socraticorum epistulae quae dicuntur scriptae sint" [Ph.D. diss., University of Münster, 1912]) assigns "Socrates'" letters to the second century C.E., but Johannes Sykutris (*Die Briefe des Sokrates und der Sokratiker* [Paderborn, 1933], 112), thinks they may be slightly earlier than the second century.

of the rejected gift occurs not only in letters[34] but also in anecdotes circulated elsewhere. For example, Diogenes Laertius reports that Xenocrates retained three thousand drachmas from a large gift made by Alexander but returned the rest, saying that Alexander needed more money "because he had more people to care for."[35]

The point of these "philosopher's demurrals" is perhaps best spelled out by Lucian, who, in the guise of Parrhesiades in the *Fisherman*, fishes off the edge of the acropolis for false philosophers, using gold and figs for bait.[36] This brings us to "Plato's" thirteenth letter, in which "Plato" seeks more and more money from Dionysius.[37] (One excuse he gives is that he may need money if his mother dies soon.) Reversing the pattern, this exception proves the rule. Unlike the letters previously discussed, "Plato's" thirteenth epistle does not mean to document a philosopher's virtuous behavior. Rather, its purpose is to vilify: the author of this anti-Platonic letter seems to have been a Pythagorean who wished to demonstrate the superiority of his school by casting aspersions upon his enemies.[38] In one of the letters of "Phalaris," the tyrant bestows elaborate gifts, including a large sum of money and twenty slave boys, on his private doctor Polyclitus, who apparently accepts with gratitude.[39] This too is explicable; the point is not to heroize the unknown doctor Polyclitus but to magnify the legendary wealth of Phalaris.

The rejection of funds by the youthful "Epicurus" in the *Letter to Mother* is admittedly on a smaller scale and is addressed not to a king but to a parent. The main point is the same, however: the philosopher asserts that he is interested not in wealth but in the pursuit of wisdom. This is not the only philosopher's letter to decline small gifts from home. In most of the thirty-six epistles attributed to "Crates," the philosopher either rejects a gift or warns his correspondents against the evils of wealth. Although his counsel takes a particularly Cynic shape, the thirtieth and thirty-second letters of the "Crates" collection fit our pat-

---

34. My catalog of "philosopher's demurrals" is not exhaustive; "Hippocrates'" letter to the King of Persia and "Pythagoras'" letter to Hieron, for example, may also be relevant.

35. 4.8. See Cicero *Tusc.* 5.32.91 and Plutarch *Mor.* 181e.

36. For the importance attached to the integration of a philosopher's lifestyle (or βίος) with his philosophy, see J. Hahn, *Der Philosoph und die Gesellschaft: Selbstverständnis, öffentliches Auftreten und populäre Erwartungen in der hohen Kaiserzeit* (Stuttgart, 1989).

37. Hercher, *Epistolographi,* 528 ff.

38. See G. Pasquali, *Le Lettere di Platone* (Florence, 1938), 217–20, cited by Wolfgang Speyer, *Die literarische Fälschung im heidnischen und christlichen Altertum: Ein Versuch ihrer Deutung* (Munich, 1971), 140. "Plato's" thirteenth letter is considered spurious by most authorities, but most who have recognized it as a late composition have not judged it to be particularly anti-Platonic. See, e.g., Ulrich von Wilamowitz, "Unechte Briefe," *Hermes* 33 (1898): 496.

39. Hercher, *Epistolographi,* 427, lxx.

tern particularly well.[40] There "Crates" tells his wife Hipparchia that he is return-
ing the tunic she has sent to him. A Cynic requires no such luxuries.

One other letter provides an even better parallel to the topos of the refused
gift as it occurs in the *Letter to Mother*. This letter is also found in the epistolary
novel about "Chion of Heraclea." "Chion's" sixth letter portrays him as a
young man who has just arrived in Athens to study with Plato in the Academy.
His parents have sent gifts and money, so he writes to thank them. "Chion" tells
them that the fish, honey, and wine will give him an opportunity to entertain his
friends and even Plato. The latter does not accept gifts, but, Chion intimates, he
might join his disciples in enjoying this produce sent from Heraclea. While
Chion is willing to accept supplies from home, money is another matter. Self-
consciously imitating Plato's behavior, Chion closes his letter as follows.

χρημάτων δὲ οὐδὲ εἷς ἔμοιγε πόθος, καὶ μάλιστα ἐν Ἀθήναις τε ὄντι
καὶ Πλάτωνι διαλεγομένῳ, ἐπεὶ καὶ ἄτοπον ἴσως, πεπλευκέναι μὲν
ἡμᾶς εἰς τὴν Ἑλλάδα, ἵνα ἧττον φιλοχρήματοι γενώμεθα, μηδὲν
δ' ἧττον καὶ ἐκ Πόντου πλεῖν πρὸς ἡμᾶς τὴν φιλοχρημοσύνην.
Χαριέστερον οὖν ποιήσεις ταῦτα πέμπων, ὅσα τῆς πατρίδος ἡμᾶς,
οὐχ ὅσα πλούτου ἀναμνήσει.

[I have no desire at all for money, especially since I am now in Athens at-
tending Plato's school. For it would be quite out of place if now, when I
have sailed to Greece in order to become less fond of money, love of
money should none the less sail to me from Pontus. Please do send me
such things as remind me of my country, not of wealth.][41]

Thus, "Chion" and young "Epicurus" who writes the *Letter to Mother* enact
a younger person's version of the philosopher's rejection of gifts. As mere students they are in no position to be offered a king's support, but they respond appropriately (that is, according to the model set by the conventional "wise man")
when their parents make similar offers. The positions the young philosophers
take regarding wealth are also appropriate for their chosen schools. The young
"Diogenes" is shown embracing the emblems of his Cynic lifestyle, while
"Chion" imitates Plato. Likewise, "Epicurus" enacts the fundamentals of Epicurean economy. From Philodemus, Plutarch, and Diogenes Laertius it is apparent that Epicurus solicited financial support from his followers.[42] The *Letter to
Mother* demonstrates how fairly he did so: he asks for small contributions

40. Hercher, *Epistolographi,* 214–15; Malherbe, *The Cynic Epistles,* 80, 82. For various explanations of the doublet, see Malherbe, 10.

41. Hercher, *Epistolographi,* 198; trans. Düring, *Chion of Heraclea,* 57.

42. See Philodemus fr. 55 (Olivieri), Plutarch 1117de, and Diogenes Laertius 10.20.

toward his frugal lifestyle, with the dues being shared so as not to be oppressive. Moreover, in the *Letter to Mother* "Epicurus" asserts that his mother should be comfortable even if he is not, thus dramatizing the principle (attributed to Epicurus by Diogenes Laertius 10.11) that friends need not keep all in common, for to do so would imply a lack of trust.

The Recurrent Theme as a Criterion against Authenticity

That a trope or pattern common to other pseudepigraphical letters occurs in a letter attributed to a philosopher or other historical figure should weigh heavily against authenticity. This judgment is not new; Bentley cited a recurrent theme in Greek epistolography as evidence against authenticity in his *A Dissertation upon the Epistles of Phalaris.* The cliché to which Bentley objected was the request for tyrants' clemency toward certain worthy (but sometimes unnamed) prisoners.[43] Clichés in the letters of any particular figure have seldom been compared with those in the rest of the large corpus of Greek epistles.[44] One could compose a list of recurrent themes as a companion to Hercher's *Epistolographi Graeci:* rejections of gifts, requests for clemency, descriptions of prodigious wealth, letters of introduction, and apologies explaining why the author left Athens would be a few of the important categories. Another category would be reserved for letters in which the addressee is not actually a contemporary of the alleged author. To my knowledge, no such list exists. Instead, suspicious letters are categorized according to the stock letter-types described by ancient epistolary theorists. The apparent assumption is that close correspondence would show that the writer had taken the basic form and theme of the letter from a common handbook. Although the extant handbooks are difficult to date securely, they are certainly postclassical.[45]

Comparing extant letters to model letters in the handbooks is seldom productive. For example, in his commentary on the letters of "Euripides," Gösswein

---

43. On the second half of "Euripides'" first letter, where the tragedian requests clemency for two men, Bentley writes: "Now, besides that the whole business has the air and visage of Sophistry, for this same is a mighty topic too in Phalaris' Epistles, it is a plain violation of good sense to petition for a man without telling his name" (422).

44. H.A. Steen's "Les clichés épistolaires dans les lettres sur papyrus greques," *Class. Med.* 1 (1938): 119–76, treats verbal formulas in real letters.

45. Recent studies assign dates between 200 B.C.E. and 300 C.E. to Pseudo-Demetrius' *Typoi Epistalikoi,* a handbook which discusses twenty-one types of letters. The *Epistolimaioi Characteres,* which discusses forty-one types, is attributed in one manuscript tradition to Libanius and in another to Proclus and was written by an unknown author in the fourth, fifth, or sixth century C.E. See Abraham Malherbe, "Ancient Epistolary Theorists," *Ohio Journal of Religious Studies* 5.2 (1977): 3–77; now published separately (Missoula, Mont., 1988).

finds that theorists have no special name for the type of letter in which money is rejected, so he is forced to conclude that the closest category available is the ἀποφαντική, the "responding" letter. Since that designation would not take the whole of "Euripides'" first letter into account, Gösswein ultimately assigns that letter to Pseudo-Libanius' forty-first category, the μικτή, or "mixed," letter: after rejecting the king's money the author moves on to another subject.[46] Düring, the editor of the letters of "Chion of Heraclea," also assigns each letter to one of Pseudo-Demetrius' or Pseudo-Libanius' categories, but none of them matches perfectly. "Chion's" sixth letter (in which he declines future gifts from his parents) is placed in the general category of εὐχαριστική, or "thank-you note." Düring himself admits that his designations "should not be taken too seriously or pressed too hard."[47]

Thus, the ancient theorists' model letter-types are not very useful for categorization of fictitious letters; nor should they be. After all, the epistolary handbooks were meant to provide advice for the writing of *real* letters. Real letter-writers rarely needed to write to Macedonian monarchs to reject large sums of money. Nor did real students often wish to decline support from their parents. Furthermore, even real letters should not agree with the handbooks in detail; the models were designed to provide only a sparse framework.[48]

More relevant to the study of fictitious letters are the discussions of prosopopoeia in the rhetorical handbooks. Most such discussions do not mention letter-writing, but the section on prosopopoeia in Aelius Theon's *Progymnasmata* (probably of the first or second century C.E.)[49] lists the letter as a medium through which a person's character can be portrayed. Theon's guidelines are both general and sensible: the words a writer wishes to attribute to another person must be appropriate to that person's age, the era, the place, the event, and the subject matter. This applies whether the person portrayed is a husband taking leave of his wife, a general addressing his troops, or Cyrus attacking the

---

46. Gösswein, *Die Briefe des Euripides,* 17–19. B. Fiore applies the categories of Pseudo-Demetrius to the corpus of Socratic letters and assigns a category to most of the letters. Although none of the letters seem to fit those categories particularly well, Fiore concludes that the Socratic collection "thus betrays a knowledge and use of the varied letter types as listed in the handbooks" (*The Function of Personal Example in the Socratic and Pastoral Epistles,* Analecta Biblica 105 [Rome, 1986], 127). Fiore's examination of the letters' use of paradigms and exempla is more fruitful.

47. Düring, *Chion of Heraclea,* 19.

48. It seems that Pseudo Demetrius' *Typoi Epistolikoi* did not even influence real letters: a comparison of both literary and real letters with that handbook reveals no decisive parallels. This is the conclusion of Clinton W. Keyes, "The Greek Letter of Introduction," *AJP* 56 (1935): 28–44.

49. George Kennedy, *The Art of Rhetoric in the Roman World* (Princeton, 1972), 616, gives the first century as a possible date.

Massagetae.[50] Spartans, for example, should say little, while Athenians must be outspoken. Older people should speak with authority, while the young should speak with simplicity and *sophrosyne*. By having the young philosophers decline gifts from their parents, rather than the gifts of kings, the author of the *Letter to Mother* and that of "Chion's" letters have followed Theon's simple rule. Both authors also invested their young philosophers with *sophrosyne:* their letters express respect for their parents and an appropriate concern for their parents' well-being.

Thus, while the "philosophers'" letters are not easily categorized according to the types of letters listed in the epistolary handbooks, they do conform to the guidelines for prosopopoeia of Aelius Theon and other rhetoricians.[51] The author of the *Letter to Mother* did not necessarily read Theon's handbook, but the correspondence suggests that character portrayal was one of our author's goals.

Since Bentley, the belief that all spurious letters are either rhetorical exercises, forgeries written for profit, or mere hoaxes has led to their neglect.[52] This attitude was fostered by Bentley's acerbic style; he meant his to be the last word on the subject, and following generations acquiesced.[53] But the explanations behind spurious letters are diverse. Whether a letter pretends to be from Socrates, Euripides, Phalaris, or Paul the Apostle, it is impossible for us to categorize it with certainty as a hoax or a practical joke. Such motives may have played a role occasionally, but proof requires unusual external evidence like that we have for Lucian's (nonextant) treatise by "Heraclitus." According to Galen, Lucian fabricated and put into circulation such a text simply for the joy of watching a learned contemporary write a commentary on it.[54] From Galen we know that competitive

---

50. These are Theon's examples.

51. See L. Spengel, ed., *Rhetores Graeci,* vol. 2 (Leipzig, 1853–56).

52. Recently, however, there has been a revival of interest, especially among scholars of early Christianity and the New Testament. See Malherbe, *The Cynic Epistles;* and Fiore, *Personal Example.* Both provide extensive bibiographies.

53. Gösswein remarks: "Wie fruchtbar und verdienstvoll auch immer die Anwendung von scharfsinniger Methode und witziger Polemik sich bewaehrte: Bentleys brillantes Werk zeitigte entschieden mehr Wirkung, als der Sache dienlich sein konnte. Denn in der Folge wagte nun—aus Furcht, sich zu kompromittieren—lange Zeit niemand mehr, der Epistolographis auch nur die geringste Aufmerksamkeit zu schenken" (*Die Briefe des Euripides,* 4).

54. For Lucian's practical joke, see G. Strohmaier, "Übersehenes zur Biographie Lukians," *Philologus* 120 (1976): 117–27. Vladimir Nabokov provides a modern parallel: because the prominent critic Georgy Adamovich dismissed Nabokov's poetry, Nabokov wrote a poem to suit Adamovich's taste and published it under the pseudonym Vasily Shishkov. As soon as Adamovich published effusive praise for the "new" poet, Nabokov revealed his trick by publishing a story entitled "Vasily Shishkov" in the same Russian émigré paper. See V. Nabokov, *Tyrants Destroyed and Other Stories* (New York, 1975), 204. See also Andrew Field, *Nabokov: His Life in Part* (London, 1977), 218.

bids for rare manuscripts sometimes inspired the production of forgeries, especially under the Ptolemies and Attalids.[55] We also know that letters from famous persons were sometimes written as part of one's rhetorical training. Theon's *Progymnasmata* attests to this practice, which was similar to the more popular *melete*. The omission of letter-writing from most discussions of prosopopoeia suggests that such epistolary exercises were not common, however, and letter-writing in general was not always included in the rhetorical curriculum.[56]

Furthermore, ever since Bentley dismissed the authors of so many Greek epistles as mere "sophists"—in Bentley's disquisition the sibilance echoes his contempt—the term *rhetorical exercise* has been used to categorize all letters whose authenticity is doubted. Sometimes this has been an intentional condemnation,[57] but more often scholarship has simply failed to notice that our letters often have serious philosophical and apologetic purposes. Practical jokers, the rhetorical schools, and the book trade cannot account for all of our fictitious letters. The explanation for their existence is more complicated than Bentley assumed.

Why Write a Letter from Epicurus?

Our testimonials to letters of Epicurus contain no reference to a *Letter to Mother*. Ancient sources do mention the existence of spurious letters, however. Philodemus lists several letters whose authenticity was doubtful, including the *Letter to Pythocles*.[58] Even more significant is Diogenes Laertius' amusing disclosure that "Diotimus the Stoic, who is hostile toward Epicurus, has cruelly slandered him by producing fifty obscene [ἀσελγεῖς] letters as Epicurus' own" (*Life of Epicurus* 10.3). Laertius' text does not make clear whether the calumnious items he then cites originated from Diotimus, but perhaps the fifty letters

---

55. Galen *Commentarius in Hippocratis De natura hominis* 1.42; 2. proem and *Commentarius in Hippocratis Epidemiorum* 3.4. See also Lucian *Pseudologista* 30.

56. See Malherbe, "Ancient Epistolary Theorists," 12.

57. For example, B.A. van Groningen ("General Literary Tendencies in the Second Century A.D. "*Mnemosyne* 18 [1965]: 50), views almost all literature of the Second Sophistic as a vacuous mass: "Literary life [in the second century] is no more than a prolongation of the school. *Non vitae, sed scholae* might have been the motto. Very few pupils became culturally adult and independent, and what the others wrote remained just school-exercises." In a more appreciative study, J. Bompaire (*Lucien écrivain: Imitation et création,* Bibliothèque des Ecoles Françaises d'Athènes et de Rome 190 [Paris, 1958]) explains Lucian's writing as the product of a basic rhetorical curriculum. Bompaire overstates his view and is refuted by, for example, Barry Baldwin, "Lucian as Social Satirist," *CQ* 11 (1961): 199–208. See also Barry Baldwin, *Studies in Lucian* (Toronto, 1973); and Bompaire's response to Baldwin in *REG* 88 (1975): 226–29. (Baldwin exaggerates Lucian's role as a satirist, but his work is an important corrective to Bompaire.)

58. Usener, *Epicurea,* 34. Arrighetti, *Opere,* 524 and appendix 1.

included the love letters to various objects of "Epicurus'" desire, including several hetairai, a married woman, and "lovely Pythocles." One of the letters to the hetaira Leontion divulged that Epicurus spent a whole mina on his daily food. Another letter seems to have revealed that Epicurus' brother was a pimp who lived with Leontion.[59]

It does not sound as though these "lewd letters" were a "rhetorical exercise," at least not in the limited sense of a training exercise. Nor was profit a likely incentive. The main purpose was to lampoon and discredit Epicurus.[60] The subject matter was an obvious choice: tenets such as "No pleasure is in itself evil" (*Principal Doctrine* 8) had often led detractors to view Epicurus as a debauched sensualist. Detractors liked to omit the second half of the saying, which warns: "but things producing certain pleasures involve troubles many times greater than their pleasures." The less informed may not have known that Epicurus regarded sexual activity (τὰ ἀφροδίσια) as natural but "unnecessary."[61]

The attribution of Diotimus' obscene letters to Epicurus was probably not meant to be taken literally,[62] but the purpose of the letters may have been quite serious. Even the most ludicrous parody can deliver trenchant criticism. Our Stoic Diotimus was not the only anti-Epicurean polemicist to resort to such tactics; Diogenes Laertius (10.3) knew of another collection of unsavory letters that some sources attributed to Epicurus but others assigned to Chrysippus. If those letters were extant, perhaps we could determine whether a Stoic fabricated them, causing Epicureans to retaliate by switching the attribution from Epicurus to Chrysippus, or whether someone with Epicurean sympathies started the process.

---

59. These letters are mentioned in Diogenes Laertius 10.4–6. Perhaps some belonged not to Diotimus' collection but to the group that Diogenes Laertius mentions was sometimes attributed to Chrysippus. The letter that mentions Epicurus' expenditures on food (10.7) may have belonged to yet another collection (exposed by Timocrates). The lack of clarity seems to be due to Laertius' method of compiling and condensing his sources, rather than to textual corruption. Several of the letters quoted by Laertius here are generally recognized as genuine works of Epicurus.

60. I suspect that some of the letters of "Diogenes the Cynic" in which he is portrayed as urinating and masturbating in public were also written as a lampoon of Cynicism. Like Epicurus' detractors, who imagined Epicurus corresponding with prostitutes and other men's wives, the anti-Cynic author of, for example, epistle 36 produced the obvious extension *ad absurdum* of the Cynic rejection of convention. I find no one who would agree with me, however: the old view that the Cynic letters were school exercises is being replaced by the claim (justified in most cases) that the letters "were composed as Cynic propaganda, to justify the Cynic *modus vivendi,* and perhaps to offset the picture of Cynics we find in such authors as Lucian" (Malherbe, *The Cynic Epistles,* 17). If some of the Cynic epistles are indeed lampoons of Cynicism, this would not affect the status of the whole collection. Wilamowitz ("Unechte Briefe") argues that every letter in a collection must be judged on its own merits because the collections contain works of various origin.

61. See the scholiast to Aristotle quoted in Usener, *Epicurea,* 456.

62. Or were they the tabloid newspapers of their day? Perhaps, like the sensational articles in *Bild* or the *National Enquirer,* they were jokes to some but coveted "news" to others.

Diotimus' rude letters offer a simple answer to the attribution question: the *Letter to Mother* could be the work of a devoted Epicurean whose intentions were diametrically opposed to those of the Stoic detractor. I suggested earlier that by the second century C.E. the theme of "the refused gift" had become a stock formula in the letters of "philosophers" that served to ennoble the supposed letter-writer. The rejection of funds would also exonerate them of any charges that they valued wealth more than wisdom or that they lived in profligate luxury. That Epicurus in particular needed to be defended is obvious from our references to Diotimus and the disgruntled Epicurean Timocrates, as well as from extant criticism in the writings of, for example, Cicero, Dio Chrysostom, and Plutarch.[63]

Diotimus the Stoic and the author of the *Letter to Mother* were not alone in choosing the medium of the pseudonymous letter for expressing scorn or respect for a philosopher. We have abundant evidence for other propagandistic letters.[64] Some, such as the anti-Epicurean letters cited by Diogenes Laertius, are polemical tracts accusing rival philosophical schools of criminal or immoral behavior. Others present idealized portraits of a group's founder or of important disciples.[65] Some were intended to lend credence to a belief by creating a supporting document.[66] Many, like the *Letter to Mother,* are also didactic and contain explanations of particular doctrines.[67]

Why Write a Letter to Epicurus' Mother?

In the *Reply to Colotes* (1123a) Plutarch poses the following rhetorical question to Colotes and to all Epicureans: "Do you people not dismiss the instinctive love of parents for their offspring, a fact accepted by all?" Elsewhere Plutarch alleges that Epicurus claims that parents and children love each other only when the promise of personal gain is involved (*On Love for Offspring* 495a).

---

63. Our source for Timocrates' exposé is Diogenes Laertius 10.6–8. For a discussion of other enemies of Epicurus, see David Sedley, "Epicurus and His Professional Rivals," in *Etudes sur l'Epicurisme antique,* ed. Jean Bollack and Andre Laks (Lille, 1976), 119–59. For a discussion of the popular prejudice against Epicureanism in Cicero's time, see Phillip De Lacy, "Cicero's Invective against Piso," *TAPA* 72 (1941): 49–58. Anti-Epicurean sentiment in Diogenes' own era (or close to it) is evident in the writings of, for example, Cleomedes, Epictetus, Plutarch, Dio Chrysostom, and Alciphron. It is also documented by Athenaeus and Lucian.

64. See Speyer, *Die literarische Fälschung,* especially 131–46, "Die einzelnen Fälschungen und ihre Motive."

65. For this trend in biography in general, see Patricia Cox, *Biography in Late Antiquity: A Quest for the Holy Man* (Berkeley, 1983).

66. Speyer notes: "Der Brief ist zugleich Selbstaussage und Dokument" (*Die literarische Fälschung,* 79). Gösswein argues that the letters of "Euripides" represent an attempt to create a document that was intended to improve Euripides' reputation (*Die Briefe des Euripides,* 23) .

67. On didactic Cynic letters, see Attridge, *First Century Cynicism.*

He elaborates his position in the essay *That Epicurus Actually Makes a Pleasant Life Impossible (Non Posse)*, where he mentions parental concern for children as one of the many honorable things that Epicureans shun (1100cd). Here the context suggests that Plutarch is presenting the gist of a critique of Epicureanism that had developed in Stoic circles: he groups their allegedly irresponsible attitude toward parenting with their refusal to recognize divine providence or to hold public office. For Plutarch these aberrations epitomize the unpatriotic stance of the Epicureans, whom he refers to as "those people who say that it is not necessary to save Greece, but rather to eat and drink." Epictetus offers a similar appraisal of Epicurean attitudes.[68]

Only within the rhetoric of anti-Epicurean polemic is it logical to equate any unconventional attitude toward the family (or any claim that parental love is not biologically or divinely ordained) with dereliction of familial duties and betrayal of country. As is often the case, we have very little firsthand knowledge of Epicurus' original position, but it appears that Epicurus' detractors have exaggerated and oversimplified the stance of Epicurus, who seems to have encouraged marriage and child-rearing in appropriate circumstances.[69] Instead of prompting a systematic philosophical response, denunciations like Plutarch's seem to have inspired ardent testimonials to the goodness of Epicurus' character, like that we find in Diogenes Laertius 10.10.

> Epicurus has plenty of witnesses to his unsurpassed kindness to all. There is his country, which honored him with bronze statues. . . . There is again his grateful devotion to his parents, his generosity to his brothers, and his gentleness towards his servants. . . . In short there is his *philanthropia* to all. Of his reverence towards the gods and his love of country it is impossible to speak adequately.[70]

Laertius' praise and Plutarch's attacks reveal an important aspect of the significance of the choice of addressee of the *Letter to Mother:*[71] by portraying the concern of the mother and the considerate reply of the son, the letter effectively

---

68. See Usener, *Epicurea,* 525 (Epictetus *Discourses* 3.7.19). See also the remarks of Cicero, Clement of Alexandria, and Lactantius quoted by Usener, 526–29. On the Stoic recommendation of marriage for the good of the city, see the fragments of Zeno, Chrysippus, and Antipater of Tarsus cited by Robert D. Brown, *Lucretius on Love and Sex* (Leiden and New York, 1987), 119.

69. See Diogenes Laertius 10.119, the interpretation of which is disputed. See C.W. Chilton, "Did Epicurus Approve of Marriage?" *Phronesis* 5 (1960): 71–74; and the brief survey in Brown, *Lucretius on Love and Sex,* 118–22.

70. My translation is influenced by Cyril Bailey's in *Epicurus,* 147.

71. See the discussion of the importance of the role of "pseudo-recipient" in Lewis R. Donelson, *Pseudepigraphy and Ethical Argument in the Pastoral Epistles* (Tübingen, 1986).

defends Epicurus against the popular charge that Epicureans have no regard for familial duties or affection.

In my view the portrayal of Epicurus' filial piety is a significant aspect of the *Letter to Mother,* but I suggest that an even more important item on its apologetic agenda is the implicit refutation of the popular view of the role of women in Epicurus' philosophical circle. Ancient and modern authorities seem to agree that the Garden of Epicurus was open to women. Later generations continued this tradition in Greece as well as in Rome, and Diogenes of Oenoanda (in the letter partially preserved in fr. 122 [Ch fr. 51]) alludes to the presence of at least one woman in his circle of Epicurean friends. In the absence of direct testimony from early Epicurean texts, we may attribute this unprecedented openness to an increase in freedom for women in Hellenistic society in general or to specific Epicurean views.[72] What concerns us here, however, is not the admission of women per se but the reaction of the outside world.

Epicurus' detractors seized on the presence of women in the Garden as material for their exposés: they could understand the inclusion of women only as evidence of "Epicurean" licentiousness.[73] To Plutarch, for example, it is self-evident that the women in the Garden were "young and attractive" (1097d), and to Cicero the presence of women is obvious proof of Epicurean turpitude. Cicero ridicules Epicurus for writing so many volumes about a woman named Themista, an aberration he associates with the failure of contemporary Epicureans to pay homage to great men such as Solon and Themistocles (*De Finibus* 3.21.68). Cicero also finds fault with Leontion, a woman of the school's first generation who became famous (or rather, notorious) for a treatise she wrote against Theophrastus. She may also have held the directorship of the Garden at one time.[74] Although Cicero's Cotta acknowledges the excellence of Leontion's prose, he calls her *meretricula,* "little prostitute," and condemns her audacity:

72. The latter seems more likely. Epicurean social theory rejected the idea that existing social hierarchies belong to a purposefully created natural order; thus, Epicureans were unlikely to endorse traditional attitudes toward gender roles. As Jane Snyder has put it, it is reasonable to conclude that Epicurus' antiteleological stand would lead him to assert: "Man was not created to serve anyone, nor woman to serve man" (*The Woman and the Lyre: Women Writers in Classical Greece and Rome* [Carbondale and Edwardsville, Ill., 1989], 102). Furthermore, Epicurus' contempt for traditional education (especially geometry and rhetoric) would have made philosophical discussion in the Garden accessible to women (and slaves) who had not had access to traditional schooling. A.J. Festugière points out that the purpose of Epicurean study differed from that of the philosophic schools that excluded women: "since [Epicurean] philosophic education no longer looks to the moulding of politicians, the circle of disciples is open to women, whether married ... or courtesans ..." (*Epicurus and His Gods* [Oxford, 155]); trans. Chilton, *Diogenes of Oenoanda,* 28.

73. See Usener, "Δημηλάτα?" in *Epicurea,* 402.

74. See Christian Jensen, "Ein neuer Brief Epikurs," *Abhandlungen der Gesellschaft der Wissenschaften zu Göttingen,* Philologisch-Historische Klasse, 3.5 (1933): 1–94.

"Of course, she writes in fine Attic style, but really! Such license the Garden of Epicurus allowed!" (*De Natura Deorum* 1.93).[75]

Cicero is not the only ancient source to accuse Epicurean women of prostitution. Other detractors enjoyed cataloging the erotic-sounding names of other first-generation Epicurean women: Mammarion, Hedeia, Erotion, Nicidion, and Boidion, most of whom the renegade Timocrates (according to Diogenes Laertius) labeled as hetairai.[76] Because our information about these women appears in sources hostile to Epicureanism or is influenced by such sources, it is difficult to separate fact from polemic. The name *Hedeia* (Pleasant), so appropriately "Epicurean," sounds suspiciously burlesque. Attic epigraphy demonstrates that the names themselves are authentic Hellenistic names, however: a Nicidion, a Hedeia, and a Boidion appear together as dedicators in an inscription at the sanctuary of the healing god Amphiaraos, and a Hedeia and a Mammarion appear as dedicators in an inventory of offerings made to Asclepius in Athens.[77] At least one of the inscriptions seems to be contemporary with Epicurus' residence in Athens, and it has been suggested that the correspondence with our lists of Epicurean hetairai may be more than coincidental.[78] The identification of the dedicators with Epicureans is extremely speculative, however: the names of women with no suspected Epicurean connections appear in the same inscriptions, and Hedeia's and Mammarion's offerings are separated by a substantial break (at least twenty-three lines) in the stone.[79]

---

75. Trans. Jane Snyder, *The Woman and the Lyre,* 103.

76. See Plutarch *Non Posse* 1097e and Diogenes Laertius 10.7. The names listed here can be translated as "Tit" (Mammarion); "Delectable" or "Pleasant" (Hedeia); "Lovey" (Erotion); "Winner," "Seductress," or possibly "Dominatrix" (Nicidion); and "Cow-eyed" (Boidion; see "Doe-eyed"). Philodemus and others mention women whose names are less insinuating: Demelate, Demetria, Philainis.

77. See Catherine J. Castner, "Epicurean Hetairai as Dedicants to Healing Deities?" *GRBS* 23 (1982): 51–57. As Castner notes, the name *Hedeia* seems to have been rather common.

78. Castner, "Epicurean Hetairai," dates both inscriptions to the era of Epicurus and focuses on the possibility that these women could make offerings to healing gods while remaining good Epicureans. Castner's position is further complicated by the fact that *Mammarion* in our texts of Diogenes Laertius is an emendation for *Marmarion.* The emendation seems to have been inspired by Philodemus' reference to a woman with the name *Mammaron,* a name that is also attested in Attic inscriptions. See Sedley, "Epicurus and His Professional Rivals," 149 n. 5.

79. See Sara B. Aleshire *The Athenian Asklepieion: The People, Their Dedications, and the Inventories* (Amsterdam, 1989). According to Aleshire, the proximity of names in the Athenian inventory indicates nothing about the chronological sequence of the dedications: the inventory "simply lists all those dedications which were in the temple at the time when it was made, shortly before 274/3 B.C., and can serve as no more than a *terminus ante quem* for the dedication listed there" (67). Aleshire concludes that the idea of visits by Epicurean hetairai to the Athenian Asklepieion is "open to serious question" (67).

In my view it is significant that the two Epicurean women's names with the best authority—*Themista* and *Leontion* (both appear in texts of Epicurus)—are also the least suggestive. Although it may have been common to endow prostitutes with animal names, Leontion's name (meaning "Little Lioness") is not necessarily erotic (cf. the masculine name *Leonteus*), and other women named Leontion do not seem to have been hetairai.[80] Themista ("Righteous"), who is not labeled as a prostitute in the ancient texts, was married to a disciple named Leonteus; their son was named Epicurus. Perhaps there were no hetairai in the Garden until Timocrates invented them in his exposé.[81] Outsiders who equated Epicureans with "pleasure seekers" would have readily accepted Timocrates' testimony.

Thus, there may not have been as many women in Epicurus' circle as our hostile sources suggest. It is still possible that some Epicurean women were originally hetairai, however. Our polemical sources are not concerned with the distinctions between "prostitutes," "loose women," and "whores"—to Plutarch and Cicero the words *hetaira* and *meretricula* seem to have all those connotations. Setting pejoratives aside, we may wonder whether some of the women who joined the Epicureans may have been working women who relied on their sexuality (and artistic talents) for economic subsistence. Perhaps the Garden offered them refuge. Epicurus' nonextant letter titled *On Occupations* discussed the humble livelihoods pursued by certain philosophers before they achieved the status of philosopher. Protagoras, for example, is said to have worked as a laborer until his ingenious device for carrying logs attracted the notice of Democritus; and Aristotle supposedly worked in the drug trade. In an innovative study, David Sedley has suggested that the purpose of these stories was not to condemn Protagoras or Aristotle but to inspire others. He offers the following modern parallel: "A New York art school used to advertise its course with a poster which read, *At the age of thirty-five Gauguin worked in a bank.* The point was not, of course, to mock Gauguin as a bank-clerk."[82] Sedley also suggests that later stories about the advancement of Mys (from slave to Epicurean philosopher) and Leontion (from courtesan to philosopher) have affinities with Epicurus' *On Occupations,* which he suggests was addressed to Mys and Leontion or to others like them.

---

80. See F. Bechtel, *Die Attischen Frauennamen* (Göttingen, 1902). Many, but not all, of the animal names listed by Bechtel belong to hetairai.

81. Sedley argues for the pervasive influence of Timocrates in "Epicurus and His Professional Rivals." The corrupt text of Diogenes Laertius (10.5.10) may suggest that Epicurus was rumored (perhaps by Timocrates?) to have had sexual relations with Themista. See Rist, *Epicurus,* 11 n. 2.

82. "Epicurus and His Professional Rivals," 126.

So perhaps Leontion actually was a prostitute before she, like Aristotle, turned from a lowly lifestyle to the life of a philosopher. Ancient gossip denied that Leontion ever changed, however. In Athenaeus' *Deipnosophistae* a dinner guest reports that when Leontion became a philosopher she did not stop being a hetaira "but consorted with all the Epicureans in the Garden, even in front of Epicurus, so that he was very worried about her, as he reveals in his letters to Hermarchus" (13.588b).

Regardless of whether Leontion was a hetaira or whether that occupation was only attributed to her by polemicizers, the story endured. Polemicizers and antiquarians continued to populate the Garden with accommodating courtesans. To generations of anti-Epicurean writers, Epicurus' relations with these women, together with the stories of Epicurus' overindulgence in food and wine, epitomized his immoral doctrine of pleasure. When Epicurus himself responds to such charges, he seems to acknowledge the logic of the association of sex and food: "For it is not endless drinking and parties and the enjoyment of boys, women, and fish and the other things supplied by a rich table that produce a pleasant life, but sober reasoning. . . ." (*Letter to Menoeceus* 132). Similarly, Diogenes of Oenoanda (fr. 29 = Ch fr. 24) includes rich food and "the pleasures of exotic sexual activity" in his list of coveted possessions that are erroneously considered necessary for happiness.

Epicurus was not only rumored to have associated with prostitutes; he was also supposed to have kept up quite a correspondence with them, as Diotimus' letters suggested. Thus, Diogenes Laertius writes of Epicurus' enemies: "They say he wrote letters to many hetairai, especially to Leontion, with whom Metrodorus was also in love" (10.6); and in Alciphron's fictional *Letters of Courtesans* Leontion is made to complain to another hetaira about a lecherous Epicurus: "I shall flee from land to land rather than put up with his interminable letters" (4.17.3).

The *Letter to Mother,* in my view, responds to such defamation by replacing the popular view of Epicurus with a favorable portrayal. Rejecting the dominant tradition, it documents another Epicurus, a man who wrote helpful letters to his mother, teaching her how to seek *ataraxia*. Not only does the letter demonstrate that Epicurus cared for his mother (perhaps the ultimate character reference), but by depicting him engaged in philosophical discussion with her, it suggests that his interest in bringing women into the Garden was completely honorable. Thus, the letter exonerates Epicurus of the charge that women were welcome in the Garden simply because they offered erotic pleasure. In Plutarch's imagination Epicurus was a source of shame to his mother, who Plutarch says grieved to see her son "making babies in the little garden";[83] the text from Oenoanda demonstrates instead that Epicurus was a source of joy and wisdom.

At this point I would like to mention one last issue concerning the gender of the addressee of the *Letter to Mother*. In chapter 1, I quoted the following from fragment 27 (NF 24) of Diogenes, which M.F. Smith once assigned to the letter.

> You will veer away from the speeches of the rhetoricians in order to listen to some of our doctrines. And from then on it is our firm hope that you will come as quickly as you can to knock at the doors of philosophy.

Diskin Clay has suggested that this fragment is addressed not to Chaerestrata but to Hermarchus: "for it puts a heavy strain on the imagination to think of Epicurus' mother as so addicted to public displays of oratory that her son felt the need to turn her away from their beguilement."[84] Perhaps the strain is not so heavy if we imagine that the *Letter to Mother* was composed not in the late fourth century B.C.E., when a woman could study neither philosophy nor rhetoric without being called a hetaira, but during Diogenes' era, when another Diogenes dedicated to a woman his "Lives and Opinions of Famous Philosophers and According to Their Sects,"[85] and when women were often visible in the public life of the Greek cities of Asia Minor, especially as magistrates and important *patronissai*.[86] An imperial date for fragment 127 would also fit well with the immense popularity of oratory in that era. Thus, Smith's first impression—that fragment 127 belongs to the *Letter to Mother*—may have been correct after all.

---

83. Plutarch contrasts the pride of the parents of a successful general with the shame of Epicurus' mother when she discovers him in the κηπίδιον, sharing a hetaira with his disciple Polyaenus (*Non Posse* 1098b).

84. "The Philosophical Inscription of Diogenes of Oenoanda: New Discoveries 1969–1983," *ANRW* II.36.4 (1990): 2542.

85. On female students of philosophy and the probable date of Diogenes Laertius, Momigliano writes: "The phenomenon of women intensely interested in pagan philosophy seems to be widespread precisely between A.D. 150 and A.D. 250" (*Greek Biography*, 170).

86. In other words, if fr. 127 (NF 24) is part of the *Letter to Mother*, the author has anachronistically attributed later customs to fourth-century Athens. On the term *patronissa*, see MacMullen, *Changes in the Roman Empire: Essays in the Ordinary* (Princeton, 1990), 342 n. 12. On eponymous magistracies held by women, see MacMullen, 165.

Fictional Biography and the Second Sophistic

When sophistic performance came into prominence in Asia Minor, so did the novel. Both genres were most in vogue under Hadrian and the Antonines.[87] B.P. Reardon has asked why two art forms that are apparently such "strange bedfellows" would enjoy popularity at the same time and apparently with the same audiences.[88] Although he ventures no explanation for this phenomenon, Reardon points out that the novel and declamation have important traits in common: both elevate rhetorical technique to an art form; and, since the early Greek novel dealt with historical themes, both are indicative of the second-century predilection for the past. While Reardon does not mention the large corpus of second-century fictional letters in his discussion of the novel, the letters demonstrate even more clearly the intersection between the novel and the declamation.[89] Both the letters and the sophists' declamations present dramatic portrayals of historical figures. Like the declamations, the letters could combine philosophy with history, biography, and storytelling.

Some scholars who accept the *Letter to Mother* as a genuine text by Epicurus have been troubled by the sound of full-grown Epicureanism coming from the mouth of a young man writing to his mother. In addition to the description of dream theory, the letter quotes or alludes to *Principal Doctrines* 1 and 2, and if more fragments turn up we may find the whole *tetrapharmakos* in the letter.[90] To account for this philosophical content, some have tried to understand the letter as a document by the mature Epicurus. This is an awkward solution because the letter-writer sounds youthful: he is still engaged in philosophical study—"daily acquiring something good and . . . advancing to a higher level of happiness"—and he still depends on his parents for support.

The contradiction between the writer's youth and his wisdom appears less extraordinary when we accept the letter as fictional and draw connections

---

87. See B.P. Reardon, "The Second Sophistic and the Novel," in *Approaches to the Second Sophistic,* ed. G.W. Bowersock (University Park, Pa., 1974), 24–25. Longus, Achilles Tatius, and Xenophon of Ephesus probably wrote in the second century; and second-century papyri attest that the works of Chariton and others were being read by then. For chronology of the novel, see B.P. Reardon, *Courants littéraires grecs des IIe et IIIe siècles après J.-C.,* Annales littéraires de L'Université de Nantes 3 (Paris, 1971), 334–37.

88. "The Second Sophistic and the Novel," 23. Others have thought that both the novel and the sophistic performance are simply signs of decay and the need to escape from reality. See F. Altheim, *Literatur und Gesellschaft im ausgehenden Altertum,* 2 vols., (Halle, 1948–50); and Altheim, *Roman und Dekadenz* (Tübingen, 1951).

89. Patricia Cox calls biography "a halfway house between history and oratory" (*Biography in Late Antiquity,* xiv).

90. The complete letter may have affinities with epistle 39 in the corpus of Socratic letters, which "sounds like a short paraphrase of the Phaedo" (Malherbe, *The Cynic Epistles,* 16).

between it and the broader realm of Greek biography. Ancient Greek historio-graphical and biographical traditions embraced fiction, as is clear from Hero-dotus' conflicting folk stories and Thucydides' speeches.[91] By the fourth cen-tury the Socratics had set philosophical biography in the "ambiguous position between fact and imagination" where it would remain throughout antiquity.[92] The fictions that developed around a sage's childhood seem to have been shaped by a convention that required that the character of a great person be evi-dent in that person as a child.[93] In postclassical biography of classical figures the idea becomes a familiar motif: Pindar fills in for his teacher and trains cho-ruses when he is a mere boy, the young Homer inherits and successfully runs a school, and Archilochus meets the muses when he is running an ordinary errand for his father.[94] We see the concept at work in an anecdote about Epi-curus' frustration with schoolteachers: according to a biographer cited by Di-ogenes Laertius (10.2), the young Epicurus first decided to study philosophy when his teachers could not explain what Hesiod wrote about Chaos. A recent study points to a trend toward an even more emphatic claim for childhood wisdom in the biographies of divine philosophers written in the first centuries of our era. Thus, Philostratus and Iamblichus portray the youthful Apollonius and Pythagoras (respectively) as fully formed sages who need education only as a sort of "fine-tuning."[95]

It is in this light that we ought to view young "Epicurus" assertions about his "godlike" state of happiness in the fourth column of the *Letter to Mother.* Our sources indicate that the deification of Epicurus began during the sage's own lifetime, then grew and persisted for generations despite the derision of out-

---

91. See C.R. Ligota, "'This Story Is Not True': Fact and Fiction in Antiquity," *Journal of the Warburg and Courtauld Institutes* 45 (1982): 1–13. The step from Thucydides' presentation of τὰ δέοντα in speeches attributed to protagonists in the Peloponnesian War to the writing of letters in the voice of historical figures had already been taken by Thucydides himself when he composed his letter from Nicias.

92. Momigliano writes that biography was invented at least a century before Socrates but "ac-quired a new meaning when the Socratics moved to that zone between truth and fiction which is so bewildering to the professional historian" (*Greek Biography,* 46).

93. This convention can be traced at least as far back as Herodotus. Cox traces the convention back to Xenophon (*Biography in Late Antiquity,* 22). It seems that fiction was especially likely to creep into a biography when the writer was treating a subject's early years. See C. Pelling, "Child-hood and Personality in Greek Biography," in *Characterization and Individuality in Greek Litera-ture,* ed. C. Pelling (Oxford, 1990). As Pelling puts it: "Everybody notices when a great man dies; it is more difficult to notice when one is born, or when one is growing up" (213).

94. See Mary Lefkowitz, *The Lives of the Greek Poets* (Baltimore, 1981), 59 (Pindar), 140 (Homer), and 27 (Archilochus).

95. See Cox, *Biography in Late Antiquity,* 22. Cox (23) suggests that the biographers of these sages dwell on the sages' educations out of a desire to portray their humanity.

siders.[96] Thus, Lucretius describes Epicurus as a god (5.8 ff.), and Diogenes
of Oenoanda refers to his Epicurean friends as "blessed" (ὦ μακάριοι [NF 10,
col. II, line 2]). In a fragment of a letter to Colotes quoted disparagingly by Plutarch (1117bc = Usener 140), Epicurus writes as though his disciples' habit
of venerating their teacher originated during a particular conversation when
Colotes, "seized with an unaccountable desire," suddenly threw himself at
Epicurus' feet. Colotes had met Epicurus early on, in Lampsacus, and precise
dating of the fragment is impossible. I hazard to suggest that the encounter
between Epicurus and the younger Colotes took place when Epicurus was regarded as his mature mentor, that is, after the purported date of the *Letter to
Mother.* To the composer of the *Letter to Mother,* however, the later deification of
Epicurus is an established fact and thus an important characteristic to document
in the young sage. When viewed alongside our author's apologetic stance
toward Epicurus' reputation for greed and sexual immorality, it is significant that
this Epicurus does not press too far his aspirations toward the divine. Cicero and
Plutarch had also mocked Epicurus' habit of collecting worshipers; here too the
Master could be defended.

What about Those Minas?

In his study on the *Letter to Mother,* Anthony Raubitschek concludes that content and language rule out the possibility that Epicurus could have been the
author.[97] He argues instead that Diogenes must have written the letter to his
own mother. The only stumbling block to accepting Diogenes' authorship was
the currency named in the third column of fragment 126 (Ch fr. 53). To fit the
mention of minas to Diogenes' authorship, Raubitschek suggested that Diogenes himself would have referred in his correspondence to the Greek standard, which was in use in Egypt and Rhodes in imperial times.[98] The necessity
for this awkward solution vanishes once we recognize that the author wanted to
write not in his own voice but in the voice of Epicurus.

Most authors of fictitious letters sought to give their compositions an air
of authenticity. To this end they incorporated into their letters well-known details from the lives of their subjects (such as the name *Cleon* in the *Letter to*

---

96. See the sources collected by Festugière, *Epicurus and His Gods,* 41.

97. "Das abschliessende Urteil über die Echtheit des Briefes könnte von der sprachlichen Seite
erst gefällt werden, wenn man nachgewiesen hat, dass trotz der Zeitspanne, die zwischen Abfas-
sung von Brief und Inschrift liegt und trotz inhaltlicher Verschiedenheit, der Brief dem Stil und
Sprachgebrauch desselben menschen entstammt, der die Inschrift abgefasst hat" ("Epikureische
Untersuchungen" [Ph.D. diss., University of Vienna, 1935], 142).

98. "Epikureische Untersuchungen," 136.

Mother) and tried to imitate their subjects' writing styles. As Bentley and Wilamowitz were quick to point out, they often made mistakes that resulted in strange anachronisms. But many epistolographers got the basics right: Pseudo-Hippocrates, for example, almost always writes in Ionic, while Pseudo-Pythagoras and Pseudo-Aristippos write in Doric.[99] Since the epistolographers took care to compose in the appropriate dialect, it is understandable that the author of the *Letter to Mother* would mention not Roman coinage but a currency appropriate for Epicurus. Since the epistolographers of late antiquity were experts on the classical Athenians, such accuracy is not surprising. Not all letter-writers were so careful, however. Bentley found that the author of "Phalaris'" epistles did not achieve accuracy in either dialect or currency.

> But should we connive at his using the Attic dialect, and say not a word of those flaws and innovations in his style, yet there is one thing still that I fear will more difficultly be forgiven him; that is, a very slippery way in telling of money. This is a tender point and will make every body shy and cautious of entertaining him.[100]

The writer of "Phalaris'" letters seems not to have understood the considerable difference between Sicilian and Attic talents. In contrast, the author of the *Letter to Mother,* whom I identify as an Epicurean of the first or second century (possibly an acquaintance of Diogenes of Oenoanda or even Diogenes himself), took care to compose a gem of an epistle that would often be accepted as Epicurus' own.

---

99.   See Sykutris, "Sokratikerbriefe," *RE* Suppl. 5 (1931): col. 985–87. Bruno Snell (*Leben und Meinungen der Sieben Weisen* [Munich, 1938]) found that the letters of the Seven Sages preserved in Diogenes Laertius were written in dialects appropriate to each sage; he attributed this to the care taken by a single author. The letters written in the voice of Darius use the formula βασιλεὺς βασιλέων Δαρεῖος, in accordance with the style of authentic Persian royal letters. See Reinhold Merkelbach, *Die Quellen des griechischen Alexanderromans* (Munich, 1954), 50.

100.   *Dissertation upon the Epistles of Phalaris,* 308.

CHAPTER 4

A Second-Century Mission for the "New Epicurus"

τὸ μηχάνημα ἐδεῖτο Δημοκρίτου τινὸς ἢ καὶ αὐτοῦ· Ἐπικούρου ἢ
Μητροδώρου ἢ τινος ἄλλου ἀδαμαντίνην πρὸς τὰ τοιαῦτα τὴν
γνώμην ἔχοντος, ὡς ἀπιστῆσαι καὶ ὅπερ ἦν εἰκάσαι. . . .

[Really the trick stood in need of a Democritus, or even Epicurus himself
or Metrodorus, or some one else with a mind as firm as adamant toward
such matters, so as to disbelieve and guess the truth . . . .]

—Lucian *Alexander the False Prophet* 17

In fragments 2 and 3 (Ch frr. 1 and 2) of his inscription Diogenes of Oenoanda explains why he has decided to inscribe philosophy on stone. Regardless of whether these fragments provided a preface to the whole inscription or to only part of it,[1] they reveal unambiguously that Diogenes' purpose was evangelical. In fragment 2 he writes:

col. II   —τούτους
     5   οὖν ὁρῶν, (πάλιν γὰρ ἐπα-
         ναλήμψομαι) διακει-
         μένους οὕτως, κατω-
         λοφυράμην μὲν αὐτῶν
         τὸν βίον καὶ ἐπεδάκρυ-
    10   σα τῇ τῶν χρόνων ἀ-

The translation of the epigraph is that of A.M. Harmon, in the Loeb edition of Lucian, *Lucian* 4 (Cambridge, Mass., 1925).

1. In *Diogenis Oenoandensis Fragmenta* (Milan, 1960), 29, A. Grilli followed William in assigning frr. 2 and 3 (Ch frr. 1 and 2) to the introduction to the *On Physics* section of the inscription. R. Philippson suggested that the fragments were a foreword to the *On Physics* and *On Ethics* together (Diogenes von Oinoanda," *PW* Suppl. 5 [1931]). The content (e.g., "I wanted, having used this stoa, to put forth in public the remedies that bring salvation") suggests instead that these fragments belong to an introduction (or conclusion) to the entire inscription.

πωλείᾳ, χρηστοῦ δέ
τινος ἡγησάμην ἀν-
δρός, ὅσον ἔστ᾽ ἐφ᾽ ἡμεῖν
τοῖς εὐσυνκρίτοις αὐ-

col. III   τ[ων]. . . .[2]

[—seeing these people, therefore (again, I shall repeat) in that condition,
I wailed over their way of life and cried over their ruined years, and I
decided that it was appropriate for any good man, as much as is in my
power, [to help] people of good judgment. . . .][3]

After a gap of unknown length Diogenes resumes in fragment 3.

col. I   οὕτω [δ, ὦ]
                 πο[λεῖται], καὶ οὐ πο[λει-]
    5   τευόμενος διὰ τῆ[ς]
         [γ]ραφῆς καθάπερ πρ[άτ]-
         των λέγω ταῦτα, δε[ι-]
         [κ]νύειν δὲ πειρώμε-
         νος ὡς τὸ τῇ φύσει
   10   συμφέρον, ὅπερ ἐσ-
         τὶν ἀταραξία, καὶ ἑνὶ
         καὶ πᾶσι τὸ αὐτό ἐσ-
         τιν. καὶ τὴν δευτέ-
         ραν οὖν ἀποδοὺς αἱ

col. II   [τί]αν τοῦ συνγράμ-
          [μ]ατος, τὸ κατεσπου-
          δασμένον ἡμῶν νῦν
          προστίθημι, ὁποῖόν
    5   ἐστιν καὶ τίν᾽ ἔχει φύ-

---

2. The text is that of C.W. Chilton, *Diogenes Oenoandensis Fragmenta* (Leipzig, 1967).

3. My translation of frr. 2 and 3 (Ch frr. 1 and 2) is influenced by Chilton's but renders only
what is preserved with a high degree of certainty. Many of the reconstructions printed in Chilton's
Teubner text (which are also used for his English translation in the Oxford edition) seem probable,
but I have omitted several uncertain passages. Thus, the third column of fr. 2 is omitted from the
translation. The first column we have of fr. 2 is also omitted; it discusses the needs of the soul as opposed to the needs of the body.

[σιν ἐξηγούμενος].
[ἐν δυ]σμαῖς γὰρ ἤδη
[τοῦ β]ίου καθεστη-
[κότε]ς (διὰ τὸ γῆρας
10   [καὶ ὅ]σον οὔπω μέλ-
[λοντ]ες ἀναλύειν
[ἀπὸ τ]οῦ ζῆν) μετὰ
[καλο]ῦ παιᾶν[ος ὑ]-
[πὲρ το]ῦ τῶ[ν ἡδέ]-

col. III   ων πληρώματος ἠ-
θελήσαμεν, ἵνα μὴ
προλημφθῶμεν, βο-
ηθεῖν ἤδη τοῖς εὐ-
5   συνκρίτοις.⁴ εἰ μὲν
οὖν εἷς μόνον ἢ δύ' ἢ
τρεῖς ἢ τέτταρες ἢ
πέντε ἢ ἕξ ἢ ὅσους,
ἄνθρωπε,⁵ βούλει τῶν
10   τοσούτων εἶναι πλείονας, μὴ πάνυ δὲ πολ-
λούς, διέκειντο κα-
κῶς, κἂν καθ' ἕ[να]
[κ]αλούμενος [πάν-]

col. IV   τα παρ' ἐμαυτὸν ἔπρατ-
τον εἰς συμβουλίαν
τὴν ἀρίστην. ἐπεὶ δέ,
ὡς προεῖπα, οἱ πλεῖστ[ο]ι
5   καθάπερ ἐν λοιμῷ

---

4. I follow H. Usener in understanding εὐσυνκρίτοις here as meaning "of good sense" or "discriminating," but J. William and others have interpreted it as meaning atomically "well compounded." Perhaps that peculiarly Epicurean interpretation is valid. See C.W. Chilton, *Diogenes of Oenoanda: The Fragments* (Oxford, 1971), 29; and D. Clay, "The Philosophical Inscription of Diogenes of Oenoanda: New Discoveries 1969–1983," *ANRW* II 36.4 (1990): 2458.

5. "Sir" translates ἄνθρωπε here. Chilton denies that the address has its usual contemptuous sense and offers instead "fellowman" or "brother" (*Diogenes of Oenoanda*, 1973). He omits it from his translation. G.N. Hoffman cites several sources where ἄνθρωπε is contemptuous, including Plutarch *Non Posse* 1103d and Lucian *Charon* 12 ("Diogenes of Oenoanda: A Commentary" [Ph.D. diss., University of Minnesota, 1976], 159).

τῇ περὶ τῶν πραγμάτων
ψευδοδοξίᾳ νοσοῦσι
κοινῶς, γείνονται δὲ
καὶ πλείονες (διὰ γὰρ
10   τὸν ἀλλήλων ζῆλον
ἄλλος ἐξ ἄλλου λαμ-
βάνει τὴν νόσον ὡς
[τ]ὰ πρόβατα), δίκαιο[ν]
[δ' ἐστὶ καὶ] τοῖς μ[εθ' ἡ]

col. V   μᾶς ἐσομένοις βοη-
θῆσαι (κἀκεῖνοι γάρ
εἰσιν ἡμέτεροι καὶ εἰ
⟨μὴ⟩ γεγόνασί πω), πρὸς
5   δὲ δὴ φιλάνθρωπον
καὶ τοῖς παραγεινομέ-
νοις ἐπικουρεῖν ξέ-
νοις ἐπειδὴ οὖν εἰς
πλείονας διαβέβη-
10   κε τὰ βοηθήματα
τοῦ συνγράμματος,
ἠθέλησα τῇ στοᾷ ταύ-
τῃ καταχρησάμενος
[ἐ]ν κοινῷ τὰ τῆς σωτη-

col. VI   ρίας προθεῖν[αι φάρμα-
κα, ὧν δὴ φαρμάκων]
πεῖραν ἡμε[ῖ]ς π[άντως]
εἰλήφαμεν. [τοὺς]
5   γὰρ ματαίως [κ]ατ[έχον-]
τας ἡμᾶς φόβους [ἀ]-
πελυσάμεθα, τῶν γε
λυπῶν τὰς μὲν κενὰς
ἐξεκόψαμεν εἰς τέ-
10   λειον, τὰς δὲ φυσικὰς
εἰς μεικρὸν κομιδῇ
συνεστείλαμεν ἐλα-
χιστιαῖον αὐτῶν τ[ὸ]
μέγεθος πο⟨ή⟩σ[αντες,]. . . .

[. . . and thus, my fellow citizens, while not meddling with politics, I am saying these things through my inscription as though I were taking action, trying to show that what is appropriate to nature—that is, *ataraxia*—is the same thing for one and all. And thus, having revealed the second purpose of my inscription, I now add how serious it is, explaining what sort it is and what is its nature.

Having reached the sunset of my life (being almost on the verge of departure from the world on account of old age), I wanted, so that I might not be too late, to help people of good sense now. Now if only one person, or two, or three or four, or five or six, or, sir, as many more than that as you wish, but not too many, were in an evil condition, calling on them even one by one, I would do what I could to give them my best advice. But since, as I have said, most people, as in a plague, are all sick with false judgment about things, and they are gaining in numbers (for, copying each other, they are catching the disease from each other like sheep), and it is right that I should help future generations, for they are mine too even if they are not yet born, and it is also philanthropic to help the foreigners among us, and since this treatise is meant to assist more people, I wanted, having used this stoa, to put forth in public the remedies that bring salvation. These remedies we have put fully to the test, for we have abolished those fears that have needlessly gripped us. And as for pains, we have totally done away with those that are unnecessary, and those pains that are natural we have reduced to the smallest measure, making their severity infinitesimal. . . .]

Pity for erring humanity is not new to Epicureanism. It was probably Epicurus himself who wrote: "Vain is the word of a philosopher that does not heal any human suffering."[6] Lucretius too was motivated by compassion for the ignorant.

> o miseras hominum mentes, o pectora caeca!
> qualibus in tenebris vitae quantisque periclis
> degitur hoc aevi quodcumquest!
>   (*De Rerum Natura* 2.14–16)

It is to save humanity from this condition that Lucretius expounds the nature of things. Like Lucretius, Diogenes views himself as an Epicurean savior—an idea he expresses neatly in his pun on Epicurus' name when he declares that he wants "to help" or "protect" (ἐπικουρεῖν), "the strangers among us" (fr. 3, [Ch

---

6. Porphyry *Ad Marc.* 31, in H. Usener, *Epicurea* (Leipzig, 1887; reprint, Rome, 1963) 221.

fr. 2], col. V, line 7). Also like Lucretius, Diogenes has adapted the Epicurean message to answer the immediate needs of his particular readers.

The purpose of this chapter is to bring out those aspects of Diogenes' message that are most indicative of his campaign against the spread of the disease of "false judgment" (ψευδοδοξία [fr. 3 (Ch fr. 2), col. IV, line 7]) among his own contemporaries in second-century Asia Minor. A good and faithful Epicurean, Diogenes strove to give a cogent and accurate presentation of Epicurus' teachings. His role as "new Epicurus" required, however, that he confront particular types of "false judgment" that Epicurus himself had not lived to see. Here Diogenes does not limit himself to a critique of Stoic positions: his message is meant for all people who are burdened by wrong ideas.

Second-Century *Pseudodoxia*

For Gibbon, Diogenes' was the happiest era humanity had ever experienced.

> If a man were called to fix the period in the history of the world during which the condition of the human race was most happy and prosperous, he would, without hesitation, name that which elapsed from the death of Domitian to the accession of Commodus. The vast extent of the Roman empire was governed by absolute power, under the guidance of virtue and wisdom. The armies were restrained by the firm but gentle hand of four successive emperors whose characters and authority commanded involuntary respect.[7]

Twentieth-century scholarship, however, has discerned a pervasive "anxiety" among the subjects of Gibbon's virtuous emperors.[8] To characterize an entire era as anxious and superstitious would be to oversimplify, and critics of Festugière and Dodds are right to point out that belief in the supernatural did not simply burst out like a jack-in-the-box during the second century.[9] Diogenes'

---

7. *Decline and Fall of the Roman Empire* (New York, 1932), 70.

8. E.R. Dodds used Auden's expression "Age of Anxiety" to refer to late antiquity in *Pagan and Christian in an Age of Anxiety* (Cambridge, 1965).

9. Peter Brown criticizes the "model of the jack-in-the-box" in "A Social Context to the Religious Crisis of the Third Century A.D.," Center for Hermeneutical Studies Colloquy 14 (Berkeley, 1975), 1–3. See also the remarks of Robin Lane Fox (*Pagans and Christians* [New York, 1987]), who calls anxiety "too vague a diagnosis" (66) and points out that one could just as easily characterize the Antonine age as an "age of anger" (65). See also the collection of essays in *Pagan and Christian Anxiety: A Response to E.R. Dodds,* ed. R.C. Smith and J. Lounibos (Lanham, Mass., 1984); and the review of that collection by Lane Fox in *JRS* 76 (1986): 304–5.

era was, however, a time of change in religious attitudes. Peter Brown has described this gradual shift in religious and spiritual outlook as a "tacit decision" to acknowledge that particular human individuals are capable of a "peculiar intimacy" with the supernatural.[10] What developed during the first centuries C.E. was not necessarily an increase in religiosity or superstition but rather a new willingness to view certain human agents as having direct and privileged contact with the divine. Among Hellenes this notion was intimately connected with the attitude toward the past discussed in chapter 1 of this study. A person capable of communicating with the divine was likely also to be viewed as the present embodiment of a classical exemplar: a "new Socrates," a "new Pythagoras," a "new Asclepius."[11] To the Epicurean Diogenes of Oenoanda this development involved grave misconceptions about the divine, especially regarding the gods' supposed interactions and communications with humanity. In the Epicurean view it also involved outright fraud on the part of the religious entrepreneurs who claimed to have direct communication with the gods.

Revealing the Divine in Oenoanda: Who Is God?

Diogenes' first task in explaining to Oenoanda the true nature of the gods is to defend Epicurus against the charge of atheism, an accusation that had wide currency in antiquity despite the fact that the extant texts of Epicurus state emphatically that the gods do exist. Epicureans like Diogenes knew that Epicurus wrote in the beginning of the *Letter to Menoeceus* (123): "First of all believe that god is a being immortal and blessed."[12] Epicurus claimed that the reason most people believe in the gods is that people can "see" the gods—not with their senses, but with their minds: "For gods there are, since knowledge of them is visible" [θεοὶ μὲν γὰρ εἰσίν· ἐναργὴς γὰρ αὐτῶν ἐστιν ἡ γνῶσις] (*Letter to Menoeceus* 123). Epicurus follows that affirmation of the existence of the gods with a statement that was less acceptable to his non-Epicurean readers: "the impious man is not he who denies the gods of the many but he who attaches to the gods the beliefs of the many." Because he denied that the gods performed the roles commonly regarded as the most obvious divine functions, Epicurus appeared to have no gods, and by Diogenes' era it had become conventional—among non-Epicureans—to regard Epicurus as an atheist.

---

10. "A Social Context," 3.

11. See Peter Brown, "The Saint as Exemplar in Late Antiquity," *Representations* 1.2 (1983): 1–5. The examples I cite are from Lucian's *Peregrinus* and *Alexander*. According to Lucian, Peregrinus fashioned himself as Proteus, Phoenix, and Heracles and was called the "new Socrates" by his Christian supporters. Before his Asclepius scheme, Alexander fashioned himself after Pythagoras.

12. Trans. C.W. Bailey, *Epicurus: The Extant Remains* (Oxford, 1926), 83.

Rather than stemming from the hostile gossip of Epicurus' Athens (as one might expect), the charge that Epicurus did not believe in the divine seems to have had its roots in philosophic discourse, possibly beginning with the second-century B.C.E. polemics of the skeptic Academic Carneades.[13] Posidonius (head of the Stoic school in Rhodes in the early first century B.C.E.) certainly suggested that Epicurus was an atheist: Cicero's Academic speaker Cotta claims that Posidonius wrote in his *On the Nature of the Gods* that Epicurus "considered the gods to be nothing at all but spoke about them only for the sake of avoiding enmity [invidiae detestandae gratia]" (*De Natura Deorum* 1.123). Posidonius could reconcile the claim that Epicurus was an atheist with texts like the *Letter to Menoeceus* by asserting that Epicurus feigned belief in the gods to avoid the hostility of the Athenians. Later generations seem not to have made even that distinction. As a recent article formulates it: "the lasting result of the polemical representation of Epicurus as an atheist was a distortion of historical fact."[14] By the second century C.E. most outsiders seem to have thought that Epicurus had simply dispensed with the gods. Lucian, for example, presents the Epicurean Damis in *Zeus: The Tragic Actor* as a nonbeliever, even though Lucian must have known that Epicureans rejected atheism; for Lucian's purposes "it was enough that they were often accused of it."[15]

Diogenes of Oenoanda confronts this misconception directly by declaring that "it is not we but other philosophers who do away with the gods" [οὐχὶ ἡ[μεῖς ἀναιρο]ῦμεν τοὺς [θεοὺς ἀλλ᾽ ἕτ]εροι] (fr. 16 [Ch fr. 11], col. I, lines 5–7). The text is in poor condition, but among those philosophers Diogenes identifies as atheists are Diagoras the Melian and Protagoras of Abdera, who "in effect held the same opinion as Diagoras but used different words so as to avoid its excessive boldness" (fr. 16). When he cites Diagoras, Diogenes is following Epicurus, who attributed atheistic views to Diagoras, as well as to Prodicus, Critias, and other classical philosophers who may also have been named in the full text of Diogenes (fr. 11). In his treatment of Protagoras, however, Diogenes is responding to later doxographical tradition by using a tactic similar to the one Posidonius used against Epicurus. Diogenes takes an accusation that was directed against Epicurus during the centuries after Epicurus' death and turns it on Protagoras, who "said that he did not know whether gods exist, which is the same as saying that he knew they did not" [ἔφησε γὰρ μὴ εἰδέναι εἰ θεοί εἰσιν. τοῦτο δ᾽ ἐστὶν τὸ αὐτὸ τῷ λέγειν εἰδέναι ὅτι μή εἰσιν] (fr. 16 [Ch fr. 11], col. II, lines 8–12).

---

13. See Dirk Obbink, "The Atheism of Epicurus," *GRBS* 30 (1989): 187–223.
14. Obbink, "The Atheism of Epicurus," 222.
15. C.P. Jones, *Culture and Society in Lucian*, (Cambridge, Mass., 1986), 40.

While Diogenes disputes the popular conception of Epicurus as an atheist, he stands firm on the issues that seem to have brought the charge against Epicurus in the first place. To those who actually read the texts, Epicurus' notions about the gods seemed so unconventional that his acceptance of traditional forms of worship struck detractors (first in philosophical circles, then more generally) as disingenuous and hypocritical. Although Epicurus affirmed that the gods exist and condoned such conventional (and pleasurable) practices as the offering of sacrifices and the celebration of cultic festivals,[16] he rejected received opinion on the nature and role of the gods. The gods of Epicurus are happy, peaceful creatures who spend their immortal lives in the *intermundia*, enjoying food, drink, and friendly conversation. For Epicurus there is no teleological order in the world, no divine providence, and no divine retribution: his gods have not created the world (but are themselves subordinate to atoms and the void) and are not the least inclined to meddle in human affairs. As *Principal Doctrine* 1 (which Diogenes quotes at the beginning of his treatise *On Ethics*) puts it: "The blessed and immortal nature knows no trouble itself nor causes trouble to any other, so that it is never constrained by anger or favor. For all such things exist only in the weak."

Diogenes takes on one of the commonplace misconceptions about the gods in fragment 19 (NF 115), where he reminds his contemporaries that the gods are happy beings whose statues should reflect their benignity. They should not be represented with weapons, "like Heracles in Homer," or "with a bodyguard of wild beasts" (col. II). Rather, we should "make statues of the gods genial and smiling, so that we may smile back at them rather than be afraid of them." Diogenes ends his discussion of statues with an exhortation: "Well, then, you people, let us reverence the gods [rightly] both at festivals and on [unhallowed occasions, both] publicly [and privately]."[17] Here Diogenes is following the teachings of Epicurus, who asked his followers to withdraw from politics but not from traditional religious practice. His suggestion about statue design seems to be completely his own, however.

Diogenes' criticism of traditional statues of the Olympians may not sound radical to modern readers, but the dream interpreter Artemidorus of Daldis supplies us with a hint of how extreme Diogenes' position was: even to dream of the gods without their traditional attributes and weapons was considered inauspicious. Diogenes' critique was also likely to offend those of his contemporaries who, during this era of great building programs, were engaged with filling their city squares and elaborate new temples with images of the gods.

---

16. See Obbink, "The Atheism of Epicurus," 200 (with notes), who cites Philodemus *De pietate.*
17. The translation and restorations are those of Smith, *The Epicurean Inscription,* 376.

Even more controversial was Diogenes' stance toward the alleged activities of the gods. One reason the Epicureans could proclaim "Death is nothing to us" (*Principal Doctrine* 2) is that they rejected all the traditional stories about punishments in Hades (and the idea of any afterlife). In a fragment of a letter that seems to belong to the course that displayed Diogenes' epistolary (fr. 73 = Ch fr. 14), the writer (Diogenes?) seems to be thanking his addressee (perhaps Epicurus?) for persuading him to laugh at "the Tityuses and Tantaluses that some people depict in Hades."[18] Plutarch's *On Superstition* and Lucian's *On Funerals* attest to widespread belief not only in the underworld but also in its divinely sanctioned punishments for the wicked. In Lucian's account of Alexander of Abonuteichus (discussed later in this chapter), the *pseudomantis* wins many friends and clients by delivering an oracle that describes Epicurus' punishment in Hades: "Of slime is his bed / And his fetter of lead" (*Alexander* 25).[19]

In fragments 20 (NF 39)and 21 (NF 40) Diogenes ridicules the idea that the world was created for gods and people, an idea familiar to us from Cicero's Stoic presentation in *De Natura Deorum* (2.62.154). Diogenes finds absurd (γελοῖον [fr. 20, col. I, line 4]) the notion that a god would be a fellow citizen to mortals. "And there is this further point too," he continues, "if he had created the world as a habitation and city for himself, I seek to know where he was living before the world was created."[20] To Diogenes the notion that a divinity created the world for himself is strange (ἄτοπα [fr. 20, col. III, line 1]); even stranger (ἀτοπώτερα [fr. 20, col. III, line 3]) is the notion that god created the world for people. In the last column Diogenes proposes to divide his discussion into two sections, one dealing with the world and one with people. We find a section of the first part of this discussion in fragment 21 (NF 40). Here Diogenes uses the sea as evidence that the world was not created for people as a divine gift.

col. I   [ἡ δὲ θάλασσα περιτ]τὰ
         [τοῦδε τοῦ κόσμου με]τέχει

col. II μέρη, χερρόνησον ποιοῦσα
         τὴν οἰκουμένην, ἄλλων
         πάλιν καὶ αὐτὴ κακῶν

---

18. Clay ("The Philosophical Inscription," 2514) suggests that Diogenes imagines Epicurus as his addressee. Other possibilities are that Diogenes is addressing his living teacher (perhaps someone at the Epicurean school in Rhodes?) or that Diogenes is exhibiting a letter sent to him by one of his own followers.

19. H.W. Fowler and F.G. Fowler, *Lucianus Samosatensus* (Oxford, 1905), 25.

20. Translation by M.F. Smith, ed., *Diogenes of Oenoanda: The Epicurean Inscription* (Naples, 1993), 376–77. Extracted quotation is from p. 377.

μεστή, καὶ ἐπὶ πᾶσιν μηδὲ
5 τὸ ὕδωρ ἔχουσα πότιμον,
ἁλμυρὸν δὲ καὶ πικρόν—ὥσ-
περ ἐπίτηδες ὑπὸ τοῦ θεοῦ
τοιοῦτο κατεσκευασμένον
ἵνα μὴ πίωσιν ἄνθρω-
10 ποι. <u>ν</u> ἡ μέντοι καλουμέ-
νη νεκρὰ θάλασσα, καὶ ἀ-
ληθῶς οὖσα νεκρά—πλεῖ-
ται γὰρ οὐδέποτε—, καὶ προσ-
αφαιρεῖταί τι τῶν ἐγγὺς

col. III   [ἀνθρ]ώπων ἧς νέμονται
γῆς· ἐγδιώκει γὰρ αὐτοὺς
ἐπεμβαίνουσα ἰταμῶς
πάνυ μέχρι πολλοῦ καὶ ἀ-
5 ναδυομένη πάλιν ἐπικλύ-
ζει, ὥσπερ παραφυλάττου-
σα μή τι τῆς γῆς ἀρότρῳ
τέμωσιν. vacat
τὰ μὲν οὖν τοῦ κόσμου τοι-
10 αῦτά ἐστιν.

[[The sea] has [excessively large] parts [of this earth] as its share, making a peninsula of the inhabited world, itself also being full of yet other evils, and, to cap all, having water which is not even drinkable, but briny and bitter—as if it had been purposely made like this by the god, to prevent men from drinking.

Moreover, the so-called Dead Sea, which is really and truly dead (for it is never sailed), even deprives the local inhabitants of part of the land which they occupy; for it chases them away to a very considerable distance with its impetuous attacks and again floods their land as it withdraws, as though being on its guard lest they may do any cleaving of the earth with a plough.

Such then are the things of the world.]]

Before Diogenes' era the name *Dead Sea* designated in Greek and Latin not the Palestinian Dead Sea but a section of the northern ocean (as does *mortuum mare* in Pliny *Naturalis Historia* 4.13.95).[21] Later in the second century, however, Pausanias, Galen, and Justin used the name Dead Sea to refer to the lake in Palestine, and Diogenes may here be following earlier sources that knew that usage.[22] Neither of the two "dead seas" appears in other Epicurean sources, and it may have occurred to Diogenes simply as a striking example to cite in his critique of teleology. I suggest, however, that if Diogenes has the "Lake of Palestine" (as Aristotle calls it) in mind, his choice may be due to Diogenes' awareness that the area was the home of Jews and Christians—people who were as convinced as the Stoics that the world was divinely created as a home for humanity. Diogenes can hardly have been unaware of Judaism, and given Paul's missionary activity in Lycia and the fact that Colossae is only fifty miles away from Oenoanda, it is difficult to imagine that Diogenes could be unaware of Christianity, the fastest-growing religious movement in second-century Asia Minor.[23] If Diogenes' reference to the Dead Sea signifies that he included the inhabitants of Palestine among the many victims of wrong ideas about the gods, Diogenes' apparent failure to name the Christians or Jews is not unusual: many Hellenes (or "Pagans") avoided naming the early Christians and did not acknowledge the seriousness of their creed.[24]

Epicurus and Divination

It was traditional in some Epicurean circles to speak of Epicurus as a font of oracular wisdom, a convention paralleled by the Epicurean willingness to call Epicurus a god (which culminates in the proem to Lucretius' fifth book: "deus

21. See T. Kappeler, "Das 'Tote Meer' bei Diogenes von Oenoanda (NF 40)," *Epigraphica Anatolica* 15 (1990): 7–18.

22. See M.F. Smith, "More New Fragments of Diogenes of Oenoanda," in *Etudes sur l'Epicurisme antique*, ed. J. Bollack and A. Laks (Lille, 1976), 292–93. Smith now agrees with Kappeler (cited in the preceding note) that Diogenes must mean the Dead Sea of the north ocean. See *The Epicurean Inscription*, 462.

23. Although the definitive history of early Christianity in Asia Minor has yet to be written, much recent material is available in, for example, Lane Fox, *Pagans and Christians;* R. MacMullen, *Christianizing the Roman Empire* (New Haven and London, 1984); and Abraham Malherbe, *Social Aspects of Early Christianity,* 2d ed. (Philadelphia, 1983).

24. Arnaldo Momigliano argues that the purpose of the work of Diogenes Laertius (who maintained an "intentional" silence on the Christians) was "to recommend Greek philosophy to those who were in danger of professing barbarous doctrines, Christian or otherwise" (*On Pagans, Jews, and Christians* [Middletown, Conn., 1987], 172–73). If the spread of Christianity distressed Diogenes of Oenoanda, his sustained polemic against Stoicism is quite appropriate. B.P. Reardon maintains that Christianity absorbed so much of Stoic philosophy that the result was merely "a change of name": Stoicism became Christianity (*Courants littéraires grecs des IIe et IIIe siècles*

ille fuit, deus" [5.8]). The tradition may have originated with Epicurus himself: one of the sources that likens Epicurus to an oracle seems to be a quotation from one of his writings. It is found in the *Sententiae Vaticanae* (29) and sounds more like an excerpt than a maxim.

Παρρησίᾳ γὰρ ἔγωγε χρώμενος φυσιολογῶν χρησμωδεῖν τὰ συμφέ-
ροντα πᾶσιν ἀνθρώποις μᾶλλον ἂν βουλοίμην κἂν μηδεὶς μέλλῃ συνή-
σειν, ἢ συγκατατιθέμενος ταῖς δόξαις καρποῦσθαι τὸν πυκνὸν παρα-
πίπτοντα παρὰ τῶν πολλῶν ἔπαινον.

[In investigating nature I would prefer to speak openly and like an oracle to give answers serviceable to all mankind, even though no one should understand me, rather than to conform to popular opinions and so win the praise freely scattered by the mob.][25]

Lucretius may have that quotation (or a similar passage) in mind when he compares himself (favorably) to the Delphic oracle in *De Rerum Natura* (5.110–13).

Qua prius aggrediar quam de re fundere fata
sanctius et multo certa ratione magis quam
Pythia quae tripode a Phoebi lauroque profatur,
multa tibi expediam doctis solacia dictis. . . .

[Yet before I essay on this point to declare destiny in more holy wise, and with reasoning far more sure than the Pythian priestess, who speaks out from the tripod and laurel of Phoebus, I will unfold many a solace for you in my learned discourse. . . .][26]

Cicero's sarcastic reference to the *Principal Doctrines* as "oracles of wisdom" (quasi oracula sapientiae [*De Finibus* 2.7.20]) also points to the Epicurean usage of the term, as does the epigram by Athenaeus that describes Epicurus' wisdom as coming "from the muses or from the sacred tripod of Pytho" (Di-

après J.-C., Annales littéraires de L'Université de Nantes 3 (Paris, 1971), 34. This is of course an overstatement, but many early Christian thinkers accepted wholeheartedly the Stoic view of morality—so much so that Tertullian, for example, refers to "Seneca saepe noster."

    25. Trans. Bailey, *Epicurus,* 111. Cicero alludes to this quotation in *De Natura Deorum* 1.66: "haec ego nunc physicorum oracula fundo." See also Diogenes Laertius 10.12 and Lucian's imitation of Epicurean language in *Alexander* 61.

    26. Trans. Cyril Bailey, ed., *Titi Lucreti Cari De rerum natura.* vol. 1 (Oxford, 1947), 439.

ogenes Laertius 10.12). Lucian (in the voice of a pro-Epicurean narrator) also imitates this Epicurean convention at the close of *Alexander the False Prophet* (61), where he calls Epicurus "truly holy and prophetic" (φεσπέσιος).[27]

Diogenes of Oenoanda departs from this tradition. Rather than praising Epicurus with language borrowed from the vocabulary of prophecy, Diogenes mentions oracles only to relegate them to the realm of *pseudodoxia* (frr. 23, 52, 53, 54 [Ch frr. 30, 31, 32 and NF 19]). In my view, Diogenes' stance (which matches that of other second-century Epicureans) is due to the massive increase in the buying and selling of oracular prophecies in Diogenes' era. The Epicurean response to this growth in business may further illuminate Plutarch's hostility toward contemporary Epicureans; Plutarch was, after all, a Delphic priest.[28]

Although the pronouncements of second-century Epicureans departed from those of Epicurus, they were completely consonant with his teachings. The Epicurean conception of the gods as beings who do not concern themselves with human affairs in any way is of course incompatible with the belief in prophecy. Diogenes Laertius reports that Epicurus stated, "Prophecy (μαντική) does not exist, and even if it did exist, things that come to pass must be counted nothing to us" (10.135), but there is no discussion of oracular shrines in the extant writings of Epicurus, and none of the titles of Epicurus' "best books" listed by Diogenes Laertius mention oracular prophecy.[29] Epicurean texts that used stronger language may have been known to Cicero, who records that "nihil tam inridet Epicurus quam praedictionem rerum futurarum" (*De Natura Deorum* 1.3.5). There is no indication, however, that Epicurus attacked oracles with the vehemence of the second-century Epicureans. Epicurus may have tolerated oracular practices in the same spirit in which he urged his students to respect the cultic practices of prayer and sacrifice.[30]

Two of the relevant passages from Diogenes' inscription are unfortunately in very poor condition,[31] and fragment 54 (Ch fr. 32)—in which Diogenes asks,

27. See also Petronius *Satyricon* 132.

28. G.W. Bowersock suggests that it is "not unreasonable" to assign to Plutarch "an important role" in this rejuvenation of Delphi ("Philostratus and the Second Sophistic," in *Cambridge History of Classical Literature,* vol. 1, *Greek Literature,* ed. P.E. Easterling and B.M. Knox [Cambridge, 1985], 666).

29. One of Epicurus' books was called Περὶ Εἱμαρμένης (On fate).

30. See my discussion of Epicurus' alleged atheism (earlier in this chapter) and Philodemus *De pietate* (Usener frr. 12 and 387). See also W. Schmid, "Götter und Menschen in der Theologie Epikurs," *RhM* 94 (1951): 155–56.

31. Frr. 52 and 53 (Ch frr. 31 and 30) preserve only a few words. Smith translates fr. 53 as follows: "Why then is [the fulfilment of] certain predictions [stronger] evidence [of the soundness of divination than their non-]fulfilment is evidence [of its unsoundness? It is illogical,] in my view. . . . [I lay down] . . ." Fr. 52 has not been rediscovered since it was recorded by Cousin in 1889.

"So if divination [μαντική] is [done away with, how] is there any other proof of destiny [εἱμαρμένη]?"—must be the conclusion of a discussion that has not yet been discovered. There is, however, one well-preserved fragment in which Diogenes mentions the treachery of ambiguous oracular responses (fr. 23 = NF 19).

οὐκ ἀναγκαῖον εἰ[πεῖν τι]
ἐπ' ἐνέδρα τῶν λάθ[ρα με]-
5   νόντων, εἰ μὴ δοκεῖ[τε]
ἀγνοεῖν ἡμᾶς ἡλίκαις
συμφοραῖς διὰ τὸ ἀμφίβο-
λον τοῦτο τῶν χρησμῶν καὶ
ποικίλως πλάγιον κέ-
10   χρηνταί τινες ἢ και-
ρὸν ἡμᾶς ἔχειν διακα-
θαίρειν ἐπὶ τοῦ παρόν-
τος οἷα Λακεδαιμόνι-
οι κακὰ πεπόνθασιν. . . .

[It [is] not necessary [to give further warning] against the things that wait secretly in ambush, unless [you] think we are ignorant of the great misfortunes some have suffered on account of this ambiguity and tricky obliqueness of the oracles, or that we have time to explain the kinds of evils the Lacedaemonians suffered. . . .][32]

As commentators have noted, it sounds as though Diogenes is referring to the famous oracle given to the Spartans when they asked Delphi if they would succeed in conquering all of Arcadia.[33] Herodotus (1.66) relates that the Spartans understood the Pythia's reply to mean that they would gain control of the Tegean plain, but the benign-sounding oracle actually led to their being enslaved there.

It has been suggested that Diogenes borrowed this and one of his other two references to Herodotus from the writings of Epicurus.[34] Given the immense

---

32. This translation is David Sedley, review of M.F. Smith, *Thirteen New Fragments of Diogenes of Oenoanda* (Vienna, 1974), *CR*, n.s., 26 (1976): 218; and D. Clay, "A Lost Epicurean Community," *GRBS* 30 (1989): 333.

33. See M.F. Smith, *Thirteen New Fragments of Diogenes of Oenoanda,* Denkschriften der österreichische Akademie der Wissenschaften, Philologisch-Historische Klasse, 117 (Vienna, 1974), 15.

34. See Smith, *Thirteen New Fragments,* 41. The other passages containing Herodotean allusions are fragments 153 (NF 27) and 139 (NF 93).

popularity of Herodotus in Diogenes' era, Epicurus' antipathy toward traditional erudition, and Diogenes' apparent membership in a family that claimed a Spartan ancestor, it is more likely that the use of Herodotus originated with Diogenes himself. The use of rhetorical prolepsis—he says there is no need to cite examples but then proceeds to give a historical exemplum—also fits Diogenes' oratorical style. Moreover, collections of riddling oracles culled from ancient literary sources are typical of Second Sophistic erudition. Dio Chrysostom, for example, in his tenth discourse, "On Servants" (24–25), has Diogenes the Cynic cite several troublesome oracles (including the well-known responses given to Oedipus and Croesus). Here, although he enjoys the opportunity to cite Herodotus and his own "native" Sparta, "Diogenes" expresses a bit of contempt for the well-worn contents of such catalogs.

The Revival of Oracular Prophecy in the Second Century

I mentioned in chapter 1 of this study that Delphi experienced a revival during the reign of Hadrian. The oracles of Asia Minor were revived around that time also. In fact, the oracle of Apollo at Didyma seems to have been more active between the years 100 and 225 C.E. than in any other period.[35] Most of the evidence for the revival is inscriptional, but the picture afforded by epigraphy is supported by architectural remains and literary accounts.[36] The emperor Trajan aided the revival by restoring the sacred way between Miletus and the temple.[37] The oracle of Apollo at Claros also experienced a similar revival.[38] Both of

35. On Didyma, see H.W. Parke, *The Oracles of Apollo in Asia Minor* (London, 1985), chapter 5, "The Imperial Roman Period: The Flowering" (69–93). On the second-century revival of oracles in Asia Minor, see Lane Fox, *Pagans and Christians,* chapter 5, "Language of the Gods" (168–261).

36. Parke (Oracles, 74) acknowledges that epigraphy was in fashion and that many people could afford to inscribe whatever they wished, so the recording of oracles may have increased at a higher rate than consultation itself. He concludes, however, that all the evidence points to a sharp increase in the prominence of the oracular centers of Asia Minor.

37. See Parke, *Oracles,* 72.

38. Louis Robert writes: "Le recours d'Alexandre à Claros avait lieu quand l'oracle d'Apollon en ce temple était dans sa plus grande gloire; de Trajan et d'Hadrien jusque dans le IIIe siècle avancé, les inscriptions, qui sont un memorial d'une consultation par telle ou telle ville, venaient couvrir murs et colonnes du tripylon et l'exedre voisine, bases honorifiques de l'époque republicaine et augusteenne, autel, marches du temple et colonnes de la façade, par dizaines et par dizaines, sans parler des stèles indépendantes *A travers l'Asie Mineure: Poètes et prosateurs, monnaies grecques, voyageurs et géographie,* Bibliothèque des Ecoles Françaises d'Athènes et de Rome 239 (Paris, 1980), 404. See also Robert's "L'oracle de Claros," in *La civilisation grecque de l'antiquité à nos jours,* ed. C. Delvoye and G. Roux (Brussels, 1967); and Parke, *Oracles,* chapter 9, "The Late-Flowering of Claros" (142–71). Lane Fox, *Pagans and Christians,* 174, provides a map that shows the many "client cities" of the oracle at Claros attested for the imperial period.

these oracular centers enjoyed imperial patronage (especially under Hadrian) and received numerous private benefactions, sometimes in the form of buildings and sculpture.[39] Both were frequently consulted concerning matters ranging from the personal to the political, by individuals as well as by delegations. Many of the oracles' responses were collected in Cornelius Labeo's *On the Oracle of Clarian Apollo* and Porphyry's *Philosophy from Oracles.*[40] Closer to Oenoanda, there were Apolline oracular centers at Patara, Sura, and Cyaneae. These sites have not been thoroughly excavated, but the evidence suggests that they too were revived in the second century.[41]

As activity increased at the shrines the critics responded. A contemporary of Diogenes named Oenomaus of Gadara also records a catalog of ancient oracular responses, but his is written as an exposé rather than as a homage to the ancient sites.[42] Oenomaus' collection is part of his *Exposure of Frauds,* a polemic that alerts people to the deceptive nature of all oracular responses. Like Diogenes of Oenoanda, Oenomaus cites notorious oracles from the distant past as proof of the unreliability of prophetic utterances.[43] The *loci classici* were not his only evidence, however: he had had firsthand experience of tricky oracles. According to his own account, he had consulted the oracle of Apollo at Claros several times and had eventually discovered that the oracle not only distributed extremely vague answers but gave the same response to different people. Oenomaus was especially angered by the fact that an oracular reply that seemed to promise him prosperity was also given to several men of comparatively low social status. Perhaps the recycling of oracles was especially common at Claros: Apollo also gave identical responses to the families of the two young lovers in Xenophon's *Ephesian Tale of Anthia and Habrocomes.*

Oracles were also a major concern of Diogeneianus, the second-century Epicurean who composed a treatise against Chrysippus' doctrine of fate.[44] Diogeneianus relies on the type of commonsense arguments that Lucian also ex-

---

39. See Parke, *Oracles,* 72–73, 76–77, 146.

40. The former may be a second-century treatise; the latter is from the third century. Julian the Theurgist's *Chaldaean Oracles* may also belong to the second century.

41. See Parke, *Oracles,* 184–97; on Patara, see Louis Robert, chap. 18, "Lucien en son temps," in *A travers l'Asie Mineure: Poètes et prosateurs, monnaies grecques, voyageurs et géographie* (Paris, 1980), 402 n. 38.

42. Oenomaus seems to have been an old man while Hadrian was emperor. Quotations of his work are preserved by Eusebius, who found his criticism of a pagan practice useful.

43. In the text preserved by Eusebius, Oenomaus cites five Herodotean oracles (including the one given to Croesus). See *Praep. Ev.* 5.20, 24, 26, and 34.

44. Diogeneianus is known only through the writings of Eusebius (*Praep. Ev.* 4.3). The second-century dating is generally accepted, but the decisive factor for Hans von Arnim's dating ("Diogenianus" no. 3, *RE* 5.1 [1905]: col. 778) is the prevalence of criticism of mantic practices in

ploits (in *Juppiter Confutatus* 12): if all events are fated and oracles can tell the future, the oracles are still useless because an event that is fated cannot be avoided.[45] Diogeneianus' treatise appears to have been primarily a theoretical discussion, but his work included a polemical attack against the use of oracular shrines. By denouncing divination by oracles Diogenes and Diogeneianus are acting as faithful Epicureans, but their loyalty does not involve the simple echoing of Epicurus. As good Epicureans, they have taken a fundamental Epicurean teaching and have applied it to a second-century need.

Here the contrast between Diogenes and Lucretius brings out a crucial aspect of Epicurean method: all Epicurean teachers must adapt Epicurus' teachings to suit the needs of their contemporaries. The passage in which Lucretius compares himself to the Pythia (*De Rerum Natura* 5.110–13; quoted earlier in this chapter) is Lucretius' only allusion to oracular shrines. The obvious explanation for the Roman poet's silence is supplied by Cicero (*De Divinatione* 2.117).

Sed, quod caput est, cur isto modo iam oracla Delphis non eduntur non modo nostra aetate, sed iam diu, ut modo nihil possit esse contemptius? . . . Quando ista vis autem evanuit? an postquam homines minus creduli esse coeperunt?

[However, the main question is this: Why are Delphic oracles not uttered now as they used to be? Why have they been silent for so long? Why are they now regarded with the utmost contempt? . . . When did their power disappear? Was it after people began to be less credulous?]

Lucretius had no need to expose oracular prophecy as a fraudulent practice, because in his era activity at Delphi, Claros, and Didyma was at a low ebb. This would also explain why Epicurus and his early followers seem not to be particularly concerned about oracles: their stance was a reasonable one to take in the Hellenistic age, when the shrines were not heavily used.

Although Lucretius passes over Delphi and its competitors, he does criticize the originally Etruscan practice of divination through interpretation of lightning. In *De Rerum Natura* 6.83–89 he launches into his scientific explanations

---

the second century. Diogeneianus' Epicureanism is generally accepted but has sometimes been questioned; on this issue, see M.I. Parente, "Diogeniano, gli epicurei e la τύχη," *ANRW* II 36.4 (1990): 2424–45; and J. Ferguson, "Epicureanism under the Roman Empire," *ANRW* II 36.4 (1990): 2289–90.

45. Eusebius *Praep. Ev.* 4.3, 138.

of lightning and thunder, lest anyone think that flashes in the sky can be interpreted as celestial messages.

> est ratio <terrae> caelique tenenda,
> sunt tempestates et fulmina clara canenda,
> quid faciant et qua de causa cumque ferantur;
> ne trepides caeli divisis partibus amens
> unde volans ignis pervenerit aut in utram se
> verterit hinc partim, quo pacto per loca saepta
> insinuarit, et hinc dominatus ut extulerit se.

[We must grasp the inner working of <the earth> and sky, we must sing of storms and flashing lightnings, of how they act and by what cause they are severally brought to pass; that you may not mark out the quarters of the sky, and ask in frenzied anxiety, whence came this winged flash, or to what quarter it departed hence, and how after tyrant deeds it brought itself forth again.][46]

In Lucretius' Roman context such criticism of augury was not only relevant but radical.[47] Few people outside Roman Epicurean circles seem to have been willing to proclaim that meteorological events were not messages from the gods, and the rejection of augury was identified so closely with Roman Epicureanism that Horace (*Odes* 1.34) claimed that he recanted his Epicureanism because of a sudden bolt out the blue. Lucretius' contemporaries did not need to be cautioned, however, about outmoded and nearly forgotten Greek oracular shrines.

Second-century Epicureans, in contrast, had to contend with more than the revival of the traditional oracular shrines. There were also entrepreneurs like Alexander "the false prophet," who invented his own "new Asclepius," a mantic snake-god named Glycon who delivered oracles (on healing as well as on more general topics) for a drachma and two obols. Our main source for Alexander's activities is the seriocomic biography presented in Lucian's *Alexander the False Prophet,* and it is significant that Lucian there adopts the voice of an earnest Epi-

---

46. Trans. Bailey, *Epicurus,* 517. Cf. *De Rerum Natura* 6.381–86.

47. For recent discussions of belief in augury and other types of Roman divination in Lucretius' era, see Mary Beard, "Cicero and Divination: The Formation of a Latin Discourse," *JRS* 76 (1986): 33–46; and Malcolm Schofield, "Cicero for and against Divination," *JRS* 76 (1986): 47–65. J.H.W.G. Liebeschuetz, in *Continuity and Change in Roman Religion* (Oxford, 1979), argues that belief in divination was strong throughout the republic and that Cicero and Lucretius "were exceptional in the radicalism of their rationalism" (29).

curean.[48] Celsus, the man to whom Lucian addresses his *Alexander,* was also an Epicurean and had himself written a book that exposed the frauds committed by sorcerers. What perturbed the Epicureans (and Lucian qua Epicurean) was not so much the religiosity or credulousness of the oracle's clients but mainly the grotesquely fraudulent (and lucrative) behavior of the human operators of the oracle. Alexander was not a completely isolated phenomenon. As Branham has shown, Lucian uses Alexander to represent a "known type" (the religious entre-preneur),[49] whom Lucian exposes by impersonating another "known type" (the enthusiastic Epicurean).

Lucian reveals that the role of Alexander's Glycon was played by a type of serpent of unusual size and gentleness that was native to Pella.[50] The launching of Glycon's career included carefully staged events, such as the "discovery" of tablets that foretold his arrival, and the birth of the snake from a goose egg. To the spectators who returned a few days later, this baby snake (having been replaced by the gigantic serpent) seemed to have grown with miraculous speed. Alexander had a humanlike linen head made for it, and when people came to see the "god," Alexander met them in a darkened room, the snake draped across his lap and around his neck, its actual head hidden in Alexander's armpit (*Alexander* 15). When the snake began its career as an oracle, his prophet, Alexander, requested that questions be submitted on sealed scrolls to give visitors the impression that only the god himself would know their questions. Lucian's impersonation of a good Epicurean is especially on target when he explains what Alexander did—or must have done—to ensure that his oracular responses were relevant to the "secret" questions: he furtively opened, read, and resealed the scrolls (using various devious methods involving hot needles, special plas-ters, and synthetic marble). To boost his credibility Alexander also resorted to espionage, to questioning the client's companions, to giving deliberately unin-telligible answers, and—when necessary—to "correcting" old oracles when events proved him wrong. For an extra fee one could buy "autophonic" oracles delivered directly by Glycon; the actual voice was that of an accomplice who spoke through a hidden tube (made from cranes' windpipes) that ran through the linen head (*Alexander* 26). Thus, Lucian dispels any faith the reader might have had in Alexander's supernatural abilities by explaining the physical

48. For Lucian's impersonation of an Epicurean, see R. Bracht Branham, *Unruly Eloquence: Lucian and the Comedy of Traditions* (Cambridge, Mass., 1989), especially chapter 4, "Sudden Glory: The Revenge of Epicurus" (179–210).

49. Branham (*Unruly Eloquence,* 183–85) compares Alexander to the first-century C.E. miracle-working doctor Thessalus.

50. The locale is one of many details in Lucian's narrative that link the rise of this Alexander with that of Alexander the Great.

realities behind Alexander's performance in a manner similar to the way Epicurus, Lucretius, and Diogenes of Oenoanda offer multiple physical explanations for meteorological events that were traditionally attributed to the actions of the gods.[51]

Alexander's authority seems to have been questioned by few people other than the Epicureans and Lucian (who, dropping the guise of gentle Epicurean, claims to have bitten the prophet's hand). Lucian maintains that Alexander urged a crowd to pelt with stones an Epicurean who revealed in public that one of Alexander's oracles had caused two men to be put to death (*Alexander* 45). Also, Alexander refused responses to anyone from Amastris in Pontus because an important citizen of that city, Lepidus, was an Epicurean with many followers. When Glycon did meet with one of Lepidus' friends, he prophesied, "Do not trust Lepidus, for a baneful fate is in waiting."[52] If we may believe Lucian, Alexander began an annual three-day festival with a proclamation against the only people who denied him homage: atheists, Christians, and Epicureans (*Alexander* 38). The Epicureans were Alexander's greatest enemies while "the followers of Plato, Chrysippus, and Pythagoras were his friends" (*Alexander* 25). We are told by Lucian that the oracle's fame spread throughout the whole empire; Glycon was consulted by men of consular and senatorial rank, and even the court of Marcus Aurelius had two lions thrown into the Danube at Glycon's bidding (*Alexander* 48).

Lucian's account of this bizarre snake oracle is extremely derisive, but external sources substantiate the main points of Lucian's story and attest to Alexander's phenomenal success.[53] As Louis Robert and others have shown, coins, statues, and inscriptional evidence lend external support to Lucian's account. Glycon's name and image appear not only on coins from Abonuteichus but also on coins from towns in Bithynia and Paphlagonia.[54] Even Lucian's claim that Alexander had sexual encounters with married women, who proudly bore his children, seems to find support in an inscription in Lydia.[55]

As the oracles gained in popularity they expanded their purview to include philosophical and theological issues. As Lane Fox puts it, "the gods' hori-

---

51. See especially Epicurus *Letter to Pythocles;* Lucretius *De Rerum Natura* 6; and Diogenes frr. 98 (NF 168) and 99 (NF 169).

52. *Alexander* 25 and 43. An inscription in Amastris (*CIG* 4149) honors "Tiberius Claudius Lepidus, Chief Priest of Pontus and President of the Metropolis of Pontus," who must be the same man. See Robert, "Lucien en son temps," 416.

53. See G.W. Bowersock, *Greek Sophists in the Roman Empire* (Oxford, 1969), 71; Jones, *Culture and Society,* 133–48; and D. Clay, "Lucian of Samosata," *ANRW* II 36.5 (1992): 3406–50.

54. See Robert, "Lucien en son temps," 393–421. See also Jones, *Culture and Society,* 138.

55. See Robert, "Lucien en son temps," 405–8.

zons had grown with their prophets' education"; one second-century Milesian prophet even called himself "successor of Plato."[56] At some shrines Apollo's utterances became increasingly Platonist, a trend that culminated in a "Delphic obituary" for Plotinus, whom the oracle identified as a recipient of divine light.[57] According to Philostratus, Apollonius of Tyana descended into the oracular shrine of Trophonius "on behalf of philosophy." When he emerged a week later, he carried with him the wisdom of Pythagoras. One of the most remarkable signs of Apollo's new expertise comes from Oenoanda itself, where the answer to the question "Who is God?" was carved on the city wall.

> Self-born, untaught, motherless, unshakable,
> Giving place to no name, many-named, dwelling in fire,
> Such is God: we are a portion of God, his angels.
> This, then, to the questioners about God's nature
> The god replied, calling him all-seeing Ether: to him, then, look
> And pray at dawn, looking out to the east.[58]

The prophets' expansion into philosophical and religious territory would have been especially alarming to nonbelievers, including the Epicureans.

Thus, the criticism of oracles voiced by Diogenes and other second-century Epicureans is hardly an outdated polemic taken directly from the teachings of Epicurus; it was instead a serious critique of contemporary practice. Oracular prophecy was undergoing a revival, and Epicureans felt called on to expose the fraud. They did not need to quote any particular Epicurean text to protest against the revival; Epicurus' teachings about the nature of divinity and the Epicurean belief that all phenomena can be explained rationally were enough. Lucian (*Alexander* 17) describes the situation well in reference to Alexander's Glycon.

> Really the trick stood in need of a Democritus, or even Epicurus himself
> or Metrodorus, or some one else with a mind as firm as adamant toward
> such matters, so as to disbelieve and guess the truth—one who, if he
> could not discover how it went, would at all events be convinced before-
> hand that though the method of the fraud escaped him, it was neverthe-
> less all sham and could not possibly happen.[59]

---

56. Lane Fox, *Pagans and Christians,* 187.

57. Lane Fox, *Pagans and Christians,* 188.

58. See Louis Robert, "Un oracle gravé à Oinoanda," *CRAI* (1971): 597; and Lane Fox's discussion in *Pagans and Christians,* 169 ff. Garth Fowden's review of Lane Fox ("Between Pagans and Christians" *JRS* 78 [1988]: 173–82) cites some errors in that account. The translation quoted here is that of Lane Fox, 169.

59. Trans. A.M. Harmon, *Lucian,* 199.

Dreaming the Gods

The belief that the "all-seeing" gods use dreams to deliver prophecies and advice was also strong among Diogenes' contemporaries, as the texts of, for example, Aristides, Artemidorus, Marcus Aurelius, and even Galen demonstrate. The *Oneirocritica* of Artemidorus of Daldis (who was born in Ephesus but named himself after his mother's town in Lydia) records hundreds of dreams that Artemidorus gathered from people of all walks of life on his travels between Rome and Asia Minor. The Olympians appear frequently in these dreams, a feature of second-century dreaming that seems to be indicative not only of the intensity of second-century religious experience but also of the mood of nostalgia discussed in chapter 1 of this study.[60]

Artemidorus' professional interest was in the prophetic power of dreams and the delicate art of interpretation.[61] Much of Artemidorus' research involved sifting the different types of predictive "god-sent" dreams (ὄνειροι) from lesser dreams (ἐνύπνια) that simply mirror the dreamer's thoughts (1.1–2) and collecting information on the correlation between dream content and eventual outcome.[62] The interpretation of god-sent dreams required skill: Artemidorus specialized in interpreting allusive (ἀλληγορικοί) dreams in light of the dreamer's cultural and social location. In the fifth and final book of the *Oneirocritica* he records ninety-five dreams that were known to have come true.

The prophetic power of dreams was closely connected with their curative powers in the second century, especially in the cult of Asclepius, whose temples supplied incubatory chambers for patients who wished to court the advice of the healing god. According to Artemidorus, the help of an interpreter is not required in the case of such divine remedies: healing gods use ordinary language and indulge only in very simple riddles (4.22). For detailed descriptions of curative dreams, we must turn to Aelius Aristides' *Sacred Tales,* which record copious information about the visitations he experienced at the Asclepieion at Pergamum.[63] There the ailing Aristides met in his dreams not only Asclepius but his favorite classical authors and Apollo, Athena, and Hermes (who once appeared disguised as Plato), as well as Sarapis and Isis. The lucidity Ar-

---

60. Writing about dreamers in the Antonine period, Lane Fox puts it thus: "As night fell, they recaptured the lost ideal of Phaeacia and the pre-Homeric past" (*Pagans and Christians,* 164).

61. See S.R.F. Price, "The Future of Dreams: From Freud to Artemidoros," in *Before Sexuality,* ed. D. Halperin et al. (Princeton, 1990), 365–87.

62. On Artemidorus' uncertainty about the exact role of the gods in the formation of dreams, see Price, "The Future of Dreams," 376–77 and 380.

63. Peter Brown ("A Social Context") suggests that Aristides' unwillingness to exploit his intimacy with Asclepius is unusual; Aristides wished to avoid being a demagogue during an era when others who felt such close contact with the gods opened their own shrines.

temidorus attributes to curative dreams is not borne out by the texts of Aristides, who often referred his more obscure dreams to the doctors and temple attendants.

For Epicureans too dreams could offer a chance to gaze on the gods. The advent of the gods in human dreams seems in fact to have been one of Epicurus' proofs not only of the existence of the gods but of their anthropomorphism.[64] While the gods may appear to people during their waking hours, the fine εἴδωλα of the gods are more likely to enter peoples' minds while the other senses are at rest. Epicureans explained the process as a variation of the mechanics of vision in general: our viewing of any object is the result of the object's constant emission of εἴδωλα, the thin, fine films that flow off all solid bodies.[65] As evidence for the existence and behavior of εἴδωλα, both Diogenes and Lucretius cite the reflections we see in mirrors (fr. 9 [NF 5]; *De Rerum Natura* 4.98–109, etc.). Vision occurs when these films act on the senses. The εἴδωλα of the gods behave somewhat differently because their especially fine structure (which reflects the fine atomic structure of the gods) is generally perceivable not by the eyes but only by the mind.

Epicurus' affirmation of the idea that the gods appear in the dreams of mortals does not extend to the notion that the gods communicate to people via dreams.[66] Human beings and objects appear in dreams in a similar way: we "see" dream images with our minds. As this notion is phrased in the *Letter to Mother,* dream visions (φαντασίαι) are "not tangible [ἁπταί] but intelligible [διανόηται]" (fr. 125 [Ch fr. 52], col. II, lines 3–4). There is no volition involved on the part of the god (or anyone else who appears in the dream), nor can dreams give us a glimpse of the future; it is all a matter of the natural movements of atoms and their films (εἴδωλα). Usually the films preserve the main characteristics of the forms from which they emanate, but sometimes the films become distorted during their journey between their source and the human mind. Such distortion can result in confused images or hallucinations, but the mind itself does not imagine such distortions.[67] Diogenes stresses this point in his treatise *Physics* (fr. 10 = Ch fr. 7), where he describes the Epicurean

---

64. See Velleius' explanation in Cicero's *De Natura Deorum* 1.46. For most of our information about Epicurean theology we depend on first-century B.C.E. sources.

65. See NF 5 and NF 6; *Letter to Herodotus* 46–49. See also Elizabeth Asmis, *Epicurus' Scientific Method* (Ithaca, N.Y., 1984), especially chapters 6 and 7.

66. On Diogenes' contribution, see D. Clay, "An Epicurean Interpretation of Dreams," *AJP* 101 (1980): 342–65.

67. See *Letter to Herodotus* 48 and the discussion of Stephen Everson, "Epicurus on the Truth of the Senses," in *Epistemology,* ed. Stephen Everson (Cambridge, 1990), 161–83, especially 176–78.

position as being located between the extreme stances held by the Stoics, on the one hand, and Democritus, on the other. He refutes the Stoic notion that some dreams are simply products of the human imagination.

col. I

κενὰ μὲν οὖν [σ]κι[α-]
5 γραφήματα τῆς δια-
νοίας οὐκ ἔστι τὰ φάσ-
ματα, ὡς ἀξιοῦσιν οἱ
Στωικοί. καὶ γὰρ εἰ μὲν οὕτως αὐτὰ λέγουσιν
10 κενὰ ὡς ἔχοντα μὲν
σωματικὴν φύσιν, λε-
πτὴν δὲ ἄκρως καὶ οὐ-
χ ὑπόπτωτον ταῖς αἰσ-
θήσεσι, τῇ ἑρμηνείᾳ

col. II

[κέχρ]ηνται κακῇ, ἐ[πεὶ]
[ἔ]δε[ι] α[ὐ]τὰ σωμ[τικὰ λ[έ]-
[γεσ]θαι καὶ λεπτὰ ὄντα.
εἰ δὲ οὕτω κενὰ ὡς οὐ-
5 δ' ὅλως ἔχοντα σωμα-
τικὴν φύσιν, ὃ δὴ καὶ
μ[ᾶλ]λον βούλονται
λέγε[ιν ἢ] τὸ πρῶτον,
πῶς οἷόν τε τὸ κενὸν
10 ἀναζωγραφε[ῖ]σθαι;
τί οὖν ἔστιν; λεπτ[ὴ]ν
μὲν ἔχει τὰ δὴ φάσμα-
τα τὴν σύνκρισιν καὶ
ἐκπεφευγυῖαν τῆς ὄψε-

col. III   [ως], κε[νὴν δ' οὔ.][68]

[Visions are not then empty figments of the imagination, as the Stoics claim. For indeed if they call them empty for the reason that although they do have a corporeal nature yet it is extremely thin and does not im-

---

68. The text I give here does not record Smith's restorations for the first lines of col. I or the continuation of col. III.

pinge on the senses, then the expression they employ is wrong since these too should have been called corporeal despite their subtlety. But if they are so thin that they do not have a corporeal nature at all—which is what they really want to say rather than the former—how can the empty be depicted? So what are they? Images do indeed have a thin constitution and one that has escaped our sight, [but they are not empty].]

Here Diogenes' rhetorical opposition of the Stoics and Democritus may seem to misrepresent Stoic views (since the Stoics were generally firm believers in the divine inspiration of dreams), but Diogenes is not claiming that the Stoics reject the mantic power of dreams. Rather, he is alluding to a Stoic claim that some dreams or visions could be simply false, with no connection to reality.[69] The Epicurean approach (here as elsewhere) is not to dismiss or deny the existence of apparently supernatural phenomena but to explain them, to bring them into the concrete realm of nature. While Diogenes' account is consonant with what we know of Epicurus' own teachings, it does not depend on any particular text of Epicurus. This is clear not only from his engagement with the Stoics but from his adoption of Stoic vocabulary: his word for vision (φάζμα) follows the usage of Chrysippus, not Epicurus.[70]

In a fragment discovered by Smith we find another piece of Diogenes' presentation of the contrast between Democritus and the Stoics. Here Diogenes has already moved on to Democritus, who held that figures who appear in dreams are real beings who actually have the power to speak with us: "So he [sc. Democritus] says that these [sc. dream visions] are not empty shapes since so much power belongs to them as well. But it is not the case, to reiterate, that if they are not void they possess sensation and the power to reason and can in truth chat [προσλαλεῖ] with us" (fr. 10, col. IV = NF 1, col. II). To Diogenes, Democritus' ideas about dreams are as incorrect as the Stoics'. In the fifth column of fragment 10 (NF 1), he writes:

> [ἀμ]ήχανον γὰρ λε-
> πτοῖς ὑμέσιν οὕτως καὶ
> στερεμνίας φύσεως βά-
> 5   θος οὐκ ἔχου[ι]ν ταῦτα προσ-

---

69. In *Stoicorum Veterum Fragmenta,* vol. 2 (Leipzig, 1903), 22, hallucinations are attributed to the melancholia or madness of the beholder.

70. See Clay, "An Epicurean Interpretation," 349 (with n. 14) and 358. The word φάζμα also appears in fr. 125 (Ch fr. 52), col. III; those who take the *Letter to Mother* as a document of Epicurus have there a precedent for Diogenes' usage.

εἶναι. οὗτοι μὲν οὖν κα-
τὰ τὸ ἐναντίον ἐπλανή-
θησαν οἵ τε Στωικο[ὶ] κ[αὶ] Δημόκριτος. οἱ μὲν γὰρ Στω-
10   ικοὶ καὶ ἣν ἔχουσι δύνα-
μιν τῶν φαντασιῶν ἀφαι-
ροῦνται. Δημόκριτος δὲ
καὶ ἣν οὐκ ἔχουσι χα[ρί]-
ζεται. ἡ δὲ φύσις τῶν ἐνυ . . .

[For it is impossible for these [s.c. abilities] to belong to thin membranes
in this way, membranes which do not possess the depth of a solid nature.
So these men, the Stoics and Democritus, have then gone astray in oppo-
site directions. For the Stoics rob dream visions of the power they possess, and Democritus bestows upon them a power they do not have. But
the nature of [dreams] . . .][71]

From a discussion of Democritus in the text of Sextus Empiricus we know that
Democritus claimed that these talking god-sent dreams can be beneficent or
malefic and can predict the future.[72] We find this discussion continued in fragment 9 (NF 5/6), but Diogenes addresses theological issues directly only at the
end of the poorly preserved sixth column (NF 6, col. II), where it seems clear
that he begins a new point with the statement "the true nature of dreams is (by
no means) that they are sent by the gods" (fr. 9, col. VI, lines 6–8).

In his treatise Ethics (fr. 43 = NF 12) Diogenes returns to Democritus'
notion that dreams can bring either good or evil.

col. II 5   τοιούτων μὲν [ἂν]
ἔχῃ μορφὴν πραγμά[των]
οἷς ἡ φύσις χαίρει, κατ[ευ]-
φραίνει μάλιστα τὴν [ψυ]-
χήν· ἂν δὲ τοιούτων [οἷς]
10   ἡ φύσις ἀλλοτριοῦ[ται],
θορύβου τινὸς πολλ[οῦ]
γεμίζει καὶ φόβου τὸ[ν]

---

71. This translation is after Chilton *Diogenes of Oenoanda;* and Clay, "The Philosophical Inscription," 2483.

72. Sextus Empiricus' discussion (DK 68 B 166) is cited in this connection by Clay in "The
Philosophical Inscription" (2489) and in "An Epicurean Interpretation" (357).

ὅλον ἄνθρωπον καὶ τ[ὸ]
πήδημα τῆς καρδία[ς. . . .

[[If these images] have the shape of the kind of things our body takes joy in, they bring very great joy to the soul. But if they have the shape of the kind of things our body finds alien, they often fill the entire person with a kind of agitation and fear and [provoke] a leaping of the heart. . . .][73]

As Clay has shown, Diogenes is here referring to Democritus' belief that the gods occupy themselves with sending either malefic or propitious dreams to sleeping mortals.[74] The happy, untroubled gods of Epicurus have no such occupation: Diogenes' readers are assured that visions and nightmares cannot tell the future, and any frightening images, whether of the gods or of our friends, are due to accidental distortion of the εἴδωλα.

Diogenes' treatment of dreams accords with the information "Epicurus" imparts to his mother in the *Letter to Mother,* which serves as an original document to support Diogenes' own treatises.[75] Having seen her son in a dream, the mother fears that the dream foretells some event that will befall him. Perhaps the dream was an obscure one (of the type in which Artemidorus specialized), and she writes to her son not to warn him but to ask for his reassurance. In the first columns of the extant text (fr. 125 = Ch fr. 52), the son responds by carefully expounding a physical account of dreams that eliminates the possibility that dreams possess any prophetic powers. Rather than scoffing at her fears (which is what the "Stoics" in fr. 10 [Ch fr. 7] would do), the son acknowledges that she has glimpsed a true image of him, even though he is so far away. While the fragments do not allow us to reconstruct the mother's dream with certainty, it sounds as though she has reported a dream in which her son appeared so still and calm that she feared the dream predicted his death. The son responds that the tranquillity she envisioned is real but is indicative not of his approaching death (or removal to the Islands of the Blest) but of his present godlike *ataraxia.* Having explained the habits of εἴδωλα, he concludes with words of encouragement: "Mother, take heart. You must not assume that visions of me are

---

73. Trans. Clay, "An Epicurean Interpretation," 356–57.
74. "An Epicurean Interpretation," 355–58.
75. In chapter 3 I argued that the *Letter to Mother* is not by Epicurus. Regardless of whether Diogenes wrote it himself or discovered it and was convinced of its authenticity, he uses it to support his own views. Other first- and second-century pseudepigraphic epistles are used in a similar way. See Wolfgang Speyer, *Die literarische Fälschung im heidnischen und christlichen Altertum: Ein Versuch ihrer Deutung* (Munich, 1971), 79: "Der Brief ist zugleich Selbstaussage und Dokument."

sinister. Instead, consider that I am daily acquiring something good and am advancing to a higher level of happiness."

If this mother's son had been a dream interpreter rather than an Epicurean, his letter would have unraveled the meaning of her dream using skills for which many of Diogenes' contemporaries earned a good wage. In his *Physics* Diogenes exposes the interpreters' trade as an example of the advantage unscrupulous people take of the victims of *pseudodoxia.* Diogenes (fr. 24 = NF 122) cites a *locus classicus,* but one that applies to the world of Artemidorus.

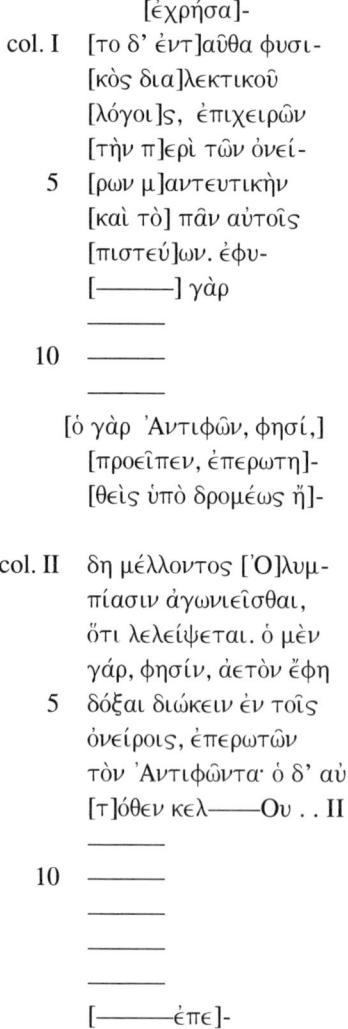

```
                  [ἐχρήσα]-
    col. I   [το δ’ ἐντ]αῦθα φυσι-
             [κὸς δια]λεκτικοῦ
             [λόγοι]ς, ἐπιχειρῶν
             [τὴν π]ερὶ τῶν ὀνεί-
        5    [ρων μ]αντευτικὴν
             [καὶ τὸ] πᾶν αὐτοῖς
             [πιστεύ]ων. ἐφυ-
             [———] γὰρ
             ─────

       10    ─────
             ─────

             [ὁ γὰρ Ἀντιφῶν, φησί,]
             [προεῖπεν, ἐπερωτη]-
             [θεὶς ὑπὸ δρομέως ἤ]-

    col. II  δη μέλλοντος [Ὀ]λυμ-
             πίασιν ἀγωνιεῖσθαι,
             ὅτι λελείψεται. ὁ μὲν
             γάρ, φησίν, ἀετὸν ἔφη
        5    δόξαι διώκειν ἐν τοῖς
             ὀνείροις, ἐπερωτῶν
             τὸν Ἀντιφῶντα· ὁ δ’ αὐ-
             [τ]όθεν κελ———Ου . . ΙΙ
             ─────

       10    ─────
             ─────
             ─────
             ─────

             [———ἐπε]-
```

col. III   ρω[τηθέντα οὐκ] ἄν-
           τικρυς εἰπεῖν τῷ
           δρομεῖ τὸν θεὸν
           ὅτι λελείψη, καὶ
     5   τὸν ἀετὸν μηδὲν
           ὀχλεῖν. εἰ μή τι δι'
           Ἀμτιφῶντα παρέ-
           [δ]ειξεν αὐτόν, ἵν' ε-
9–14   broken off

col. IV   Ι[
           μ[
           εἰς υΙΙ
           πρὸς γὰ[ρ
     5   πραγμα[
           ὡς μαρ[τυροῦσιν ὅ]-
           ν[ε]ιρ[οι
8–14   broken off

[In this case a natural philosopher [used arguments] of a dialectician, attempting the art of divination concerning dreams [and] wholly [trusting] them. For . . . [Antiphon, he says, predicted, when he was consulted by a runner,] who was just about to compete for a prize at Olympia, that he would be beaten. For the runner, he says, said, when consulting Antiphon, that he thought that an eagle was giving chase in his dreams. And Antiphon [at once told him to remember that an eagle always drives other birds before it and is itself last. However, he says that another interpreter declared, when he was consulted,] that the god did not say at all to the runner "you will be beaten," and that the eagle is no cause for anxiety. If, thanks to Antiphon, he [sc. the runner] had not shown him [sc. the interpreter] up, so that [he was able to see that the dream could be interpreted in entirely different ways, he would not have suspected that he was receiving unreliable advice.] . . . For . . . matter . . . as dreams testify . . .][76]

A passage in Cicero's *De Divinatione* suggests (unless the name Antiphon there is a gloss) that Antiphon's work treated interpretation as an art.[77] Antiphon seems to have defended the role of the well-trained interpreter: dreams as

76. Trans. Smith, *The Epicurean Inscription,* 378–79.
77. 1.177 in Arthur Stanley Pease, ed., *De Divinatione* vol. 1 (Urbana, Ill., 1920).

well as oracles come from the gods, but they require skilled interpreters, just as poems need commentators, and just as raw materials (supplied by the gods) need skilled workers (*De Divinatione* 1.117). If Cicero is describing Antiphon's work, Antiphon has a second-century counterpart in Artemidorus, who asserts that the gods cannot be expected to speak clearly in dreams; an interpreter is needed to explain the gods' hints and riddles (*Oneirocritica* 4.71). Artemidorus even included advice (for his son) on how to impress other dream interpreters (*Oneirocritica* 4). This brings us to another aspect of the Epicurean position on oneiromancy and divination. For Epicureans, the *pseudodoxia* of the believer is only part of the problem. If there is no such thing as prophecy, there can be no prophets. Both dream interpretation and oracular prophecy require a human charlatan who profits from the ignorance of his clients.[78]

In the second-century world of the oraclemongers, dream interpreters, "new Asclepiuses," and "new Pythagorases," the "new Epicurus" faced a heavy task. Diogenes' criticism of dreams and oracles was not simply an academic discussion lifted from the books of Epicurus. It was an attack on a type of *pseudodoxia* that his contemporaries especially favored. Perhaps Diogenes saved a few of his neighbors from spending their money at Claros, but most kept their confidence in prophets. It was not long after Diogenes' death that the Clarian oracle's very un-Epicurean answer to the question "Who is God?" was inscribed over a gateway in his own city.

A Dream of an Age of Gardening and Philosophy

Diogenes and the other second-century Epicureans who dissented against popular belief in prophecy and divination held an eccentric and even subversive position. Caster saw the Epicureans as lone rebels against mysticism and irrationality in general, a stance that earned them Lucian's admiration. In Caster's view, the Epicureans made their assault against the religiosity of the second century because they felt the traditional Epicurean compassion, and Lucian joined them because he was an intellectual snob.[79] Lucian and the Epicureans were not completely alone: Oenomaus of Gadara was a Cynic, and Dio

---

78. As Smith has suggested ("Diogenes of Oenoanda, New Fragments 122–124," *AS* 34 [1984]: 45), frr. 24 (NF 122) and 23 (NF 19) are connected in subject; Diogenes views dream interpreters and oraclemongers in the same light.

79. In *Lucien et la pensée religieuse de son temps* (Paris, 1937), Caster writes "Avec les Epicuriens, nous entrons dans un milieu tout à fait rebelle à la religiosité du siècle. . . . ils représentent les inadaptes, les irréductibles" (84); "Lucien déteste le mysticisme, mais ce n'est pas l'effet d'une pitié fraternelle, c'est un trait de délicatesse académique" (102).

Chrysostom also expressed Cynic views when he discussed ambiguous oracles in his discourse *On Servants*. Even Artemidorus, whose *Oneirocritica* offers dream interpretations not at all consonant with Epicurean doctrine, warns his readers against the false prophets among them.[80] Still, although Diogenes' presentation of Epicureanism was in harmony both with the revival of ancient Greek culture and with the second-century enthusiasm for civic architecture, his notions of the divine were not in keeping with those of his contemporaries. Nor does Diogenes seem to have effected much of a change, if we take the dismantling of Diogenes' stoa within a few generations of its construction as an indication of the local response.

Diogenes expected more of his fellow citizens. In chapter 1 of this study I mentioned that Diogenes intended his message of liberation from *pseudodoxia* to reach both friends and strangers, Greek and Barbarian (frr. 30 and 32 = Ch frr. 25 and 26). One other recently discovered fragment of the inscription gives us a glimpse of his hope in a future Golden Age when every person on earth would live the life of the happy Epicurean gods. The passage comes from the end of Diogenes' "Ethics" (fr. 56 = NF 21)[81] where Diogenes writes:

col. I

    τότε ὡς ἀληθῶς ὁ τῶν
5 θεῶν βίος εἰς ἀνθρώπους
    μεταβήσεται. δικαιο-
    σύνης γὰρ ἔσται μεστὰ
    πάντα καὶ φιλαλληλίας,
    καὶ οὐ γενήσεται τειχῶν
10 ἢ νόμων χρεία καὶ πάν-
    των ὅσα δι' ἀλλήλους
    σκευωρούμεθα. περὶ δὲ
    τῶν ἀπὸ γεωργίας ἀναν-
    καίων, ὡς οὐκ ἐσομέ-

---

80. To this short list of dissenters against belief in prophecy and divination Graham Anderson would add some of the Greek novelists: "It must be stressed that Lucian is not in any way exceptional even in his approach to religion in the second century. He does not embody a one-man crusade of rationalism and outspokenness against the abuses of his day: several of the Greek novelists are just as rationalistic in their approach to the gods and their dupes" ("Lucian: A Sophist's Sophist" *YCS* 27 [1982]: 80).

81. As Smith and Clay observe, the appearance of a previously unknown (but incomplete) *Principal Doctrine* that deals with justice (the topic treated in the last *Principal Doctrines* recorded by Diogenes Laertius) makes it likely that fr. 56 (NF 21) belongs to the latter part of *On Ethics*. See Clay, "The Philosophical Inscription," 2507.

col. II νων ἡμ[εῖν τότε δούλων]
         καὶ γὰρ ἀ[ρόσομεν αὐτοὶ]
         καὶ σκάψ[ομεν, καὶ τῶν φυ]-
         τῶν ἐπιμελ[ησόμεθα],
5   και ποταμο[ὺς παρατρέ]-
         ψομεν, καὶ τα[-------]
         ἐπιτηρήσο[μεν----]
         μεν ἃ μὴ τῷ[-----]
         μενοι καιρο[------],
10   καὶ διακόψει [κατὰ τὸ]
         δέον τὸ συνε[χῶς συνφι]-
         λοσοφεῖν τοια[ῦτα· τὰ]
         γὰρ γεωργή[ματα ὧν ἡ]
         φύσις χρήζει [παρέξει]

[then truly the life of the gods will pass to human beings. For all things will be full of justice and mutual love, and there will be no need of fortifications or laws and all the things we contrive on account of one another. And as for the necessities derived from agriculture,

as we shall have no [slaves then], for indeed we [ourselves shall plow] and dig and tend [the plants] and [divert] rivers and watch . . . not . . . time . . . , and such activities will interrupt as necessary the continuous [shared] study of philosophy; for the farming operations [will provide us with] the things our nature wants.[82] fr. 56 (NF 21)]

No other Epicurean text looks ahead to this peaceful era of philosophy and cooperative gardening, and nowhere do we find any indication that Epicurus hoped that the Garden might grow from an urban retreat into a global utopia. Epicurus also had doubts about the ability of ordinary people to engage in philosophy (especially if they did not happen to speak Greek).[83] Diogenes' radical concept of an Epicurean Golden Age does accord, however, with many of the essentials of Epicureanism. It fits, for example, with Epicurus' praise for the

---

82. This translation is based on Smith, *The Epicurean Inscription,* 394–95.

83. See David Sedley's review of Smith. Smith's new restoration of this fragment (*The Epicurean Inscription,* 243) has Diogenes preface the passage with a remark about the inability of ordinary people to attain wisdom, but I am not entirely convinced by Smith's suggested additions to the text.

simple pleasures and with his rejection of the idea that there is any telelogical order in the world or that there is any divine sanctioning of human social structures. It also harmonizes with the later idealized portrait of Epicurus as a man who *symphilosophized* with the slave Mys, the hetaira Leontion, and his own mother.[84] If more of Diogenes' will turns up in the environs of Oenoanda, we may discover whether Diogenes made provisions for the upkeep of the stoa or for a Garden in Oenoanda, or whether he wished his friends simply to wait for the Golden Age, when everyone would be his or her own Epicurus.

---

84. On Mys and the other slaves as "cophilosophers" of Epicurus, see Diogenes Laertius' 10.10: αὐτοὶ συνεφιλοσόφουν αὐτῷ.

Epilogue

One wonders how many visitors fulfilled Diogenes' expectations and not only ventured to Oenoanda but also paused to read the inscription addressed "to all Greeks and barbarians." Considering the respect ancient Greek culture was enjoying during this era, it is unlikely that Diogenes was disappointed in the number who came and read. Unlike the orations given in nearby Smyrna by such famous sophists as Heracleides, Scopelian, and Polemo, Diogenes' inscription surely did not attract a large influx of people from all corners of the Hellenized world. It was probably admired by the same people who enjoyed Oenoanda's other cultural offerings, however. Despite its size and location, Oenoanda possessed a theater and hosted a theatrical festival as well as athletic contests.[1] The extensive travel of the sophists, athletes, magicians, peddlers, and philosophers during the peaceful times of the empire makes Diogenes' hope for foreign visitors to Oenoanda seem realistic, despite Oenoanda's remote location. In fact, since Oenoanda was located on the route joining Lycia to the north, it was not as isolated in Diogenes' time as it is now.[2] Nor was Oenoanda totally unimportant: it was the home of one of Lycia's most distinguished families, whose members included Lyciarchs, high priests, Roman senators, and consuls, some of whom were "personally known to the emperors for the most excellent reasons."[3]

The site of Oenoanda has not been excavated, and there seems to be little hope for an excavation in the near future.[4] This is unfortunate, because most of Diogenes' inscription is probably still buried in Oenoanda and its environs. Despite the lack of an excavation, however, we have learned much about Diogenes and his city from the survey of Oenoanda conducted in recent years by the British School of Archaeology at Ankara and from the prompt publication

---

1. For inscriptional evidence for festivals, see G. Cousin, "Voyage en Carie," *BCH* 24 (1900): 344–45; and Michael Wörrle, *Stadt und Fest im kaiserzeitlichen Kleinasian: Studien zu einer agonistischen Stiftung aus Oinoanda* (Munich, 1988).

2. See D. Magie, *Roman Rule in Asia Minor,* 2 vols. (Princeton, 1950), 538.

3. C. Julius Demosthenes is so described. See Wörrle, *Stadt und Fest.*

4. As this book was going to press, M.F. Smith (letter to author, December 1995) expressed optimism that permission for an excavation may be granted after all.

of new fragments by M.F. Smith. I hope I have shown that Diogenes has also benefited from the recent growth of interest in the Greek cultural life of Asia Minor in the first centuries of this era. My aim has been to place Diogenes firmly in the world so well described in diverse ways by many scholars, including Graham Anderson, Barry Baldwin, Glen W. Bowersock, E.L. Bowie, R. Bracht Branham, Maud W. Gleason,[5] Christian Habicht, C.P. Jones, B.P. Reardon, and Louis Robert. By viewing Diogenes in his own environment, I hope that I have also made a small contribution to our understanding of the history of Epicureanism, which has too often been portrayed as a system that tolerated no innovation or development.

If we cannot look forward (with Diogenes) to a Golden Age of godlike existence, perhaps we can hope at least for an excavation in Oenoanda. New fragments (both of Diogenes' inscription and of others) and new information about the physical context of his stoa within his city will surely reveal yet more clearly Diogenes' connection with his cultural milieu in second-century Oenoanda and in the world at large.

---

5. Gleason's *Making Men: Sophists and Self-Presentation in Ancient Rome* (Princeton, 1995) appeared too late for me to use.

Select Bibliography

Diogenes of Oenoanda

Arrighetti, A. "Il Nuovo Diogene di Enoanda." *Atene e Roma,* n.s., 23 (1978): 161–72.
Casanova, A. "Diogene d'Enoanda oggi." *Prometheus* 9 (1983): 111–38.
———, ed. *I frammenti di Diogene d'Enoanda.* Studi e testi 6. Florence, 1984.
Chilton, C.W., ed. *Diogenes Oenoandensis Fragmenta.* Leipzig, 1967.
———. *Diogenes of Oenoanda: The Fragments.* Oxford, 1971.
Clay, D. "Sailing to Lampsascus: Diogenes of Oenoanda New Fragment 7." *GRBS* 14 (1973): 49–59.
———. "An Epicurean Interpretation of Dreams." *AJP* 101 (1980): 342–65.
———. "A Lost Epicurean Community." *GRBS* 30 (1989): 313–35.
———. "The Philosophical Inscription of Diogenes of Oenoanda: New Discoveries 1969–1983." *ANRW* II 36.4 (1990): 2446–2559.
———. "Lucian of Samosata: Four Philosophical Lives (Nigrinus, Demonas, Peregrinus, Alexander Pseudomantis)." *ANRW* II 36.5 (1992): 3406–50.
Cousin, G., ed. "Inscriptions d'Oenoanda." *BCH* 16 (1892): 1–70.
Grilli, A., ed. *Diogenis Oenoandensis Fragmenta.* Milan, 1960.
Heberdey, R., and E. Kalinka, eds. "Die philosophische Inschrift von Oinoanda." *BCH* 21 (1897): 346–443.
Smith, M.F. "Fragments of Diogenes of Oenoanda, Discovered and Rediscovered." *AJA* 74 (1970): 51–62.
———. "Observations on the Text of Diogenes of Oenoanda." *Hermathena* 110 (1970): 52–78.
———. "New Fragments of Diogenes of Oenoanda." *AJA* 75 (1971): 357–89.
———. "New Readings in the Text of Diogenes of Oenoanda." *CQ* 22 (1972): 159–62.
———. "Two New Fragments of Diogenes of Oenoanda." *JHS* 92 (1972): 147–55.
———. *Thirteen New Fragments of Diogenes of Oenoanda.* Denkschriften der österreichische Akademie der Wissenschaften, Philologisch-Historische Klasse, 117. Vienna, 1974.
———. "Seven New Fragments of Diogenes of Oenoanda." *Hermathena* 118 (1974): 110–29.
———. "More New Fragments of Diogenes of Oenoanda." In *Etudes sur l'Epicurisme antique,* ed. J. Bollack and A. Laks, 279–381. Lille, 1976.
———. "Fifty-Five New Fragments of Diogenes of Oenoanda." *AS* 28 (1978): 39–93.
———. "Eight New Fragments of Diogenes of Oenoanda." *AS* 29 (1979):69–89.
———. "Diogenes of Oenoanda, New Fragments 115–121." *Prometheus* 8 (1982): 193–212.

————. "A Bibliography of Work on Diogenes of Oenoanda (1892–1981)." In *Syzetesis: Studi sull' epicureismo greco e romano offerti a Marcello Gigante,* 683–95. Naples, 1983.

————. "Diogenes of Oenoanda, New Fragments 122–124." *AS* 34 (1984): 43–57.

————. "Lucretius and Diogenes of Oenoanda." *Prometheus* 12 (1986): 193–207.

————, ed. *Diogenes of Oenoanda: The Epicurean Inscription.* Naples, 1993.

Usener, H. "Epikureische Schriften auf Stein." *RhM* 47 (1892): 414–56.

William, J., ed. *Diogenis Oenoandensis Fragmenta.* Leipzig, 1907.

The Second Sophistic

Ameling, W. *Herodes Atticus.* 2 vols. Hildesheim, Zurich, and New York, 1983.

Anderson, Graham. *Theme and Variation in the Second Sophistic. Mnemosyne* Suppl. 41. Leiden, 1976.

————. "Lucian's Classics: Some Short Cuts to Culture." *BICS* 23 (1976): 59–68.

————. "Patterns in Lucian's Quotations." *BICS* 25 (1978): 97–100.

————. "Lucian: A Sophist's Sophist." *YCS* 27 (1982): 61–92.

————. *Philostratus: Biography and Belles Lettres in the Third Century a.d.* London, Sydney, and Dover, N.H., 1986.

————. *The Second Sophistic: A Cultural Phenomenon in the Roman Empire.* London and New York, 1993.

Avotins, I. "The Date and the Recipient of the *Vitae Sophistarum* of Philostratus." *Hermes* 106 (1978): 242–47.

Baldwin, Barry. "Lucian as Social Satirist." *CQ* 11 (1961): 199–208.

————. *Studies in Lucian.* Toronto, 1973.

————. "The Second Century from Secular Sources." *Second Century 1* (1981): 173–89.

Betz, Hans Dieter. "Lukian von Samosata und das Christentum." *Novum Testamentum* 3 (1959): 226–37.

Bompaire, J. *Lucien écrivain: Imitation et création.* Bibliothèque des Ecoles Françaises d'Athènes et de Rome 190. Paris, 1958.

Boulanger, A. "Lucien et Aelius Aristide." *RPh,* n.s., 47 (1923): 144–51.

Bowersock, G.W. *Greek Sophists in the Roman Empire.* Oxford, 1969.

————. "Greek Intellectuals and the Imperial Cult in the Second Century A.D." In *Le culte des Souverains dans l'empire romain,* Entretiens Hardt 19, 177–206. Geneva, 1973.

————. *Julian the Apostate.* London and Cambridge, Mass., 1978.

————, ed. *Approaches to the Second Sophistic.* University Park, Pa., 1974.

Bowie, E.L. "Greeks and Their Past in the Second Sophistic." *Past and Present* 46 (1970): 166–209.

————. "The Importance of Sophists." *YCS* 27 (1982): 29–59.

Branham, R. Bracht. *Unruly Eloquence: Lucian and the Comedy of Traditions.* Cambridge, Mass., 1989.

Caster, M. *Lucien et la pensée religieuse de son temps.* Paris, 1937.

————. *Etudes sur Alexandre ou le faux prophète de Lucien.* Paris, 1938.

Champlin, E. *Fronto and Antonine Rome.* Cambridge, Mass., 1980.

Habicht, Christian. *Die Inschriften des Asklepieions.* Altertümer von Pergamon 8.3. Berlin, 1969.

―――. *Pausanias' Guide to Ancient Greece.* Berkeley, 1985.

Hall, Jennifer A. *Lucian's Satire.* New York, 1981.

Holford-Strevens, L. *Aulus Gellius.* London, 1988.

Householder, F.W. *Literary Quotation and Allusion in Lucian.* New York, 1941.

Jones, C.P. *Plutarch and Rome.* Oxford, 1971.

―――. "Two Enemies of Lucian." *GRBS* 13 (1972): 475–87.

―――. *The Roman World of Dio Chrysostom.* Cambridge, 1978.

―――. *Culture and Society in Lucian.* Cambridge, Mass., 1986.

Keil, J. "Vertreter der zweiten Sophistik in Ephesos." *JOAI* 40 (1953): 5–26.

Macmullen, R. *Enemies of the Roman Order.* Cambridge, Mass., 1966.

―――. *Paganism in the Roman Empire.* New Haven, 1981.

Magie, D. *Roman Rule in Asia Minor.* 2 vols. Princeton, 1950.

Millar, F. *The Emperor in the Roman World.* London, 1977.

Moles, J.L. "The Career and Conversion of Dio Chrysostom." *JHS* 99 (1979): 79–100.

Oliver, J.P. *The Civic Tradition and Roman Athens.* Baltimore, 1983.

Reardon, B.P. *Courants littéraires grecs des IIe et IIIe siècles aprés J.-C.* Annales littéraires de L'Université de Nantes 3. Paris, 1971.

Robert, Louis. *A travers l'Asie Mineure: Poètes et prosateurs, monnaies grecques, voyageurs et géographie.* Bibliothèque des Ecoles Françaises d'Athènes et de Rome 239. Paris, 1980.

―――. *Documents D'Asie Mineure.* Athens, 1987.

Russell, D.A. *Greek Declamation.* Cambridge, 1983.

―――, ed. *Antonine Literature.* Oxford, 1990.

Stadter, Philip. *Arrian of Nicomedia.* Chapel Hill, N.C., 1980.

Wörrle, Michael. *Stadt und Fest im kaiserzeitlichen Kleinasian: Studien zu einer agonistischen Stiftung aus Oinoanda.* Munich, 1988.

Index

Diogenes of Oenoanda appears in subentries simply as "Diogenes" except where he is likely to be confused with another Diogenes.